Quicken® 2000 For Windows® For Dummies®

D0128135

Some cool date-editing tricks

If the selection cursor is on a Date field, you can do these things:

Press	What Happens
+	Adds one day to the date shown
–	Subtracts one day from the date shown
y	Changes the date to the first date in the year shown
r	Changes the date to the last date in the year shown
m	Changes the date to the first date in the month shown
h	Changes the date to the last date in the month shown

Windows tricks for Quicken for Windows — and for just about any other Windows program, too

- ✔ To quickly move to list-box entries that begin with a particular letter, press that letter.

- ✔ To select a list-box entry and choose a dialog box's suggested command button, double-click the entry.

- ✔ To move the insertion bar to the beginning of a field, press Home.

- ✔ To move the insertion bar to the end of a field, press End.

- ✔ To close a window or dialog box, click its Close button in the upper-right corner. (The Close button is the little box with an X in it.)

- ✔ To minimize a window, shrinking it into a tiny, little picture in Windows, click the first button in the upper-right corner — the one that looks like an underline. (Windows then places the minimized program on the taskbar.)

- ✔ To maximize the Quicken desktop in Windows so that it fills the entire monitor screen: If the middle button in the upper-right corner of the application window shows one window, click it. If it shows two, the desktop is already maximized.

- ✔ To do a Help Yelp, press F1. Works just about anywhere. Don't press this button in a crowded theater, though.

- ✔ To start another application in Windows, click the Start button.

- ✔ To switch to another application, click its button on the taskbar.

- ✔ To change any document's window size, position the mouse pointer on the window border and then drag the border. (If you can't see the border because the window has been maximized, click the middle button in the upper-right corner with two windows in it.)

...For Dummies®: Bestselling Book Series for Beginners

Quicken® 2000 For Windows® For Dummies®

Cheat Sheet

Speedy shortcuts that'll save you scads of time

Shortcut	Why You Want to Try Really Hard to Remember This
Ctrl+S	Displays the Split Transaction Window so that you can use more than one category to describe a payment or deposit
Crtl+X	Cuts out the selected text in a field and moves it to the Windows Clipboard (so that you can paste it into some other field)
Ctrl+C	Copies the selected text in a field to the Windows Clipboard (so that you can paste it into some other field)
Ctrl+V	Pastes what is on the Clipboard into the selected field
Ctrl+Z	Undoes your last action
Ctrl+P	Prints the contents of the active window (well, *almost* always)
F1	For those times when you just have to say, "Aaagh! Help! Help!"
Ctrl+K	Displays the Financial Calendar (so that you can work with and create scheduled transactions such as regularly occurring bills and deposits)
Ctrl+B	Puts you in the fast lane to back up your data
Ctrl+A	Displays the Account List
Ctrl+W	Displays the Write Checks window

The four Quicken toolbar buttons for busy people

The Quicken toolbar in the upper-right corner of the application window contains four buttons that you click to do things really fast.

Use This Button	Quicken Does This
Online	Displays the One Step Update Download Selection window so you can download all the Internet information you want in one step.
Print	Displays the Print dialog box you can use to specify how you want to print whatever you're currently viewing.
Calc	Displays the Quicken calculator.
Back	Returns you to the area you last visited.

Three things that every Quicken user should do

✔ Use the Retirement Planner to estimate when and how you can retire.

✔ Create a category list that makes tracking your spending and tax deductions easy.

✔ Balance bank accounts each month — with only a few minutes of effort — by clicking the Reconcile button in the register window.

IDG BOOKS WORLDWIDE

...For Dummies®: Bestselling Book Series for Beginners

TM

References for the Rest of Us!®

BESTSELLING BOOK SERIES

Are you intimidated and confused by computers? Do you find that traditional manuals are overloaded with technical details you'll never use? Do your friends and family always call you to fix simple problems on their PCs? Then the ...*For Dummies*® computer book series from IDG Books Worldwide is for you.

...*For Dummies* books are written for those frustrated computer users who know they aren't really dumb but find that PC hardware, software, and indeed the unique vocabulary of computing make them feel helpless. ...*For Dummies* books use a lighthearted approach, a down-to-earth style, and even cartoons and humorous icons to dispel computer novices' fears and build their confidence. Lighthearted but not lightweight, these books are a perfect survival guide for anyone forced to use a computer.

"I like my copy so much I told friends; now they bought copies."

— Irene C., Orwell, Ohio

"Quick, concise, nontechnical, and humorous."

— Jay A., Elburn, Illinois

"Thanks, I needed this book. Now I can sleep at night."

— Robin F., British Columbia, Canada

Already, millions of satisfied readers agree. They have made ...*For Dummies* books the #1 introductory level computer book series and have written asking for more. So, if you're looking for the most fun and easy way to learn about computers, look to ...*For Dummies* books to give you a helping hand.

®

IDG BOOKS
WORLDWIDE

QUICKEN® 2000 FOR WINDOWS® FOR DUMMIES®

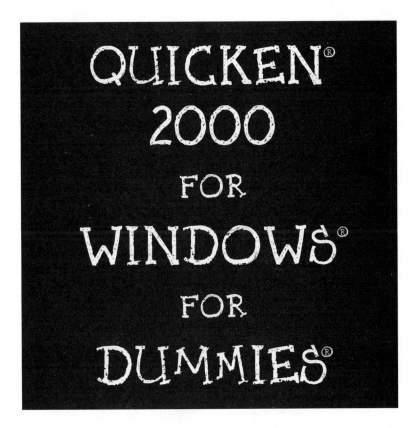

QUICKEN® 2000 FOR WINDOWS® FOR DUMMIES®

by Stephen L. Nelson

IDG Books Worldwide, Inc.
An International Data Group Company

Foster City, CA ◆ Chicago, IL ◆ Indianapolis, IN ◆ New York, NY

Quicken 2000® For Windows® For Dummies®

Published by
IDG Books Worldwide, Inc.
An International Data Group Company
919 E. Hillsdale Blvd.
Suite 400
Foster City, CA 94404
www.idgbooks.com (IDG Books Worldwide Web site)
www.dummies.com (Dummies Press Web site)

Library of Congress Catalog Card No.: 99-66344

ISBN: 0-7645-0607-2

Printed in the United States of America

10 9 8 7 6 5 4 3 2 1

1O/QR/QZ/ZZ/IN

Distributed in the United States by IDG Books Worldwide, Inc.

Distributed by CDG Books Canada Inc. for Canada; by Transworld Publishers Limited in the United Kingdom; by IDG Norge Books for Norway; by IDG Sweden Books for Sweden; by IDG Books Australia Publishing Corporation Pty. Ltd. for Australia and New Zealand; by TransQuest Publishers Pte Ltd. for Singapore, Malaysia, Thailand, Indonesia, and Hong Kong; by Gotop Information Inc. for Taiwan; by ICG Muse, Inc. for Japan; by Intersoft for South Africa; by Eyrolles for France; by International Thomson Publishing for Germany, Austria and Switzerland; by Distribuidora Cuspide for Argentina; by LR International for Brazil; by Galileo Libros for Chile; by Ediciones ZETA S.C.R. Ltda. for Peru; by WS Computer Publishing Corporation, Inc., for the Philippines; by Contemporanea de Ediciones for Venezuela; by Express Computer Distributors for the Caribbean and West Indies; by Micronesia Media Distributor, Inc. for Micronesia; by Chips Computadoras S.A. de C.V. for Mexico; by Editorial Norma de Panama S.A. for Panama; by American Bookshops for Finland.

For general information on IDG Books Worldwide's books in the U.S., please call our Consumer Customer Service department at 800-762-2974. For reseller information, including discounts and premium sales, please call our Reseller Customer Service department at 800-434-3422.

For information on where to purchase IDG Books Worldwide's books outside the U.S., please contact our International Sales department at 317-596-5530 or fax 317-596-5692.

For consumer information on foreign language translations, please contact our Customer Service department at 1-800-434-3422, fax 317-596-5692, or e-mail rights@idgbooks.com.

For information on licensing foreign or domestic rights, please phone +1-650-655-3109.

For sales inquiries and special prices for bulk quantities, please contact our Sales department at 650-655-3200 or write to the address above.

For information on using IDG Books Worldwide's books in the classroom or for ordering examination copies, please contact our Educational Sales department at 800-434-2086 or fax 317-596-5499.

For press review copies, author interviews, or other publicity information, please contact our Public Relations department at 650-655-3000 or fax 650-655-3299.

For authorization to photocopy items for corporate, personal, or educational use, please contact Copyright Clearance Center, 222 Rosewood Drive, Danvers, MA 01923, or fax 978-750-4470.

About the Author

Stephen L. Nelson is a CPA with a master's degree in finance. As corny as it sounds, Steve truly enjoys writing books that make using personal computers easier and more fun. In fact, a substantiated rumor says Steve has written more than 70 computer books.

Steve is the best-selling author on the Quicken product, having sold something like 700,000 books about Quicken.

ABOUT IDG BOOKS WORLDWIDE

Welcome to the world of IDG Books Worldwide.

IDG Books Worldwide, Inc., is a subsidiary of International Data Group, the world's largest publisher of computer-related information and the leading global provider of information services on information technology. IDG was founded more than 30 years ago by Patrick J. McGovern and now employs more than 9,000 people worldwide. IDG publishes more than 290 computer publications in over 75 countries. More than 90 million people read one or more IDG publications each month.

Launched in 1990, IDG Books Worldwide is today the #1 publisher of best-selling computer books in the United States. We are proud to have received eight awards from the Computer Press Association in recognition of editorial excellence and three from Computer Currents' First Annual Readers' Choice Awards. Our best-selling *...For Dummies®* series has more than 50 million copies in print with translations in 31 languages. IDG Books Worldwide, through a joint venture with IDG's Hi-Tech Beijing, became the first U.S. publisher to publish a computer book in the People's Republic of China. In record time, IDG Books Worldwide has become the first choice for millions of readers around the world who want to learn how to better manage their businesses.

Our mission is simple: Every one of our books is designed to bring extra value and skill-building instructions to the reader. Our books are written by experts who understand and care about our readers. The knowledge base of our editorial staff comes from years of experience in publishing, education, and journalism — experience we use to produce books to carry us into the new millennium. In short, we care about books, so we attract the best people. We devote special attention to details such as audience, interior design, use of icons, and illustrations. And because we use an efficient process of authoring, editing, and desktop publishing our books electronically, we can spend more time ensuring superior content and less time on the technicalities of making books.

You can count on our commitment to deliver high-quality books at competitive prices on topics you want to read about. At IDG Books Worldwide, we continue in the IDG tradition of delivering quality for more than 30 years. You'll find no better book on a subject than one from IDG Books Worldwide.

John Kilcullen
Chairman and CEO
IDG Books Worldwide, Inc.

Steven Berkowitz
President and Publisher
IDG Books Worldwide, Inc.

Eighth Annual Computer Press Awards 1992

WINNER
Ninth Annual Computer Press Awards 1993

WINNER
Tenth Annual Computer Press Awards 1994

Eleventh Annual Computer Press Awards 1995

IDG is the world's leading IT media, research and exposition company. Founded in 1964, IDG had 1997 revenues of $2.05 billion and has more than 9,000 employees worldwide. IDG offers the widest range of media options that reach IT buyers in 75 countries representing 95% of worldwide IT spending. IDG's diverse product and services portfolio spans six key areas including print publishing, online publishing, expositions and conferences, market research, education and training, and global marketing services. More than 90 million people read one or more of IDG's 290 magazines and newspapers, including IDG's leading global brands — Computerworld, PC World, Network World, Macworld and the Channel World family of publications. IDG Books Worldwide is one of the fastest-growing computer book publishers in the world, with more than 700 titles in 36 languages. The "...For Dummies®" series alone has more than 50 million copies in print. IDG offers online users the largest network of technology-specific Web sites around the world through IDG.net (http://www.idg.net), which comprises more than 225 targeted Web sites in 55 countries worldwide. International Data Corporation (IDC) is the world's largest provider of information technology data, analysis and consulting, with research centers in over 41 countries and more than 400 research analysts worldwide. IDG World Expo is a leading producer of more than 168 globally branded conferences and expositions in 35 countries including E3 (Electronic Entertainment Expo), Macworld Expo, ComNet, Windows World Expo, ICE (Internet Commerce Expo), Agenda, DEMO, and Spotlight. IDG's training subsidiary, ExecuTrain, is the world's largest computer training company, with more than 230 locations worldwide and 785 training courses. IDG Marketing Services helps industry-leading IT companies build international brand recognition by developing global integrated marketing programs via IDG's print, online and exposition products worldwide. Further information about the company can be found at www.idg.com. 1/24/99

Author's Acknowledgments

Hey, reader, a lot of people spent a lot of time working on this book to help make Quicken easier for you. You should know who these people are in case you ever meet them in the produce section of the local grocery store squeezing cantaloupes.

The editorial folks are Colleen Esterline (the project editor) and Laura Moss (the acquisitions editor). Thanks also to Lee Musick for his technical assistance and superb attention to detail. Thanks also to the production staff of Tom Missler, Maridee V. Ennis, Shelley Lea, Nancy Price, Marianne Santy, Toni Settle, Betty Kish, Angela F. Hunckler, Brent Savage, Mary Jo Weis, Brian Torwelle, Jill Piscitelli, Dave McKelvey, Maggie Ubertini, Karena Porter, Tracy K. Oliver, Amy M. Adrian, Kate Jenkins, and Dan Whetstine.

Publisher's Acknowledgments

We're proud of this book; please register your comments through our IDG Books Worldwide Online Registration Form located at http://my2cents.dummies.com.

Some of the people who helped bring this book to market include the following:

Acquisitions, Editorial, and Media Development

Project Editor: Colleen Williams Esterline

Acquisitions Editor: Laura Moss

Technical Editor: Lee Musick

Associate Permissions Editor: Carmen Krikorian

Media Development Coordinator: Megan Roney

Editorial Manager: Rev Mengle

Editorial Assistants: Beth Parlon, Jamila Pree

Production

Project Coordinator: Tom Missler

Associate Project Coordinator: Maridee Ennis

Layout and Graphics: Amy M. Adrian, Angela F. Hunckler, Kate Jenkins, Barry Offringa, Dave McKelvey, Tracy K. Oliver, Karena Porter, Jill Piscitelli, Brent Savage, Brian Torwelle, Maggie Ubertini, Mary Jo Weis, Dan Whetstine

Proofreaders: Betty Kish, Nancy Price, Marianne Santy, Toni Settle

Indexer: Steve Rath

Special Help Richard Graves, Suzanne Thomas, Alison Walthall

General and Administrative

IDG Books Worldwide, Inc.: John Kilcullen, CEO; Steven Berkowitz, President and Publisher

IDG Books Technology Publishing Group: Richard Swadley, Senior Vice President and Publisher; Walter Bruce III, Vice President and Associate Publisher; Steven Sayre, Associate Publisher; Joseph Wikert, Associate Publisher; Mary Bednarek, Branded Product Development Director; Mary Corder, Editorial Director

IDG Books Consumer Publishing Group: Roland Elgey, Senior Vice President and Publisher; Kathleen A. Welton, Vice President and Publisher; Kevin Thornton, Acquisitions Manager; Kristin A. Cocks, Editorial Director

IDG Books Internet Publishing Group: Brenda McLaughlin, Senior Vice President and Publisher; Diane Graves Steele, Vice President and Associate Publisher; Sofia Marchant, Online Marketing Manager

IDG Books Production for Dummies Press: Michael R. Britton, Vice President of Production; Debbie Stailey, Associate Director of Production; Cindy L. Phipps, Manager of Project Coordination, Production Proofreading, and Indexing; Shelley Lea, Supervisor of Graphics and Design; Debbie J. Gates, Production Systems Specialist; Robert Springer, Supervisor of Proofreading; Laura Carpenter, Production Control Manager; Tony Augsburger, Supervisor of Reprints and Bluelines

◆

The publisher would like to give special thanks to Patrick J. McGovern, without whom this book would not have been possible.

◆

Contents at a Glance

Cartoons at a Glance

By Rich Tennant

"You may want to talk to Phil – he's one of our more aggressive financial planners."

page 7

"WE TOOK A GAMBLE AND INVESTED ALL OUR MONEY IN A RACE HORSE. THEN IT RAN AWAY."

page 55

"Our plan is to buy the rest of it when we pay off our college loan."

page 309

"IT SAYS HERE IF I SUBSCRIBE TO THIS MAGAZINE, THEY'LL SEND ME A FREE DESK-TOP CALCULATOR. DESKTOP CALCULATOR?! WHOOAA – WHERE HAVE I BEEN?!!"

page 177

Arthur inadvertently replaces his mouse pad with a Ouija board. For the rest of the day, he receives messages from the spectral world.

page 273

Fax: 978-546-7747 • E-mail: the5wave@tiac.net

Table of Contents

Introduction

• •

*Y*ou aren't a dummy, of course. But here's the deal. You don't have to be some sort of techno-geek or financial wizard to manage your financial affairs on a PC. You have other things to do, places to go, and people to meet. And that's where *Quicken 2000 For Windows For Dummies* comes in.

In the pages that follow, I give you the straight scoop on how to use Quicken for Windows, without a lot of extra baggage, goofy tangential information, or misguided advice.

About This Book

This book isn't meant to be read cover to cover like some John Grisham page-turner. Rather, it's organized into tiny, no-sweat descriptions of how to do the things you need to do. If you're the sort of person who just doesn't feel right not reading a book from cover to cover, you can, of course, go ahead and read this thing from front to back.

I can recommend this approach, however, only for people who have already checked the TV listings. There may, after all, be a *Hardball with Chris Matthews* rerun on.

About the Author

If you're going to spend your time reading what I have to say, you deserve to know my qualifications. So let me take just a minute or so to tell you about Stephen Nelson.

I have an undergraduate degree in accounting and a master's degree in finance and accounting. I am also a certified public accountant (CPA).

I've spent the last dozen years helping businesses set up computerized financial management systems. I started with Arthur Andersen & Co., which is one of the world's largest public accounting and systems consulting firms. More recently, I've been working as a sole proprietor. When I wasn't doing financial systems work, I served as the controller of a small, 50-person computer software company.

Oh yeah, one other thing. I've used Quicken for my business and for my personal record-keeping for several years. (I also use QuickBooks for my other business, but that's another story you'll need to get *QuickBooks For Dummies* to hear about.)

None of this information makes me sound like the world's most exciting guy, of course. I doubt that you'll be inviting me to your next dinner party. Hey, I can deal with that.

But knowing a little something about me should give you a bit more confidence in applying the stuff I talk about in the pages that follow. After all, I am talking about something that's extremely important: your money.

How to Use This Book

I always enjoyed reading those encyclopedias my parents bought for me and my siblings. I could flip open, say, the E volume, look up Elephants, and then learn just about everything I needed to know about elephants for a fifth-grade report: where elephants lived, how much they weighed, and why they ate so much.

You won't read anything about elephants here. But you should be able to use this book in the same way. If you want to learn about something, look through the table of contents or index and find the topic — printing checks, for example. Then flip to the correct chapter or page and read as much as you need or enjoy. No muss. No fuss.

If you want to find out about anything else, you can, of course, just repeat the process.

What You Can Safely Ignore

Sometimes I provide step-by-step descriptions of tasks. I feel very badly that I have to do this. So to make things easier for you, I highlight the tasks with bold text. That way you'll know exactly what you're supposed to do. I also often provide a more detailed explanation in regular text. You can skip the regular text that accompanies the step-by-step descriptions if you already understand the process.

Here's an example that shows what I mean:

1. **Press Enter.**

   Find the key that's labeled Enter. Extend your index finger so that it rests ever so gently on the Enter key. In one sure, fluid motion, press the Enter key using your index finger. Then release the key.

Okay, that's kind of an extreme example. I never go into that much detail. But you get the idea. If you know how to press Enter, you can just do that and not read further. If you need help — say with the finger depression part or something — just read the nitty-gritty details.

Can you skip anything else? Let me see now. . . . You can skip the paragraphs with the Technical Stuff icon next to them. See the "Special Icons" section for an example of the Technical Stuff icon. The information I've stuck in those paragraphs is really only for those of you who like that technical kind of stuff.

For that matter, I guess you can also safely ignore the stuff in the Tip paragraphs. But if you're someone who enjoys trying things another way, go ahead and read the Tips, too.

What You Should Not Ignore (Unless You're a Masochist)

Don't skip the Warnings. They're the ones flagged with the picture of the 19th-century bomb. They describe some things you really shouldn't do.

Out of respect for you, I'm not going to put stuff in these paragraphs such as "Don't smoke." I figure that you're an adult. You can make your own lifestyle decisions.

So I'll reserve the Warnings for more urgent and immediate dangers — things akin to "Don't smoke while you're filling your car with gasoline."

Three Foolish Assumptions

I assume just three things:

- ✔ You have a PC with Microsoft Windows 95, Windows 98, or Windows NT.
- ✔ You know how to turn it on.
- ✔ You want to use Quicken.

The Four Flavors of Quicken

Okay. I lied. I'm going to assume one more thing: You own or somehow have access to a copy of Quicken.

You may be interested to know that Quicken comes in four versions. It doesn't really matter which one of the four versions you have. Quicken works in basically the same way for all four, and this book applies to all of them. But because each of the four versions has a few unique features, you may find that your screen doesn't look exactly like the screens shown in this book. You may, for example, have a few buttons that you don't see in the figures I show you. Don't worry if this happens. It probably means that you're working with a different version than I am.

Just to let you know, I used the Deluxe version to write this book. You can determine this because at the top of some of the figures it says "Quicken Deluxe 2000" in the application window title bar. If you have a different version, it will say something different at the top of your screen.

How This Book Is Organized

This book is organized into five mostly coherent parts.

Part I: Zen, Quicken, and the Big Picture

Part I covers some up-front stuff you need to take care of. I promise I won't waste your time here. I just want to make sure that you get off on the right foot.

Part II: The Absolute Basics

This second part of the book explains the core knowledge you need to know to keep a personal or business checkbook with Quicken: using the checkbook, printing, reporting on your finances, using Online Banking, balancing your bank accounts, and using the Quicken calculators.

Some of this stuff isn't very exciting compared to *The Jerry Springer Show,* so I'll work hard to make things fun for you.

Part III: Home Finances

Part III talks about the sorts of things you may want to do with Quicken if you're using it at home: credit cards, loans, mutual funds, stocks, and bonds. You get the idea. If you don't ever get this far — hey, that's cool.

If you do get this far, you'll find that Quicken provides some tools that eliminate not only the drudgery of keeping a checkbook, but also the drudgery of most other financial burdens.

While I'm on the subject, I also want to categorically deny that Part III contains any secret messages if you read it backwards.

Part IV: Serious Business

The Serious Business section helps people who use Quicken in a business.

If you're pulling your hair out because you're using Quicken in a business, postpone the hair-pulling — at least for the time being. Read Part IV first. It tells you about preparing payroll, tracking the amounts that customers owe you, and other wildly exciting stuff.

Part V: The Part of Tens

By tradition, a ...*For Dummies* book includes "The Part of Tens." It provides a collection of ten-something lists: ten answers to frequently asked questions about Quicken, ten ways not to become a millionaire, ten things to do when you next visit Acapulco, and so on.

Appendices

It's an unwritten rule that computer books have appendices, so I included three. Appendix A gives you a quick and dirty overview of Windows, for those new to the world of Windows. Appendix B summarizes how you can access financial information on the World Wide Web from Quicken. Appendix C is a glossary of key financial and Quicken terms.

Conventions Used in This Book

To make the best use of your time and energy, you should know about the following conventions I use in this book.

When I want you to type something, such as **Hydraulics screamed as the pilot lowered his landing gear**, I put it in bold letters. When I want you to type something that's short and uncomplicated, such as **Hillary**, it still appears in bold type.

By the way, with Quicken, you don't have to worry about the case of the stuff you type. If I tell you to type **Hillary**, you can type **HILLARY**. Or you can follow e. e. cummings's lead and type **hillary**.

Whenever I describe a message or information that you see on the screen, I present it as follows:

```
Surprise! This is a message on-screen.
```

You can choose menus and commands and select dialog box elements with the mouse or the keyboard. To select them with the mouse, you just click them. To select them with the keyboard, you press Alt and the underlined letter in the menu, command, or dialog box. For example, the letter F in File and the letter O in Open are underlined so that you can choose the File⇨Open command by pressing Alt+F, O. (I also identify the keyboard selection keys by underlining them in the text.) You can choose many commands by clicking icons on the iconbar as well.

Special Icons

Like many computer books, this book uses icons, or little pictures, to flag things that don't quite fit into the flow of things. ...*For Dummies* books use a standard set of icons that flag little digressions, such as:

This icon points out nerdy technical material that you may want to skip (or read, if you're feeling particularly bright).

Here's a shortcut to make your life easier.

This icon is just a friendly reminder to do something.

And this icon is a friendly reminder *not* to do something . . . or else.

Where to Next?

If you're just getting started, flip the page and start reading the first chapter.

If you have a special problem or question, use the table of contents or the index to find out where that topic is covered and then turn to that page.

Part I
Zen, Quicken, and the Big Picture

The 5th Wave   By Rich Tennant

"You may want to talk to Phil - he's one of our more aggressive financial planners."

In this part . . .

When you go to a movie theater, some prerequisites are necessary for the show to be truly enjoyable. And I'm not referring to the presence of Pamela Anderson or Mike Myers. Purchasing a bucket of popcorn is essential, for example. One should think strategically both about seating and about soda size. And one may even have items of a, well, personal nature to take care of — such as visiting the little boys' or girls' room.

I mention all this stuff for one simple reason. To make getting started with Quicken as easy and fun as possible, you have to complete some prerequisites, too. And this first part of *Quicken 2000 For Windows For Dummies* — "Zen, Quicken, and the Big Picture" — talks about these sorts of things.

Chapter 1

Setting Up Shop

● ●

In This Chapter

▶ Installing Quicken

▶ Touring Quicken

▶ Setting up your bank accounts and credit card accounts if you're a first-time user

▶ Retrieving existing Quicken data files

● ●

*1*f you have never used Quicken, begin here. The next section tells you how to install Quicken (if you haven't already) and how to start the program for the first time.

You also find out how you go about setting up Quicken accounts to track banking activities — specifically, the money that goes into and out of a checking or savings account.

If you have already begun to use Quicken, don't waste any time reading this chapter unless you want the review. You already know the stuff it covers.

By the way, if you have Windows, I assume that you know a little bit about it. No, you don't have to be some sort of expert. Shoot, you don't even have to be all that proficient. You do need to know how to start Windows applications (such as Quicken). It'll also help immensely if you know how to choose commands from menus and how to enter stuff into windows and dialog boxes.

If you don't know how to do these kinds of things, flip to Appendix A. It provides a very quick and rather dirty overview of how you work in Windows. Read the stuff in the appendix, or at least skim it, and then come back to this chapter. And that reminds me, when I say Windows, I mean Windows 95, Windows 98, Windows NT, or Windows 2000. Quicken 2000 won't run on Windows 3.1, so if you want to run the latest version, I'm afraid it's time to upgrade.

Installing Quicken

You install Quicken the same way you install any program in Windows. If you already know how to install programs, you don't need any help from me. Stop reading here, do the installation thing, and then start reading the next section, "Setting Up Your First Accounts."

If you do need help installing Quicken, let me give you the step-by-step instructions:

To install Quicken in a flash

Installing Quicken from a CD-ROM is as easy as one, two . . . well just one, two, actually:

1. **Insert the CD-ROM into the CD-ROM drive.**

   In a short amount of time, Quicken asks if you'd like to install the program onto your hard disk. You'll see a dialog box like the one in Figure 1-1 if you're a new Quicken user — or one just ever so slightly different if you're upgrading to Quicken 2000.

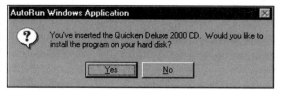

   Note: If nothing happens when you put the CD-ROM into the CD-ROM drive, don't panic! Just leave the CD-ROM in and follow the instructions in the section "To install Quicken the somewhat cumbersome way."

2. **Click the Yes button.**

   The installation program asks you a few questions. For example, it asks you where you want to install the program. Unless you know for sure that you don't want to install it in the suggested location, go ahead and go with the default Quickenw folder. (If the installation program asks if it can create this folder for you, let it do so.) The installation program also asks whether you want to perform an Express or Custom installation. Unless you want to spend time figuring out which features you'll use and muck about storing all of the bits and pieces of Quicken in different places, just go with the Express installation. Click Next after answering each question.

3. **After the installation is complete, click Finish.**

   Quicken restarts your computer. You're done.

To install Quicken the somewhat cumbersome way

If your computer didn't pick up on the AutoRun install program on the Quicken CD-ROM, don't worry, I'll walk you through the steps of installing the Quicken by hand:

1. **Click the Start button.**

   Note: The Start button, as you may already know, appears in the lower-left corner of the Windows *desktop.* (The desktop is what you see after you turn on your computer.) So that you can't possibly miss it, Windows some-times features a moving pointer that, after you turn on your computer, repeatedly points to the Start button. The following message also flashes:

   ```
   Click here to start programs, click here to start programs.
   ```

2. **Choose Settings⇨Control Panel from the Start menu.**

   Windows displays the Control Panel window. As you may know, the Control Panel provides a whole bunch of tools you use for fiddling with and fine-tuning your computer (see Figure 1-2).

Figure 1-2:
The Control
Panel
window.

3. Double-click the Add/Remove Programs icon.

Windows displays the Add/Remove Programs Properties tool (see Figure 1-3).

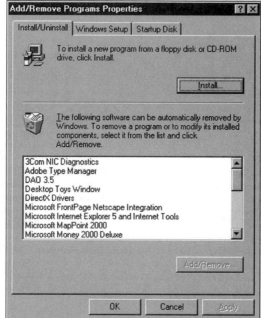

Figure 1-3:
The
Add/Remove
Programs
Properties
box with the
Install/
Uninstall tab
showing.

4. Select the Install/Uninstall tab if it isn't already selected.

5. Make sure your CD-ROM is in the CD-ROM drive.

6. Click the Install button.

Windows displays a dialog box that tells you it's about to look for the program you want to install.

7. Click the Next button.

Windows looks at the CD-ROM and finds the Quicken installation program, in this case INSTALL.EXE. Windows displays another dialog box asking, basically, "Gee, what do you think I ought to do now?"

8. Click the Finish button.

Windows starts installing Quicken. Occasionally, the installation program asks you a question. Answer the question and click Next. After the installation is complete, click Finish, and Quicken restarts your computer. You're done.

Setting Up Your First Accounts

If you've used a previous version of Quicken, the program asks if you want to convert your data to the new version. Do this. After you've upgraded from the older version, all your accounts should be ready to rock. Instead of showing you the New User Setup window, Quicken asks whether you would like to set up your accounts for online services. See Chapter 6 if you want more information on the online features and how to set them up.

After you install Quicken, your first job is to set up a bank account and tell Quicken how you want it to track your finances. This setup stuff isn't hard to do; you just need to find your most recent bank statement or — better yet — your last bank statement from the previous year.

You start Quicken the same way you start any Windows application. For example, you can click the Start button and then choose Programs➪Quicken➪ Quicken 2000. (Or you can double-click the Quicken shortcut on the Windows desktop.) Quicken starts, and you may first see the Software Registration dialog box. You, like me, may find this registration business irritating, but you have to do it. So click the Next button and then follow the instructions. Note that you don't see the software registration dialog box if you've already been using Quicken and so have (presumably) already registered the software.

Once you complete the registration process, you see the Quicken application window. If you're a new user of Quicken, you'll also see the Quicken New User Setup dialog box (see Figure 1-4).

Figure 1-4:
The Quicken
New User
Setup dialog
box.

Inside the dialog box (partial transcription of screenshot):

Quicken New User Setup

Welcome to Quicken's New User Setup.

New User Setup will now help you set up your checking account.

It will get you started in only 5 minutes.

Click Next to continue

Cancel   Help   Next

With your bank statement in hand and the Quicken New User Setup dialog box on-screen, follow these steps:

1. **Click the Next button so that Quicken moves to the second screen of the Quicken New User Setup dialog box.**

   Quicken displays a bunch of questions that you answer by clicking Yes and No buttons. Are you married? Do you have children? Do you own a house? And so on. Answer the questions and then click Next.

2. **Tell Quicken the name you want to use for the account.**

   You do so by typing a name into the Account Name text box (see Figure 1-5). By the way, you can be as general or as specific as you want. But remember, brevity is a virtue; be as concise as you can. The reason is that Quicken uses your account name to label the tabs on the Quicken program window. (I'll show this to you in a minute, but go ahead and flip ahead to Figure 1-8 if you just can't wait that long.)

3. **Select your bank from the Financial Institution drop-down list box.**

   If your financial institution isn't listed, enter its name in the box. If the account isn't held at a bank (for instance in the case that you store your money in a coffee can in your basement), leave the financial institution box empty.

Figure 1-5:
Adding an
account for
a new user.

4. **Click the Next button.**

   Quicken displays some new information that asks whether you have the bank statement that you're going to use for setting up the new account.

The best way to get started

Quicken wants you to use your last bank statement to set up the bank account you track. In this way, when you start using Quicken, your financial records are synchronized with the bank's records.

But I want to suggest something slightly different to you. Go back farther than just to the beginning of the previous month (which is what you do when you use your last bank statement). Go back to the beginning of the year and use the last bank statement of the previous year — even if it's now several months after the beginning of the year. Now, I'm not trying to waste your time. But let me point out two big advantages to having a complete year's data in Quicken. Tracking and tallying your tax deductions and planning your finances will be easier.

By the way, going back to the beginning of the year isn't as hard as you may think. Quicken provides a bunch of different tools to help you enter several months' worth of data in a very short time, as you can see in this chapter and the two or three that follow.

5. **Tell Quicken whether you have the last bank statement.**

   This part is pretty simple. If you do, click the Yes button and then click the Next button. If you don't, click the No button and then click the Next button. (If you click No, Quicken doesn't do any more setup stuff for the checking account.)

6. **Enter the ending bank statement date, using your bank statement.**

   If you indicate that you have the bank statement handy, Quicken asks for the ending statement date, which is the date you start using Quicken. Enter the date in MM/DD/YY fashion.

   "Geez, Steve," you're now saying to yourself, "What's MM/DD/YY fashion?" Okay. Here's an example. If your bank statement is dated July 1, 2000, enter **7/1/00**.

7. **Enter the ending bank statement balance, using your bank statement.**

   This balance is whatever shows on your bank statement. This balance is also the amount of money in your account on the date you begin your financial record-keeping. If you have $4.16 in your checking account, type **4.16** into the Statement Ending Balance text box.

8. **After you enter the bank statement balance, click the Next button.**

   Quicken displays a message in the Quicken New User Setup dialog box that tells you that you just set up a bank account. Click Done. Quicken removes the New User Setup dialog box and displays the My Finances QuickTab of the Quicken window. Click the hyperlink for the account you just set up to display the account's register (see Figure 1-6).

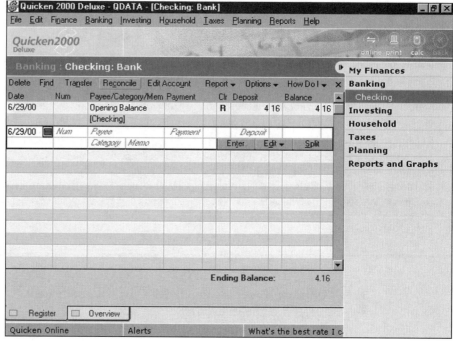

Figure 1-6:
The Quicken
program
window
shows your
new check-
ing account.

Steve's Overview

You don't need to know much about the mechanics of the Quicken interface — the way its windows work — to begin working with Quicken. But I want to make a couple of quick comments.

Quicken changes the way its document windows look

First, Quicken doesn't use document windows the way that other Windows applications do. Quicken basically turns document windows into pages that you leaf through by clicking the window tabs that appear along the bottom edge of the program window. In Figure 1-6, for example, you see window tabs for a Register window and an Overview window.

Along the right edge of the program window, Quicken displays words, which, apparently just to confuse users, it also calls tabs — specifically, QuickTabs and Feature tabs (see Figure 1-6). Figure 1-6, for example, shows several QuickTabs along the right edge of the window: My Finances, Banking,

Investing, Household and so on. These tabs are in boldface and are always available. The figure also shows a Feature tab for Checking indented under the Banking QuickTab. Feature tabs are available for features in the program that you've previously visited but not closed.

You can hide Quicken's tabs by clicking the arrow on the left side of the My Finances QuickTab. To redisplay the tabs, just click this arrow again. Note that later in the book, some figures won't show tabs. This is to give more room to the area of the screen I want you to see.

While this QuickTab versus Feature tab business is mighty confusing at first, it actually works really well. In a nutshell, Quicken arranges all of its features — whistles, bells, or whatever else you want to call them — into *centers*. There's the Banking center, for example. And the Investing center. And the Household center. You get the picture. Each of these *centers* gets its own QuickTab. Okay. So far, so good. If you use a feature within one of these centers, Quicken adds a Feature tab underneath the QuickTab. In Figure 1-6, for example, the Checking Feature tab appears because by setting an account during the New User Setup program described a page or so ago, you use the Checking feature. If you want to look at what's available in a particular center, you click its QuickTab. If you want to use a particular feature, you either need to find it within a center or if you've used the feature before, click its Feature tab.

Account register

After you get past the QuickTab and Feature tab confusion, you're pretty much on your way with Quicken. To see the account register window that you'll spend most of your time working with, click the Register window tab for the register you want to open and look at or click the Banking QuickTab and then the Checking Feature tab. Quicken displays the account register (refer to Figure 1-6).

You basically use this account register to keep track of all your financial affairs.

Setting up Quicken if you've used Quicken before

Suppose that you're a Quicken veteran. An old hand. A longtime friend. Well, anyway, you get the idea.

Can you use the existing files you've been working on? Sure you can, as long as you've been using Quicken or Microsoft Money. In fact, if the Quicken installation program can find a version of old Quicken files on your disk, it'll skip all the New User Setup stuff and just begin using your existing files.

If you've been using Quicken for Macintosh, you're going to have to export your data from the Macintosh before you can read it in the Windows version. However, there are about a million things more fun to do than exporting Quicken data from a Mac to Windows. See the section in Chapter 18 on importing data from an old accounting system for a brief discussion on the procedure and some suggestions for better ways to spend your time.

If Quicken doesn't find the old files, you need to specifically open the files. But if you have this problem, you should be able to solve it yourself. What has happened, if you find yourself in this boat, is that you've moved or messed around with the Quicken (or Money) files with some other program, such as the Windows Explorer. If you did that, presumably you had a reason. And, more to the point, you should know where you put the files.

Using the File⇨Open command

Use File⇨Open to select and open your existing Quicken files. Here's how:

1. **Choose File⇨Open from the menu bar.**

   Use your mouse or press Ctrl+O. Figure 1-7 shows the Open Quicken File dialog box that appears after you choose the command. Quicken uses this dialog box to ask the burning question, "Hey, buddy, what file you wanna open?"

Open Quicken File	
Look in: Quickenw	

   hpbank hptax ~qw~link.qdt
   hpbiz inet Qdata.qdf
   hpcar Qsapi
   hphome snap
   hpinvest sounds
   hpplan ttforms

   File name: _____ OK
   Files of type: Quicken Files (*.QDF;*.QDB;*.QDT) Cancel
   Help

   Figure 1-7:
   The Open
   Quicken File
   dialog box.

2. **Tell Quicken in which folder the files are stored.**

   If the correct folder isn't the one already shown in the Look In box in the Open Quicken File dialog box, tell Quicken what the correct drive is. Click the down arrow at the end of the Look In box. After you do, Quicken drops down a list of the disk drives and folders your computer has. (This is why the little Look In box is called a drop-down list box.)

After the list of drives and folders appears, click the one that stores your Quicken files. Quicken closes the drop-down list box and displays your selection in the list box beneath the Look In box.

3. **Select the file from the list box.**

After you tell Quicken on which disk and in which folder you stored your data files, the Quicken files in that location appear in the list box. Just click the file you want.

4. **Click OK after you find the file.**

Quicken opens the file and displays the active account in the register window. (Quicken also displays its Reminders window to show any unprinted checks or scheduled transactions.)

Note: If the file you're opening was created in a previous version of Quicken, Quicken converts the data to the Quicken 2000 format.

What if you can't find the Quicken file?

Uh-oh. This is a problem. But don't worry. You're not out of luck. What you need to do is to look through each of the folders on the disk. Or, if you have more than one hard disk, look through each of the folders on each of the hard drives.

Bummer, huh? Maybe I should bring up a point here. If you're a new user, your best bet is really to just go with whatever an application program (such as Quicken) suggests. If Quicken suggests that you use the QUICKENW directory — this is the suggestion for Windows versions of Quicken, by the way — just do it. If Quicken suggests that you use drive C, just do it. If Quicken suggests that you take all your money, put it in a coffee can, and bury the can in your backyard . . . whoa, wait a minute. Bad idea.

Maybe I can suggest a better rule. Hmmm. . . . How about this? Although you shouldn't follow suggestions blindly, you also shouldn't ignore Quicken's suggestions unless you have a good reason. And "Just because," "I don't know," and "For the heck of it" aren't very good reasons.

Starting Quicken for the second time

The second time you start Quicken — and every subsequent time — things work pretty much the same way as the first time. Click the Quicken icon, which you'll see on the desktop. Or, if you like doing things the hard way, click Start and then choose Programs⇨Quicken ⇨Quicken 2000. The only real difference is that you won't, of course, have to step through any of the new user setup stuff.

Oh, and one other thing — when you restart Quicken it will display the My Finances center. Note that this is the same *center* (also known as a Quicken Activity Center and a Financial Center) that Quicken displays if you click the My Finances QuickTab (see Figure 1-8).

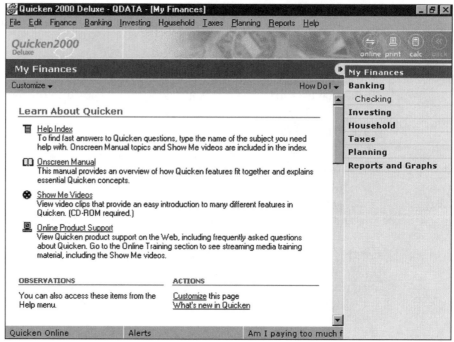

Figure 1-8:
The My
Finances
center.

In a nutshell, the My Finances center works like a web page with hyperlinks you click to move to different features of the Quicken program. (A *hyperlink* is just a piece of text or a picture you can click.) For example, if you look closely at the picture shown in Figure 1-8, you'll see the underlined phrase "What's new in Quicken" under the heading Actions in the My Finances window. If you click this bit of text, Quicken displays another window that tells you what's new in the latest version of Quicken.

You can scroll down the My Finances window to see more information — and you should do this. Quicken serves up a financial smorgasbord on the My Finances window, supplying you with all sorts of information. Once you've collected a bit of data with Quicken, for example, you'll be able to use the My Finances window to see account balances.

Chapter 2

Introduction to the Big Picture

- -

In This Chapter

▶ Distilling Quicken down to its very essence

▶ Setting up additional bank accounts

▶ Adding categories

▶ Removing categories

▶ Modifying categories

▶ Understanding classes

- -

*B*efore you spend a bunch of time and money on Quicken, you have to understand the big picture. You need to know what Quicken can do. You need to know what you actually want to do. And, as a practical matter, you need to tell Quicken what you want it to do.

Boiling Quicken Down to Its Essence

When you boil Quicken down to its essence, it does six things:

✔ **It lets you track your tax deductions.**

This feature makes preparing your personal or business tax return easier for you or your poor accountant, Cratchit.

✔ **It lets you monitor your income and outgo either on-screen or by using printed reports.**

Usually this stuff is great fodder for discussions about the family finances.

✔ **It lets you print checks.**

This device is mostly a time-saver, but it can also be useful for people who are neat freaks.

✔ **It lets you track the things you own (such as bank accounts, invest-ments, and real estate) and the debts you owe (such as home mortgage principal, car loan balances, and credit card balances).**

These things are really important to know.

✔ **It helps you make better personal financial planning decisions about such matters as retirement, your children's future college costs, and your savings and investments.**

I think this stuff is really neat.

✔ **It gives you the opportunity to pay bills electronically and, in some cases, even do all your banking electronically.**

This stuff is pretty neat, too, but I have some reservations that I discuss in Chapter 6, which deals with online banking in-depth.

Tracking tax deductions

To track your tax deductions, make a list of the deductions you want to track. To do so, pull out last year's tax return. Note which lines you filled in. This method works because there's a darn good chance that the tax deductions you claimed last year will also be the tax deductions you'll claim in the future.

I cover the Quicken categories, which you use to track your tax deductions, just a little bit later in this chapter.

Monitoring spending

At our house, we (my wife, Sue, and I, your humble author) use Quicken to monitor our spending on the mundane little necessities of life: groceries, clothing, baby food, cable television, and, well . . . you get the picture.

To keep track of how much we spend on various items, we also use the Quicken categories. (Is the suspense building?)

If you want to monitor a particular spending category, decide up front what the category should be before you begin recording your data.

Your list of spending categories, by the way, shouldn't be an exhaustive list of super-fine pigeonholes such as "Friday-night Mexican food," "Fast food for lunch," and so on. To track your spending on eating out, one category named something like "Meals" or "Grub" usually is easiest.

In fact, I'm going to go out on a limb. You can probably get away with half a dozen categories, more or less:

- ✔ Household items (food, toiletries, cleaning supplies)
- ✔ Car
- ✔ Rent (or mortgage payments)
- ✔ Utilities (electric, water, cable television)
- ✔ Entertainment and vacation
- ✔ Clothing
- ✔ Work expenses

If you want to, of course, you can expand this list. Heck, you can include dozens and dozens of categories. My experience, though, is that you'll probably use only a handful of categories.

Printing checks

You can use Quicken to print checks. This little trick provides a couple of benefits: It's really fast if you have several checks to print, and your printed checks look very neat and darn professional.

To print checks, you need to do just two things. First, look through the check supply information that comes with Quicken and pick a check form that suits your style. Then order the form. (The check forms that come with remittance *advices* — or check stubs — work well for businesses.)

Preprinted check forms aren't cheap. If you're using Quicken at home with personal-style checks (such as those that go in your wallet), using computer checks may not be cost effective. Even if you're using Quicken for a business and you are used to buying those outrageously expensive business-style checks, you'll still find computer checks a bit more expensive.

I'm pretty much a cheapskate, so I don't use printed checks at home (although I do use them in my business). I should admit, however, that I also don't write very many checks.

By the way, I've checked around. Although you can order Quicken check forms from other sources (such as your local office supplies store), they're about the same price from Intuit (the maker of Quicken). If you want to order from Intuit, you can refer to the catalog that came in the packaging. You can also visit Intuit's Web site, Quicken.com (www.quicken.com).

Tracking bank accounts, credit cards, and other stuff

You must decide which bank accounts and credit cards you want to track. In most cases, you want to track each bank account you use and any credit card on which you carry a balance.

You may also want to track other assets and liabilities. *Assets* are just things you own: investments, cars, a house, and so on. *Liabilities* are things you owe: margin loans from your broker, car loans, a mortgage, and so on.

Shoot, I suppose that you could even track the things your neighbor owns — or perhaps just those things you especially covet. I'm not sure that this is a very good idea, though. (Maybe a healthier approach is to track just those things that you've borrowed from your neighbor.)

Planning your personal finances

Your computer's computational horsepower makes it the ideal tool for doing complicated calculations. So maybe you're not very surprised that Quicken comes with five powerful calculators that let you make smarter borrowing choices, better mortgage-refinancing decisions, more accurate savings and investment calculations, and extremely helpful retirement and college savings calculations.

I believe that these financial planning tools are the most valuable features that Quicken offers. I'm just sorry that I have to wait until Chapter 10 to talk about them.

Banking online

If you want, you can tell Quicken that it should do the work of electronically paying some person or merchant. In other words, at the same time as you describe some check to Quicken — you do so by entering stuff into a window — you can say to Quicken, "I not only want you to record this check for me, but I also want you to pay for me."

If your bank supports online banking, you may also be able to move money between your accounts and get up-to-date statements electronically. Ask your bank for details about this service if you're interested.

To perform this sort of online banking, you need to have a modem. And you need to do a certain amount of paperwork. But the Quicken Online Banking features can save you scads of time. And the features are very easy to use.

Basically, all you do is use Quicken in the usual way — which is what I talk about in the chapters that follow — and then click a couple of extra buttons.

Setting Up Additional Accounts

When you begin working with a new Quicken file, you are prompted to set up an account. You probably set up a checking account, as this is probably your most active bank account. If you want to track any additional accounts — for example, a savings account — you must set them up, too.

Setting up another account

To set up an additional checking, savings, or money market account, you give the account a name and then its balance as of a set date. Here's how:

1. **Display the Banking center.**

   To do this, and you might even remember this from Chapter 1, click the Banking QuickTab (this is just the word "Banking" on the right edge of the window). Quicken displays the Banking center, as shown in Figure 2-1.

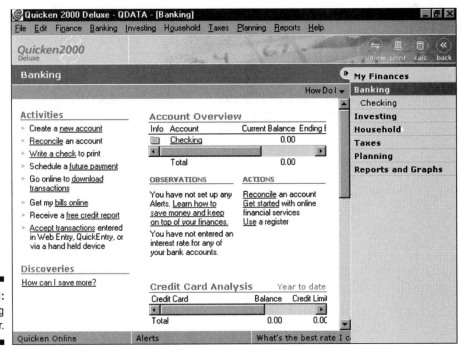

Figure 2-1:
The Banking center.

2. **Click the new account hyperlink.**

   The new account hyperlink appears in the upper-left corner of the Banking center window. The words new account are underlined. When you click, Quicken displays the Create New Account dialog box, shown in Figure 2-2.

Create New Account

Choose the type of account to create.

Banking & Cash	Investments	Home & Business
◉ Checking	○ Brokerage	○ House (with or w/o Mortgage)
○ Savings	○ IRA or Keogh	○ Vehicle (with or w/o Loan)
○ Credit Card	○ 401(k)	○ Asset
○ Money Market	○ Dividend Reinvestment Plan	○ Liability
○ Cash	○ Other Investment	

* If you are trying to set up a security such as a stock or bond, you should probably choose Brokerage. Click help for more information.

✗ Cancel   ? Help   ▷ Next

Figure 2-2:
The Create
New
Account
dialog box.

You can also display the Create New Account dialog box by choosing File⇨New, clicking the New Quicken Account option button, and clicking OK.

3. **Select the type of account.**

   Tell Quicken which type of account you want to set up by clicking one of the account buttons. (I'm assuming that at this point you want to set up either a checking or savings account.) When Quicken displays the Checking Account Setup dialog box, click the Summary tab (see Figure 2-3).

   Wondering about those other accounts? If the suspense is just killing you, you can skip ahead to later chapters in this book. Chapter 11 describes how you can set up and use Credit Card accounts. Chapter 12 describes how to set up and use Liability accounts. Chapters 13 and 14 describe how to set up and use Investment accounts, including 401(k) accounts. Chapter 15 describes how to set up and use a Cash account. And, finally, Chapter 17 describes how to set up and use Assets accounts. (Money market accounts work just like checking accounts.)

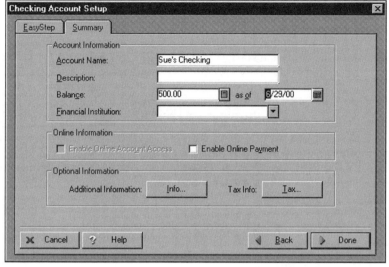

Figure 2-3:
The
Summary
tab of the
Checking
Account
Setup dialog
box.

4. **Name the account.**

   Move the cursor to the Account Name text box and enter a name.

5. **Move the cursor to the Description text box and describe the account in more detail if necessary.**

   The name you give your accounts may be the only description you need. I only name my accounts; I don't describe them. However, if you have several different accounts or especially if you have multiple accounts at the same bank, you may want to provide a description of the account by using the Description text box.

6. **Click the Balance text box and enter the bank account balance.**

   Use the number keys to enter the balance. The folks at Intuit, by the way, really want you to use the balance from your bank statement. If you have terrible financial records — for example, you haven't reconciled your account since George Bush left office — this idea is probably good advice. If you have neat, accurate financial records, go ahead and use your check register balance.

   By the way, if you do use the bank statement balance as your starting balance, be sure to enter all the transactions that cleared or will clear after the bank statement balance date. (This should make sense, right? If a check or deposit isn't reflected in the bank statement figure, you must enter it later.)

7. Enter the account balance date.

Enter the date that you're going to start keeping records for the bank account with Quicken. Move the cursor to the As Of text box and type the month number, a slash, the day number, a slash, and the year number. If you start on January 1, 2000, for example, type **1/1/00**. Or, if this is way too complicated for you, click the button at the end of the As Of text box so that Quicken displays a pop-up calendar. Then click the date. Use the << and >> buttons to move back and forth a month at a time.

Note: If you want to keep your transaction records for tax purposes, of course it makes sense to track whatever accounts you can from the first of the year, assuming you have all of the necessary statements or your own records of all the transactions.

8. Name the bank.

This step is optional, but if you'll be using Quicken's online banking capability, activate the Financial Institution drop-down list box and select the name of the bank. If you don't see your bank listed, your bank doesn't do the online banking thing.

9. Indicate whether you want to use the Quicken Online Banking or Online Bill Payment features.

If you want to use the Online Banking feature, mark the Enable Online Account Access check box. If you want to use the Online Bill Payment feature, mark the Enable Online Payment check box. After you click one of these boxes, Quicken changes the name of the Done button to Next. (Chapter 6 describes the Quicken online banking and bill-paying services.)

10. Collect a bit more information if you want.

If you click the Info button, Quicken displays a dialog box into which you can record a bunch of other information about the bank account you're setting up: the name of the bank, your account number, the name of the person whom you deal with at the bank, and so on. You can fill in this stuff if you want a reasonably convenient place to store this information. Otherwise, don't bother. I don't.

11. If the account's interest is tax-deferred, click the Tax button.

You may need to indicate whether an account's interest income is tax-deferred and whether transfers into or out of the account are tax-deductible. To do so, click the Tax button. Quicken displays the Tax Schedule Information dialog box, which lets you describe any tax implications of moving money to or from this account or of earning interest on the money in this account. Mark the Tax-Deferred Account check box to indicate that the interest earned on this account isn't taxable. Use the Transfers In and Transfers Out drop-down list boxes to describe which line of your tax return any transfers into or out of this account should be reported on. *Note:* Just for the record, it's highly unlikely that this tax schedule stuff applies to a simple bank account.

12. Choose Done or Next.

> If you didn't choose to use Quicken's Online Account Access or Online Payment features, the Done button is in the lower-right corner of the screen. After you click this button, Quicken redisplays the Account List window — just like the one shown in Figure 2-1. This time, however, the window lists an additional account — the one you just created.

> If you indicated in Step 9 that you want to use the Online Account Access or Online Payment features, Quicken changes the name of the Done button to Next. After you click the Next button, Quicken displays a dialog box that asks for the name of the bank, its routing number, your account number, the bank account type, and your Social Security number. The sign-up and welcome letter that you receive from your bank provides the bank name and routing numbering information. (Hopefully, you know the account type you've just created — probably a checking account. And you should know your Social Security number, right?)

Hey, Quicken, I want to use that account!

In Quicken, you work with one account at a time. The logic is quite simple: You record income and expenses for a particular account — a specific checking account, savings account, and so on.

You use the Banking center window (refer to Figure 2-1) to tell Quicken which account you want to work with because it provides clickable hyperlinks you can use to move to the account.

To display the Banking center window, click the Banking QuickTab. (If you're experiencing a sense of déjà vu right now, it's probably because I describe these techniques earlier in the chapter, too.) Let me also mention that you can also use Banking menu to get to the Banking Activity window. To do this, click the Banking menu and then click the Banking center command.

After you display the Banking center, select the account you want by clicking the mouse. Quicken selects the account and displays the register window.

Whipping Your Category Lists into Shape

When you set up Quicken, you tell it which of the predefined home categories you want to use and whether you need to use business categories.

The predefined categories lists may be just what you want. Then again, they may not. Table 2-1 shows the all-inclusive home categories list, and Table 2-2 shows the business categories list. If you tell Quicken to use all of the home and business categories, your actual category list combines the categories shown in Table 2-1 and those shown in Table 2-2.

Your categories list may vary slightly from the ones shown in Tables 2-1 and 2-2. Quicken may customize your starting categories list based on your answer to questions it asks in the New User Setup dialog box.

Take a minute to look through both lists. If you find categories you don't need, cross them off the list in the book. You can delete them in a minute or so on your computer. If you need categories you don't see, add them at the bottom of the list. You can add them in about two minutes or so.

✔ To track a certain income or spending item for income tax purposes, you need a Quicken category.

✔ To track a certain income or spending item because you're just interested in knowing how much you spend on it (for example, renting VCR tapes), you need a Quicken category.

✔ To budget by categories (because you need a category for any income or spending item that you want to budget), you need a Quicken category.

Table 2-1 The Category List for Married Homeowners with Children

Categories	Descriptions
Income Categories	
Bonus	Bonus money you receive
Div Income	Dividend income
Gift Received	Gift received
Interest Inc	Interest income
Invest Inc	Investment income
Other Inc	Other income
Salary	Salary income

Categories	*Descriptions*	
Income Categories		
Salary Spouse	Salary income for your spouse	
Tax Refund	That check you get back from the tax man if you withhold more than you owe	
Unemployment Inc	Unemployment benefits	
Expense Categories		
Auto	Automobile expenses	
	Fuel	Auto fuel
	Insurance	Auto insurance
	Registration	Auto registration, plates, or license tabs
	Service	Auto service
Bank Charge	Banking fees	
Cash	Miscellaneous cash purchases	
Charity	Charitable donations	
Childcare	Childcare	
Clothing	Clothing	
Dining	Dining out	
Education	Education	
Entertainment	Entertainment	
Gifts Given	Gift expenses	
Groceries	Groceries	
Household	Miscellaneous household expenses	
Housing	Housing	
Insurance	Insurance	
Interest Exp	Interest expense	

(continued)

Table 2-1 *(continued)*

Categories	Descriptions	
Expense Categories		
IRA Contrib	Individual Retirement Account contribution	
IRA Contrib Spouse	Individual Retirement Account contribution for spouse	
Medical	Medical expense	
	Doctor	Doctor and dental visits
	Medicine	Medicine and drugs
Misc	Miscellaneous	
Mortgage Int	Mortgage Interest	
	Bank	Mortgage interest paid to a financial institution
	Individual	Mortgage interest paid to a private individual (and not reported on form 1098)
Recreation	Recreation expense	
Rent	Housing rent	
Subscriptions	Subscriptions	
Tax	Taxes	
	Fed	Federal income tax
	Medicare	Medicare tax
	Other	Miscellaneous taxes
	Property	Property tax
	SDI	State Disability Insurance
	Soc Sec	Social Security tax
	State	State income tax
Tax Spouse	Employment taxes for your spouse	
	Fed	Federal income tax
	Medicare	Medicare tax
	Soc Sec	Social Security tax
	State	State income tax

Categories	Descriptions	
Expense Categories		
Utilities	Water, gas, electric — and, oh yeah, cable	
	Cable TV	Cable television
	Gas and electric	Gas and electricity
	Telephone	Telephone
	Water	Water
Vacation	Vacation expenses	
	Lodging	Motel/Hotel costs
Travel	Transportation expense	

Table 2-2	The Predefined Business Categories	
Categories	**Descriptions**	
Income Categories		
Consulting	Consulting revenue	
Finance Charge	Finance charge revenue	
Gr Sales	Gross sales revenue	
Other Inc	Other income such as interest income	
Services	Service revenue	
Expense Categories		
Ads	Advertising expenditures	
Bad Debt	Bad debt expenses	
Car	Car and truck	
Commission	Sales commissions	
Discounts	Discounts given expense	
Dues and Subscriptions	Dues and subscription expense	
Insurance, Bus	Business insurance premiums	

(continued)

Table 2-2 *(continued)*

Categories	Descriptions		
Expense Categories			
Int Paid	Interest and financing expense		
Late Fees	Late payment fees . . . ouch		
Legal-Prof Fees	Legal and professional fees . . . ouch again		
Licenses and Permits	Licenses, permits, and other stuff like that		
Meals & Entertn	Meals and entertainment		
Miscellaneous, Bus	Miscellaneous business expense		
Office	Office expenses		
Postage and Delivery Expense	Postage, courier, and delivery		
Printing and Reproduction	Printing, photocopying, and reproduction		
Rent on Equipment	Rent-Vehicle, machine, equipment		
Rent Paid	Rent paid		
Repairs	Repairs		
Returns	Returns and allowances		
Supplies, Bus	Business supplies		
Tax, Business	Taxes and licenses		
	Fed	Federal taxes	
	Local	Local taxes	
	Property	Property taxes	
	State	State taxes	
Travel, Bus	Business travel		
Utilities, Bus	Business utilities		
Telephone, Bus	Telephone bills		
Wages	Wages, salaries, and job credits		

Subcategories . . . yikes, what are they?

You surely didn't buy Quicken so that you could spend all day Saturday sitting at your computer instead of taking the kids to the zoo. I realize this, and want to make Quicken easier for you to use. In order to do so, I figure I should tell you which Quicken features you can ignore if you're feeling a bit overwhelmed. Subcategories are among those things I think you can ignore.

"Subcategories?" you say. "Yikes! What are they?"

Subcategories are categories within categories. If you look at the Taxes expense category in Table 2-1, for example, you'll notice a bunch of categories that follow the Tax category and are slightly indented: Fed (federal tax), Medicare (Medicare tax), Other (miscellaneous taxes), Prop (property tax), Soc Sec (Social Security tax), and State (state tax).

When you use subcategories, you can tag a transaction that pays, for example, federal taxes; you can further break down this category into subcategories such as federal income tax, Medicare tax, and Social Security tax. If you want to see a list of the ways you've spent your money, Quicken summarizes your spending both by category and, within a category, by subcategory. On a Quicken report, then, you can see this level of detail:

```
Taxes
Federal Tax      900
Medicare Tax     100
Soc Sec Tax      700
Total Taxes    1,700
```

No doubt about it, subcategories are useful tools. But they make working with Quicken a little more complicated and a little more difficult. As a practical matter, you usually don't need them. If you want to track a spending category, it really belongs on your list as a full-fledged category. For these reasons, I'm not going to get into subcategories here.

If you get excited about the topic of subcategories later on — after you have the hang of Quicken — you can peruse the Quicken documentation for more information.

If you *do* want to use the Quicken subcategories, don't delete the subcategories shown in Table 2-1. If you *don't* want to use the subcategories, go ahead and delete them. (I tell you how to remove categories later in this chapter.)

Category groups . . . double yikes!

Groups are a recent invention of the Intuit development people. Category groups, which were known as supercategories in the last version of Quicken, combine categories into sets that you can use in reports and in your budgeting. Sure, they're sort of cool, but you don't need to worry about them if you're just starting with Quicken.

If you're just dying to know more about Category groups, you can refer to the Quicken online help.

Four tips on categorization

I have just four tips for categorizing:

- ✔ **Cross off any category you won't use.**

  If you don't pay state income taxes in the state you live in, for example, get rid of the state tax category. Extra, unneeded categories just clutter your list. I think it's great if you can get down to just a handful of categories.

- ✔ **Don't be afraid to lump similar spending categories together.**

  Take your utilities expense, for example. If you pay water, natural gas, electricity, and sewer, why not use a single Utilities category? If you pay different utility companies for your water, natural gas, electricity, and sewer, you can still see what you spend on just electricity, for example, even with a single catch-all category for utilities.

- ✔ **Be sure to categorize anything that may be a tax deduction.**

  Categorize medical and dental expenses, state and local income taxes, real estate taxes, personal property taxes, home mortgage interest and points, investment interest, charitable contributions, casualty and theft losses, moving expenses, unreimbursed employee expenses, and all those vague, miscellaneous deductions. (By the way, the foregoing is the complete list of itemized deductions at the time this book was written.)

- ✔ **Don't sweat this category stuff too much.**

  In spite of the preceding three tips, don't let these category lists or the work of customizing them scare you. If you want to spend a few minutes cleaning the list up, hey, that's great. If not or you're starting to get nervous, just skip ahead to the next section of this chapter — the one that discusses Quicken's Classes feature.

Ch-ch-changing a category list

Okay, you should now be ready to fix any category list problems. Basically, you need to do three things: add categories, remove categories, and change category names and descriptions.

Adding categories you'd love to use

Adding categories is a snap. Here's all you have to do:

1. **Choose Finance⇨Category & Transfer List.**

   Quicken displays the Category & Transfer List window (see Figure 2-4). This window lists the categories available and the accounts you've set up.

2. **Click the New button on the Category & Transfer List window.**

   The New button, by the way, is the first button on the left. Quicken, dutifully following your every command, displays the Set Up Category dialog box (see Figure 2-5). You probably aren't surprised that you use this puppy to describe the new category.

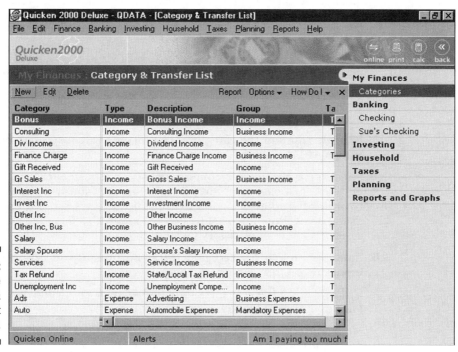

Figure 2-4:
The
Category &
Transfer List
window.

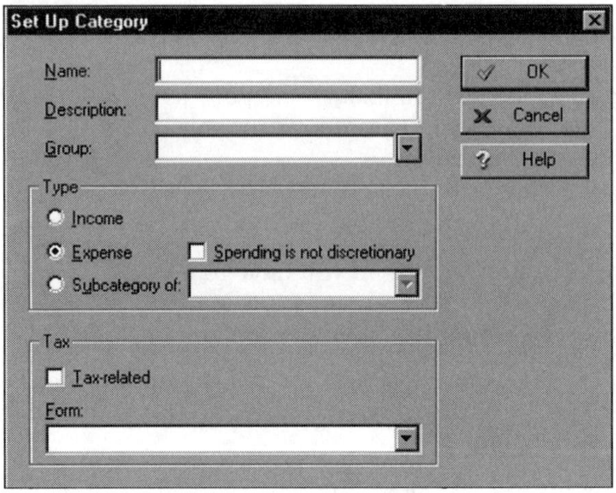

Figure 2-5:
The Set Up
Category
dialog box.

3. **Enter a short name for the category.**

   Move the cursor to the Name text box and type a name. Although you can use up to 15 characters, use as short a name as possible to clearly identify the category. Why? Because you use this category name every time you want to tag a transaction to fall into the category.

4. **Enter a description for the category.**

   Move the cursor to the Description text box and then describe the category. Quicken uses the category description on reports that show the category. If you don't add a description, Quicken just uses the category name. You don't need a description, obviously, if your category name is, well, adequately descriptive.

5. **Indicate whether the category is an income category or an expense category.**

   Select the appropriate Income, Expense, or Subcategory of option button — just click your furry little friend, the mouse. If you've totally blown off my admonition not to use subcategories just yet, use the dialog box's drop-down list to indicate into which income or expense category a new subcategory falls.

6. **Indicate whether the category tracks an amount you will use on an input line on next year's tax return.**

   By *line,* I mean the actual tax form line — such as the line on the 1040 form that tracks alimony.

   Move the cursor to the Tax-Related check box and then select the check box if the category is tax-related or deselect the check box if the category isn't tax-related. Just to clear up any confusion, vacationing in Hawaii probably isn't a tax deduction — even if your neighbor promises it is. Then identify the form and line by opening the Form drop-down list box and selecting one of its entries.

7. Click OK.

Quicken adds the new category to the Category & Transfer List window, shown in Figure 2-4, and then redisplays the window. Now that you understand the stuff in the Category & Transfer List window, note that it shows the category name, its type, the notation that a category is tax-related, and, golly darn, even its description.

Removing categories you loathe

Removing categories takes only a couple of keystrokes. With the Category & Transfer List window displayed, use the arrow keys or click the mouse to select the category you want to remove. Then click Delete. Quicken displays a message that asks you to confirm your decision. Assuming that you want to remove the selected category, click OK. Otherwise, press Esc or click Cancel.

Changing category names and descriptions

You can change a category name, its type, its description, and its tax-related setting if you later discover you've made some mistake, such as misspelling a word in a description.

To do so, display the Category & Transfer List window, as shown in Figure 2-4. Use the arrow keys or click your mouse to select the category you want to change. Then select the category and click the Edit button. Quicken displays a dialog box that has text boxes and option buttons describing the selected category's information: its name, description, type, and tax-related settings.

Make the changes you want by replacing text box contents or changing option button settings. Then click OK to save your changes and return to the Category & Transfer List window.

Do You Need a Little Class?

Categories aren't the only way you can summarize your financial records. Quicken provides a second tool, called *classes,* which also lets you summarize transactions in some way in addition to the way you summarize transactions with categories.

I have mixed feelings about classes, and I'll tell you why. For my business, I used to use them — with good success — to track the types of gross income that my business produces (writing, consulting, teaching, and so on) and the types of expenses my business incurs in these activities. (In fact, Writing, Consulting, and Teaching are the names of three of my classes.)

Classes present a couple of problems, however. First, you can't budget by classes. (Before you say, "Ah, Steve, I don't want to budget," please read the next chapter.) Second, you need to remember to tag transactions with their classes. (Quicken doesn't remind you to include classes but does remind you to include a category.)

Because I honestly don't think you'll use it now, I'm not going to describe how you use classes. But if you get really comfortable with the Quicken categories and you want a way to organize your financial information across categories, consider using the Quicken classes. You can turn to Quicken's online help to get the information you need.

Chapter 3
Maximum Fun, Maximum Profits

● ●

In This Chapter
▶ Deciding whether you need a budget
▶ Tips for personal budgets
▶ Tips for business budgets
▶ Setting up a budget manually
▶ Setting up a budget automatically

● ●

1 don't think a budget amounts to financial handcuffs, and neither should you. A budget is really a plan that outlines the way people need to spend their money to achieve the maximum amount of fun or the way businesses need to spend their money to make the most profit.

Should You Even Bother?

A budget, as you probably know, is just a list of the ways you earn and spend your money. And if you create a good, workable categories list with Quicken (see Chapter 2), you're halfway to a good, solid budget. (In fact, the only step left is to specify how much you earn in each income category and how much you spend in each expense category.)

Does everybody need a budget? No, of course not. Maybe at your house you're already having a bunch of fun with your money. Maybe in your business you make money so effortlessly that you really don't plan your income and outgo.

For the rest of us, though, a budget improves our chances of getting to wherever it is we want to go financially. In fact, I'll stop calling it a budget. The word has such negative connotations. I know — I'll call it a *Secret Plan.*

Serious Advice about Your Secret Plan

Before I walk you through the mechanics of outlining your Secret Plan, I want to give you a few tips.

Your personal Secret Plan

You can do four things to make your Secret Plan more likely to work:

✓ **Plan your income and expenses as a family.**

With this sort of planning, two heads are invariably better than one. What's more, though I don't really want to get into marriage counseling here, a family's budget — oops, I mean Secret Plan — needs to reflect the priorities and feelings of everyone who has to live within the plan. Don't use a Secret Plan as a way to minimize what your spouse spends on clothing or on long-distance telephone charges talking to relatives in the old country. You need to resolve clothing and long-distance charges issues before you finalize your Secret Plan.

✓ **Include some cushion in your plan.**

In other words, don't budget to spend every last dollar (or if you're German, every last Deutschmark). If you plan from the start to spend every dollar you make, you undoubtedly have to fight the mother of all financial battles: paying for unexpected expenses when you don't have any money.

✓ **Regularly compare your actual income and outgo to your planned income and outgo.**

This part of your plan is probably the most important and also the part that Quicken helps you with the most. As long as you use Quicken to record what you receive and spend, you can print reports showing what you planned and what actually occurred.

✓ **Make adjustments as necessary.**

When you have problems with your Secret Plan — and you will — you'll know that your plan isn't working. You can then make adjustments, by spending a little less calling the old country, for example.

Two things that really goof up Secret Plans

Because I am talking about you-know-what, let me touch on a couple of things that really goof up your financial plans: windfalls and monster changes.

Your business Secret Plan

The tips for personal Secret Plans also apply to businesses. But I have a special tip for small businesses using Quicken. (I'm going to write very quietly now so that no one else hears. . . .)

Here's the secret tip: Go to the library, ask for the Robert Morris & Associates survey, and look up the ways that other businesses like yours spend money.

This survey is really cool. Robert Morris & Associates surveys bank lending officers, creates a summary of the information these bankers receive from their customers, and publishes the results. For example, you can look up what percentage of sales the average tavern spends on beer and peanuts.

Plan to take an hour or so at the library. It takes a while to get used to the way the Robert Morris & Associates information is displayed. The survey won't actually have a line on the tavern's page labeled "beer and peanuts," for example. It'll be called "cost of goods sold" or some similarly vague accounting term.

Remember to make a few notes so that you can use the information you glean to better plan your own business financial affairs.

The problem with windfalls

Your boss smiles, calls you into his office, and then gives you the good news. You're getting a bonus: $5,000! "About time," you think to yourself. Outside, of course, you maintain your dignity. You act grateful but not gushy. Then you call your husband.

Here's what happens next. Bob (that's your husband's name) gets excited, congratulates you, and tells you he'll pick up a bottle of wine on the way home to celebrate.

On your drive home, you mull over the possibilities and conclude that you can use the $5,000 as a big down payment for that new family van you've been looking at. (With the trade-in and the $5,000, your payments will be a manageable $200 a month.)

Bob, on his way home, stops to look at those golf clubs he's been coveting for about three years, charges $800 on his credit card, and then, feeling slightly guilty, buys you the $600 set. (Pretend that you're just starting to play golf.)

You may laugh at this scenario, but suppose that it really happened. Furthermore, pretend that you really do buy the van. At this point, you've spent $6,400 on a van and golf clubs, and you've signed up for what you're guessing will be another $200-a-month payment.

This turn of events doesn't sound all that bad now, does it?

Here's the problem: When you get your check, it's not going to be $5,000. You're probably going to pay roughly $400 in Social Security and Medicare taxes, maybe around $1,500 in federal income taxes, and then probably some state income taxes. Other money may be taken out, too, for forced savings plans (such as a 401(k) plan) or for charitable giving. After all is said and done, you'll get maybe half the bonus in cash — say $2,500.

Now you see the problem, of course. You have $2,500 in cold, hard cash, but with Bob's help, you've already spent $6,400 and signed up for $200-a-month payments.

In a nutshell, you face two big problems with windfalls. Problem one is that you never get the entire windfall — yet spending as if you will is quite easy. Problem two is that windfalls, by their very nature, tend to get used for big purchases (often as down payments) that ratchet up your living expenses. Boats. New houses. Cars.

Regarding windfalls, my advice to you is simple:

- ✔ Don't spend a windfall until you actually hold the check in your hot little hand. (You're even better off to wait, say, six months. That way Bob can really think about whether he needs those new golf clubs.)
- ✔ Don't spend a windfall on something that increases your monthly living expenses without first redoing your budget.

The problem with monster income changes

If your income changes radically, planning a budget becomes *really* hard. Suppose that your income doubles. One day you're cruising along making $35,000, and the next day, you're suddenly making $70,000. (Congratulations, by the way.) I'll tell you what you'll discover, however, should you find yourself in this position. You'll find that $70,000 a year isn't as much money as you may think.

Go ahead. Laugh. But for one thing, if your income doubles, your income taxes almost certainly more than quadruple.

One of the great myths about income taxes is that the rich don't pay very much or that they pay the same percentage. Poppycock. If you make $30,000 a year and you're an average family, you probably pay about $1,500 in federal income taxes. If you make $200,000 a year, you'll pay about $45,000 a year. So if your salary increases by roughly 7 times, your income taxes increase by about 30 times. I don't bring this fact up to get you agitated about whether it's right or fair to make the rich pay more; I bring it up so that you can better plan for any monster income changes you experience.

Another thing — and I know it sounds crazy — but you'll find it hard to spend $70,000 smartly when you've been making a lot less. And if you start making some big purchases such as houses and cars and speedboats, you'll not only burn through a great deal of cash, but you'll also ratchet up your monthly living expenses.

Monster income changes that go the other way are even more difficult. If you've been making, say, $70,000 a year and then see your salary drop to a darn respectable $35,000, it's going to hurt, too. And probably more than you think. That old living-expenses ratcheting effect comes into play here, of course. Presumably, if you've been making $70,000 a year, you've been spending it — or most of it.

But other reasons contribute — at least initially — to making a monster salary drop very difficult. You've probably chosen friends, clothing stores, and hobbies that are in line with your income.

Another thing about a monster salary drop is sort of subtle. You probably denominate your purchases in amounts related to your income. Make $35,000 and you think in terms of $5 or $10 purchases. But make $70,000 a year and you think in terms of $10 or $20 purchases. This observation all makes perfect sense. But if your income drops from $70,000 down to $35,000, you'll probably still find yourself thinking of those old $20 purchases.

So what to do? If you do experience a monster income change, redo your Secret Plan. And be particularly careful and thoughtful.

Living with creature comforts

To conclude this Secret Plan business, I'll make a philosophical digression.

If you provide yourself and your family with the creature comforts — a cozy place to live, adequate food, and comfortable clothes — more stuff doesn't make the difference that you think.

I don't mean to minimize the challenges of raising a family of four on, say, $14,000 a year. But, hey, in my business I see a fair number of wealthy people. What continually surprises me is that when you get right down to it, someone who makes $300,000 or $600,000 a year doesn't live a better life than someone who makes $30,000.

Sure, they spend more money. They buy more stuff. They buy more expensive stuff. But they don't live better. They don't have better marriages. Their kids don't love them more. They don't have better friends or more considerate neighbors. But you already know all this. I know you do.

Setting Up a Secret Plan

Okay, now you're ready to set up your budget — er, I mean, Secret Plan.

Introducing Budget window

To get to the window in which you enter your budget, choose the Planning➪Budgeting command. Quicken displays a message box that says something about creating your first budget. Just press Enter. Don't even worry about reading the message. Quicken next displays the Budget window, and it should look like the window shown in Figure 3-1.

Note: One weird little point I'll mention here. If you've been using Quicken for a while before you tangle with this budget stuff, Quicken creates a starting budget based on transactions in your accounts for the month prior to the current month. This setup means, then, that the Budget window won't only show zeros.

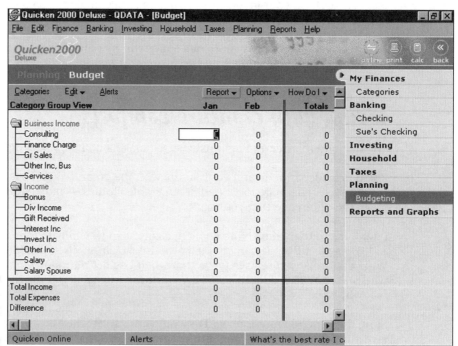

Figure 3-1:
The Budget window.

If the Budget window doesn't look like the one shown in Figure 3-1, follow these three simple steps:

1. **Click the Categories button so that Quicken displays the Select Categories to Include dialog box.**

2. **Click the Mark All button.**

3. **Click OK.**

The window is not very complicated. The income and expense categories — including the ones that you created earlier — appear along the left edge of the screen. Any categories with subcategories (if you have these) contain subtotals for the total inflows and for the total outflows.

Across the top of the screen is a row of command buttons that makes your budgeting job easier. (I describe the more useful commands just a little later in this chapter and provide brief descriptions of those that aren't quite as useful.)

Entering budgeted amounts the simple way

Here's the two-step way to enter budgeted amounts — not to be confused with the Texas Two-Step:

1. **Select the amount you want to budget.**

   Select the budgeted income or expense amount that you want to enter either by using the arrow keys or by clicking the amount with the mouse. For example, to select the January Salary budget field, click its number with the mouse. Or use the arrow keys to move the square and select the field. (You're doing this stuff so that you can enter the budgeted amount.)

2. **Enter the budgeted amount.**

   Type the amount you've budgeted and press Enter. Suppose that you've already selected the January Salary budget field and now need to enter a value. Say that you take home $3,000 a month. To use this figure as the January Salary budget, type **3000**.

After you press Enter, Quicken updates any subtotals and grand totals that use the salary income amount, as shown in Figure 3-2. For example, look at the Total Income subtotal at the bottom of the screen. And look at the Totals column along the right edge of the window.

Since we're talking about the Budget window's geography, I'll mention one other thing here: Notice the Edit button. (It's the second one from the left.) Later in the chapter, I tell you about all the cool things it lets you do.

You need to scroll the screen to the right to see months near the middle and end of the year. Unless you're using a really short categories list, you need to scroll down to see categories (usually expense categories) that aren't at the top of the list.

The easiest way to scroll is by using the mouse to click and drag on the scroll bars. If you don't already know how to do this, you can experiment (probably the most fun) or you can flip to Appendix A.

If you don't want to use the mouse or you just need to be different, you can use the old arrow keys, too. To scroll the screen right, just press the Tab key. To scroll the screen back, or left, press Shift+Tab. To scroll the screen up and down, use the PgUp and PgDn keys.

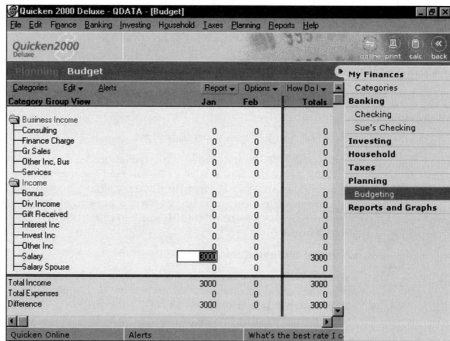

Figure 3-2:
The Budget window showing salary income for January.

The list of categories doesn't scroll off the screen. You know what else? The Totals column doesn't scroll off the screen either. Quicken leaves these elements frozen in the window so that you can tell which column and row is which and how things are going.

Entering budgeted amounts the fast way

It just figures, doesn't it? You have the simple way and then you have the fast way, and "never the twain shall meet."

If monthly budgeted amounts are the same over the year

Take the following steps if your monthly budget stays the same over the course of the year:

1. **Enter the first month's figures (as I describe earlier).**

   You do this as described in the "Entering budgeted amounts the simple way" section.

2. **Click the Edit button.**

   Quicken displays a menu of commands.

3. **Choose Fill Columns.**

   If you click Yes in the dialog box that appears, Quicken takes your January budget numbers and copies them into February, March, April, and through the rest of the year.

What if you make a mistake? What if you fill some row with a bunch of goofy numbers? No problem. Move the selection cursor to that row, click the Edit button, and choose Clear Row.

If budgeted amounts are the same as last year

If you used Quicken for record keeping in the prior year, you can copy the actual amounts from the previous year and use these as part or all of the current year's budget.

To do so, click the Edit button and choose Autocreate. Quicken displays the Automatically Create Budget dialog box, as shown in Figure 3-3. You can then tell Quicken what it should copy from last year.

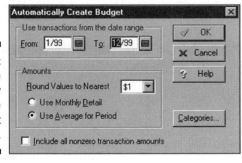

Figure 3-3:
The
Automatically
Create
Budget
dialog box.

Here's how to use this dialog box:

1. **Indicate which months you want to copy.**

   Use the From and To text boxes to indicate from which months in the previous year actual category totals should be copied. If you want to copy the entire previous year's totals and it's now 2000, for example, specify these entries as **1/99** and **12/99**.

2. **Indicate whether the actual category totals should be rounded.**

   Want to round the actual category totals? No problem. Just use the Round Values to Nearest drop-down list box to indicate how much rounding you want: to the nearest $1, to the nearest $10, or to the nearest $100.

3. **Use category averages (optional).**

   To use the average actual spending in a category for the months identified in the From and To text boxes, indicate that you want to use averages for the period. To do so, select the Use Average for Period option button. If you leave the Use Monthly Detail option button selected, Quicken doesn't calculate and use averages; it just uses the actual monthly amounts from the previous year as the budgeted monthly amounts for the current year.

4. **Limit the categories automatically budgeted (optional).**

   To tell Quicken that you want only some of your categories automatically budgeted, click the Categories button. Quicken displays the Select Categories to Include dialog box (see Figure 3-4). Indicate which categories should be automatically budgeted by clicking them. To mark or unmark a category, click the category. To mark all the categories, click Mark All. To unmark all the categories, click Clear All. After you select the categories that you want to include as part of the automatic budget creation, click OK. Quicken closes the Select Categories to Include dialog box.

5. **Click OK.**

   Quicken uses the information that you enter on the Automatically Create Budget dialog box and the previous year's actual category totals to completely fill in the Budget window.

If a single category's monthly budget is the same over the year

Hey, you're on a roll now. So suppose that a single category's monthly budget is the same over the year.

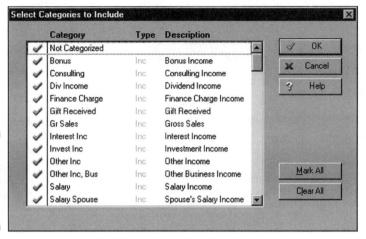

Figure 3-4:
The Select
Categories
to Include
dialog box.

To create a budget, enter the first month's budget figure (as I describe earlier). Click the Edit button and choose Fill Row Right. If you choose Yes, Quicken takes the budget number for the selected category and copies it into the following months — probably February, March, April, and so on — through the rest of the year.

You can use Fill Row Right to copy budget amounts forward from months besides January. For example, if your rent runs $500 a month from January through June and then $600 from July through December, enter **500** into the January Rent field and use the Fill Row Right command to fill the rest of the year. Then enter **600** into the July Rent field. If you choose Fill Row Right again, Quicken copies 600 forward to August, September, October, November, and December.

If you want to budget biweekly amounts

Sometimes budgeting amounts on a monthly basis doesn't make much sense because you actually receive or spend on a biweekly basis. What if you're paid every two weeks? Or what if your bowling league meets every other Thursday? See the dilemma? You won't really know how many two-week periods a given month has unless you look at a calendar and start counting with your fingers.

Lucky for you, Quicken provides a handy tool for budgeting those sorts of biweekly amounts: the Two-Week Command, which appears on the Quicken Edit button's menu. To use this command, select the category that you want to budget biweekly and then choose the command. Quicken displays the Set Up Two-Week Budget dialog box. Coincidentally, this dialog box appears in Figure 3-5.

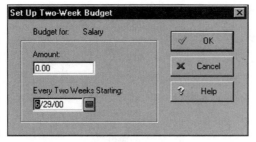

Figure 3-5:
The Set Up
Two-Week
Budget
dialog box.

Enter the biweekly amount in the Amount text box. Enter the first date you'll receive or spend the amount in the Every Two Weeks Starting text box and then click OK.

After you finish entering your budget

After you enter your Secret Plan, either the simple way or the fast way (if you're the adventurous type), you don't have to do anything special to save your work. When you leave the Budget window or close it, Quicken automatically saves your work for you.

If you want to revert to the previously saved version of the budget, click the Options button and then choose the Restore command.

I talk more about using the budget in later chapters (such as Chapter 7, for example). If you want to print a *hard copy* (Computerese for *paper*) of the budget, click the Print button and press Enter. If you have a printing question, go to Chapter 5.

You're not going to use the Secret Plan for a while. But don't worry. In Chapter 5, I explain how to print reports, including a report that compares your actual spending with your budget. Stay tuned. Same time. Same place.

More about the Options button

The Options button, which I mention in the previous section, provides some useful commands. Quick as a bunny, then, I want to describe what you do with this button's commands.

After you click the Options button, Quicken displays the Options menu. Because I thought you just may be interested in what this baby looks like, I include it as Figure 3-6. See? The bulleted list that follows describes what the mysterious commands do.

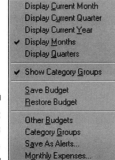

Display Current Month
Display Current Quarter
Display Current Year
✔ Display Months
Display Quarters

✔ Show Category Groups

Save Budget
Restore Budget

Other Budgets
Category Groups
Save As Alerts...
Monthly Expenses...

Figure 3-6:
The Options
menu.

✔ **Display Current Month.** Tells Quicken that you want to budget for the current month. Quicken determines which month is the current one by looking at the system date on your computer.

✔ **Display Current Quarter.** Tells Quicken that you want to budget for the current quarter. Again, Quicken determines which quarter is the current one by looking at the system date that Windows maintains.

✔ **Display Current Year.** Tells Quicken that you really are a Big Picture person (or business) and that you'll be budgeting for the year, so it should display the current year. (If you flip-flop between months, quarters, and years, Quicken automatically converts the budget figures for you.)

✔ **Display Months.** Tells Quicken that you want to budget by the month, so it should display columns for each month. Quicken budgets by the month unless you tell it to do otherwise, so this command is already checked unless you told Quicken to budget using some other time unit.

✔ **Display Quarters.** Tells Quicken that you want to budget by the quarter.

✔ **Show Category Groups.** This command works like a toggle switch. It tells Quicken that either you do want to budget by category group or you don't want to budget by category group. You can turn the command off and on by choosing the command.

✔ **Save Budget.** Saves your most recent set of changes to a budget.

✔ **Restore Budget.** Undoes your most recent set of unsaved changes to a budget.

✔ **Other Budgets.** Displays the Manage Budgets dialog box, which I describe in the paragraphs that follow this bulleted list.

✔ **Category Groups.** Displays the Assign Category Groups dialog box so that you can set up category groups. I'm assuming that you won't be working with category groups in this book. In fact, I advise that you don't in Chapter 2. But, you're your own man or woman. And that means you make your own decisions.

✔ **Save As Alerts.** Displays the Save Budget Alerts Options dialog box, which lets you tell Quicken that it should alert you whenever your actual spending begins to approach the budgeted amount. The dialog box, as you would expect, provides a bunch of buttons and boxes you use to tell Quicken how it should alert.

✔ **Monthly Expenses.** Displays the Set Up Alerts dialog box that you use to tell Quicken it should alert you whenever you've spent more than an indicated amount for a category. Note that the indicated amount for this command isn't based on the budgeted amount but on an amount you specify using the Set Up Alerts dialog box.

When you choose the Other Budgets command, the Manage Budgets dialog box appears (see Figure 3-7). The Manage Budgets dialog box is pretty neat. It lets you create more than one budget. To do so, you display the Manage Budgets dialog box, click the Create button, and then, when prompted, give the new budget a unique name. Something really clever. Whenever you want to use that budget, you display the Manage Budgets dialog box, click the budget you want to work with, and then click the Open button.

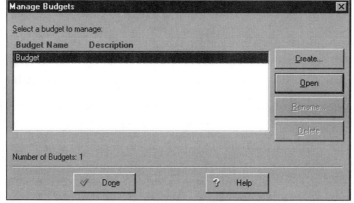

Figure 3-7:
The
Manage
Budgets
dialog box.

Wanna budget with a spreadsheet?

By using the Edit button's Copy All command — remember that a menu appears when you click the Edit button — you can copy the budget information shown in the Budget window to the Clipboard. (The clipboard is a temporary storage device you use to move information between and within Windows programs.) After the budget information is there, you can start a Windows spreadsheet program such as Excel and use Edit⇨Paste to paste the budgeting stuff stored on the Clipboard into the spreadsheet. If you're familiar with a Windows spreadsheet, such as Excel, go ahead and try it. You might like it — if you want to use the spreadsheet program to analyze the data.

Part II
The Absolute Basics

The 5th Wave   By Rich Tennant

"WE TOOK A GAMBLE AND INVESTED ALL OUR MONEY IN A RACE HORSE. THEN IT RAN AWAY."

In this part . . .

Okay, you're ready for the show to start (which is good). This part — "The Absolute Basics" — covers all the nitty-gritty details of using Quicken to keep your personal and business financial records. Whether you're just starting to use the Quicken program or you've just come from Part I, you'll find the stuff covered here dang important — dare I say essential — to using Quicken in even the most basic way.

Chapter 4

Checkbook on a Computer

● ●

In This Chapter

▶ Recording checks

▶ Recording deposits

▶ Recording transfers

▶ Splitting categories

▶ Deleting and voiding transactions

▶ Memorizing transactions

● ●

*T*his is it. The big time. You're finally going to do those everyday Quicken things: entering checks, deposits, and transfers. Along the way, you'll also use some of the neat tools that Quicken provides for making these tasks easier, more precise, and faster.

Getting Started

Okay. I'm going to start at the very beginning. After you install Quicken and set up your first account (or two), you see the My Finances window whenever you start Quicken (see Figure 4-1). "What's the Quicken My Finances window?" you ask. Good question. Basically, it looks and works (sort of) like a web page that provides clickable hyperlinks to some of the most popular features of Quicken and supplies little interesting tidbits of financial trivia. (If you worked with the previous version of Quicken, you may remember this page by another name, the Quicken Home Page.)

You actually won't work much with the My Finances window. It's really just a starting point from which you move to Activity Centers or Account Detail windows. But because I'm not going to talk more about it in the pages of this book, I did want to just mention that it's worth poking your head around it. You can to Quicken's online help, for example, by clicking one of the Learn About Quicken hyperlinks at the top of the My Finances window. (These hyperlinks are shown in Figure 4-1.) Scroll further down the window, and you'll see alert messages (perhaps based on your budgeting instructions to Quicken) and a list of accounts you've set up. You'll also see a potpourri of other hyperlinks you can use to explore various Quicken features. And that's all I'm going to say.

Finding Your Checkbook

To enter checkbook transactions, use the Register window (see Figure 4-2). If you can see a Feature tab that names the bank account you want to work with, you can click it to display the Register window. (If you don't see the account's Feature tab, you can choose Banking➪Bank Accounts, and then choose the account you want to work with.)

Figure 4-2 shows the account name and type — Checking — at the top of the Register window.

The starting balance you specified as part of setting up the account is the first amount that Quicken lists. In Figure 4-2, for example, the starting balance is $4.16. Bummer.

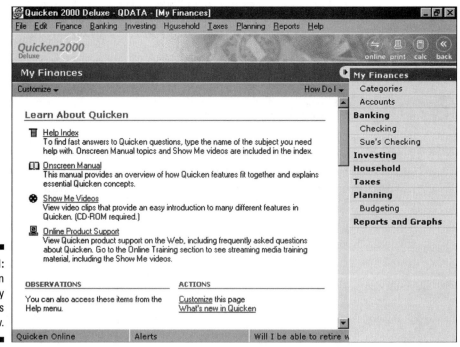

Figure 4-1:
The Quicken
My
Finances
window.

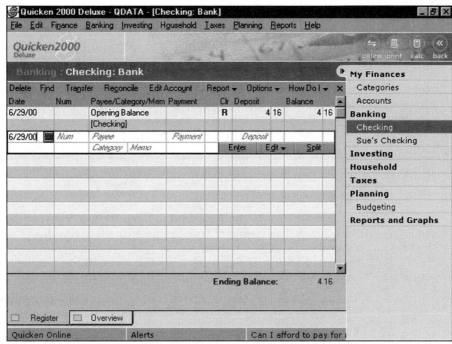

Figure 4-2:
The Register
window.

Recording Checks

First things first: You can enter checks by using either the Register window (refer to Figure 4-2) or the Write Checks window, which I describe in Chapter 5.

You use the Register window for the checks that you don't want to print or pay electronically with Quicken; you use the Write Checks window to enter the checks that you do want to print or pay electronically by using Quicken. (This rule isn't etched in stone, but it does make things easier for you, so it's the rule that I'm going to follow.)

Entering a check into the register

Entering a check in the Register window is a simple matter of describing to whom you wrote the check and how much you paid. Suppose, for the sake of illustration, that you paid $25.50 to the cable television company for your monthly cable service. Here's how you enter this check:

Interested in online banking and bill payment?

If you want to know more about how online payment and banking work, read Chapter 6. For now, however, do pay attention to how the Quicken register works. Everything you read about in this chapter will help you more easily use the Quicken Online Account Access feature.

1. Enter the check date.

Move the cursor to the Date field in the next empty row of the register (if it isn't already there) and type the date by using the MM/DD format. You enter July 14, 2000, for example, as **7/14**. You usually don't have to type the year because Quicken retrieves the current year number from the little clock inside your computer.

You can adjust the date in a Date field by using the + and - keys. The + key adds one day to the current date; the - key subtracts one day from the current date.

2. Enter the check number.

Move the cursor (or tab) to the Num field and type the check number. Alternatively, move the cursor to the Num field, and then when Quicken displays a list box of entries, such as ATM, Deposit, EFT, Next Check Number, Print Check, Send Online Payment, and Transfer Funds, select Next Check Number — if you want. Quicken then fills in the number with its guess as to the new check number — one more than the old check number. If this guess is right, of course, you can just leave it in place. If it isn't right, type over what Quicken guessed with the correct number or use the + or - key to increase or decrease the check number.

3. Enter the payee.

Move the cursor to the Payee field. Type the name of the person or business you're paying. If the cable company's name is Movies Galore, for example, type **Movies Galore**. (In the future, however, you can probably select payee names from the list box.)

4. Enter the check amount.

Move the cursor to the Payment field and type the check amount — **25.50** in this example. You don't have to type the dollar sign, but you do have to type the period to indicate the decimal place and cents.

5. Enter the category.

Move the cursor to the Category field. Quicken displays a drop-down list box of category names from your Category & Transfer List. You can select one of these categories by using the arrow keys or the mouse. Or, if you're the independent type, just type the name yourself. For example, you may categorize a payment to your cable as **Utilities**.

If you go with the typing approach and you're not a super-fast typist, Quicken can probably guess which category you're entering before you enter it. When you start typing **Ut**, for example, Quicken fills in the rest of the category name, "ilities," for you ("Ut" + "ilities" = "Utilities"). This feature is called *QuickFill,* and I talk about it in a bit more detail in the section "Working with a kooky (and clever) little thing named QuickFill."

6. Enter a memo description (optional).

Move the cursor to the Memo field and describe the specific reason that you're paying the check. You may identify the cable payment as the June payment, for example. If you are using Quicken for a business, you should use this field to identify the paid invoice — usually by entering the actual invoice number you are paying. You don't have to enter anything into this field, by the way.

7. Click Enter.

Click the Enter button that appears in the transaction's row of the register. This option tells Quicken that you want to record the transaction into your register. Quicken beeps in acknowledgment, calculates the new account balance, and moves the cursor to the next slot, or row, in the register.

Figure 4-3 shows the cable television check recorded into the register. You can't see it in the figure, but the amount in the Balance field after the $25.50 check shows in red. This *red ink* indicates that you've overdrawn your account. I don't need to tell you what that means: overdraft charges.

TIP

A neat little trick

You can expand and edit the list box of Num entries that Quicken displays. If you want to add some new Num entry to the drop-down list box, for example, do the following:

1. Click the Edit List button, which appears at the bottom of the list.

Quicken displays the Edit Num List dialog box.

2. Click the New button and then complete the dialog box that Quicken displays.

You can also edit any new Num entries you add by using the Edit Num List dialog box.

I won't spend any more time here describing how this works, so if you want to figure it all out, just experiment. You can't hurt anything.

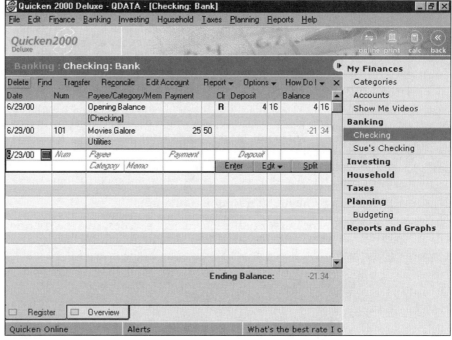

Figure 4-3:
The Quicken register after recording the check to Movies Galore.

Packing more checks into the register

Normally, Quicken displays several rows of information about each check that you enter. It also displays several rows of information about each of the other types of transactions you enter, too. If you want to pack more checks into a visible portion of the register, click the Options button (which appears in the top-right corner of the Register window) and then choose the One-Line Display command from the menu that Quicken displays. After you do, Quicken displays all the information in the register in a single-line format except the Memo field (see Figure 4-4). To return to the double-line format, click the Options button and choose One-Line Display again.

What if you need to change a check that you've already entered? Say you make a terrible mistake, such as recording a $52.50 check as $25.20. Can you fix it? Sure. Just use the arrow keys or click the mouse to highlight the check transaction that you want to change. Use the Tab and Shift+Tab keys to move the cursor to the field you want to change. (You also can select the field by clicking the mouse.) Then make your fix. Click the Enter button when you finish or press Enter on the keyboard.

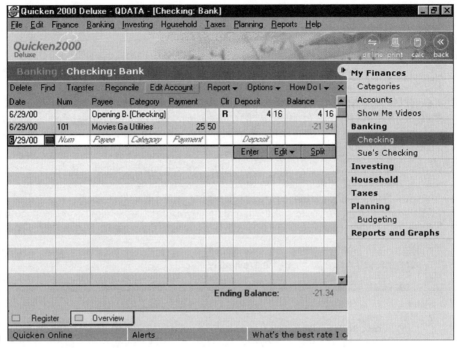

Figure 4-4:
How the
register
looks with
the One-
Line Display
format.

If you click the Options button, you'll notice that it also displays a bunch of commands that begin with the word *Sort*. These commands all work the same basic way. They let you reorganize the transactions shown in the register in some new way: by date, amount, check number, and so forth.

Don't worry. I'm not going to spend your precious time telling you things like the Sort By Date command sorts transactions by their date or that the Sort By Amount (Largest First) command sorts transactions by descending size of the transaction amount.

Working with a kooky (and clever) little thing named QuickFill

Here's kind of a funny quirk about Quicken. If Quicken can guess what you're typing into a field, it fills in the rest of the field for you. Earlier in this chapter, I mention how this works when you type category names. But it gets even better than that.

Memorized transactions

Quicken provides another feature — memorized transactions — which is almost obsolete now that the QuickFill feature exists. Just because you may have heard about this tool, however, I'll quickly describe how it works.

A *memorized transaction* is simply one that you've stored on a special list. (To store the transaction, you select it in the register, click the Edit button, and then choose the Memorize Transaction command.)

To later use or abuse one of the memorized transactions, you display a list of the previously memorized transactions by choosing Banking⇨Memorized Transaction List. When Quicken displays the list, just select the one you want to reuse and click Use.

A memorized transactions list is a handy tool. But if you're feeling a little overwhelmed, don't spin your wheels trying to get up to speed on the feature. QuickFill almost always does the job for you because — get this — it automatically grabs memorized transactions from the list for you.

The second time you use a payee name, for example, Quicken knows that it's the second time. Quicken also figures that, "Hey, some stuff from the last Movies Galore transaction will probably be the same for this transaction." So guess what Quicken does if you press Tab to accept the payee name Quicken supplies after you type the first few letters of the name? It uses the last transaction's information to fill in all the current transaction's fields.

This feature isn't as dumb as it sounds. In fact, it's a real time-saver. Suppose that you did write a $25.50 check to Movies Galore for your June cable television bill. When you type **Movies Galore** to record the next month's cable television check, the amount will probably be the same. The complete payee name will certainly be the same, and the category will also be the same. So Quicken fills in all these fields, too.

QuickFill doesn't do everything for you, however. You still need to make sure that the date and check number are correct. If Quicken quickfills a field with the wrong information, just replace the wrong information with what's right.

Recording Deposits

Guess what? Recording a deposit works almost the exact same way as recording a check works. The only difference is that you enter the deposit amount in the Deposit field rather than enter the check amount in the Payment field.

Entering a deposit into the register

Suppose that you receive a $100 birthday gift from your elderly aunt, Enid. Here's how you record this deposit into the register:

1. **Enter the deposit date.**

   Move the cursor to the Date field of the next empty row of the register (if it isn't already there) and type the date. Use the MM/DD format. You enter July 15, 2000, for example, as **7/15**. As with check dates, you have to enter the year only if the current year number, which Quicken retrieves from the little clock inside your computer, is wrong.

   You can adjust the date in a Date field in Quicken by using the + and - keys. The + key adds one day to the current date; the - key subtracts one day from the current date.

2. **Enter the code** DEP **(for deposit) into the Number field.**

   Are you the meticulous type? Then go ahead and move the cursor to the Num field. In the drop-down list box that Quicken displays, select Deposit.

3. **Enter the name of the person from whom you received the deposit.**

   In this case, move the cursor to the Payee field and enter **Aunt Enid.** (I don't mean to sound presumptuous, but, well, the next time Aunt Enid sends you birthday money, you'll be able to select her name from the Payee drop-down list box.)

4. **Enter the deposit amount.**

   Move the cursor to the Deposit field and type **100**. Don't type the dollar sign — or any other punctuation. (If Aunt Enid sweats money and sometimes passes out $1,000 gifts, for example, you record the deposit as 1000 — not 1,000 or $1,000.)

5. **Enter the category.**

   You know how this works by now. Move the cursor to the Category field and select the appropriate category. Alternatively, if you like living on the edge, try typing in the category name. You may describe Aunt Enid's check as **Gift Received**. (This income category is on the standard home category list.) You can describe a customer receipt as Gr Sales.

   To add a category, enter a name in the Category field and move to another field. When Quicken doesn't recognize the category name it asks you if you want to add the category. Click Yes and Quicken displays the Set Up Category dialog box. Refer to Chapter 2 if you have questions about how this works.

6. **Enter a memo description (optional).**

   Move the cursor to the Memo field and describe something like the reason for the deposit. Aunt Enid's money may be described as **birthday gift**. If you're a business depositing a customer's check, though, use this entry to identify the invoice the customer is paying.

7. **Click Enter.**

   This command tells Quicken that you want to record the transaction in your register. Quicken beeps in protest but then adds the transaction.

Figure 4-5 shows the check register after you enter Aunt Enid's thoughtful gift. Your account is no longer overdrawn — so you have that going for you. Maybe before you go any further, you should call Aunt Enid to thank her.

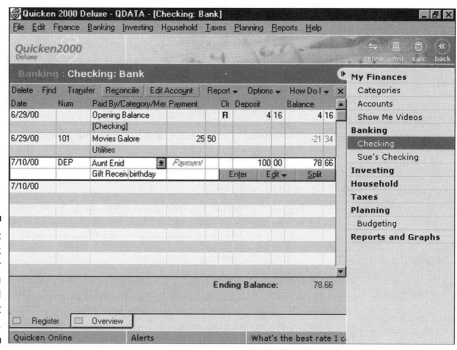

Figure 4-5:
A check register after you record your first deposit.

Quicken also includes a Paycheck Wizard that you can use to describe the taxes withheld from your paychecks and categorize the deductions from your paycheck. That much said, however, you probably don't even need to keep track of these amounts unless, for some reason, you want precise estimates of the income taxes you pay. (Keep in mind, though, that you need to use the data from your W-2 form, and not your Quicken data, when you prepare your taxes.) If you do decide to use the Paycheck Wizard, just choose the Taxes➪Tax Activities➪Set up my Paycheck command. Quicken launches the Paycheck Wizard, which asks you a few general questions about your deductions and then provides a dialog box similar to a Split Transaction window where you can enter and categorize your deductions. For more information about Splitting Transactions, refer to the "Splitting Transactions" section later in this chapter.

Changing a deposit you've already entered

Big surprise here — changing a deposit works just like changing a check. First, use the arrow keys or click the mouse to select the deposit. Use the Tab and Shift+Tab keys to move the cursor to the field you want to change. Tab moves the cursor to the next field. Shift+Tab moves the cursor to the previous field. (You also can select the field by clicking the mouse.) Then make your fix and click Enter.

Recording Account Transfers

Account transfers occur when you move money from one account, such as your savings account, to another account, such as your checking account. But jeepers, why am I telling you this? If you have one of those combined savings and checking accounts, you probably do this sort of thing all the time.

Oh, now I remember why I brought this up — Quicken makes quick work of account transfers as long as you already have *both* accounts set up.

If you don't have the second account set up, you need to do that first. If you don't know how, flip back to Chapter 2.

Entering an account transfer

Buckle up. I'll speed through the steps for recording an account transfer. For the most part, you record an account transfer the same way you record a check or deposit.

Suppose that you want to record the transfer of $50 from your checking account to your savings account. Maybe you want to set aside a little money — *little,* presumably, being a key adjective — to purchase a gift for your generous Aunt Enid.

Here's what you need to do:

1. **Enter the transfer date.**

   Move the cursor to the Date field. Then type the date that you move the money from one account to another.

2. **Flag the transaction as a transfer.**

   Move the cursor to the Num field. When Quicken displays a drop-down list box, select the Transfer entry.

3. **Enter a description of the transaction.**

   Use the Description field to describe the transfer — for example, **birthday**. You know how this works by now, don't you? You just move the cursor to the field. Then you pound away at the keyboard. Bang. Bang. Bang.

4. **Enter the transfer amount.**

   You enter amounts that you transfer out of an account in the Payment field, and you enter amounts that you transfer into an account in the Deposit field. So move the cursor to the right field *(right* as in *right and wrong,* not *right and left);* then enter the transfer amount.

5. **Indicate the other account.**

   Move the cursor to the Category field (which has a modified name of Transfer Account) and when Quicken drops down a list box of accounts, select the other account.

6. **Enter a memo description (optional).**

   Enter more information about the transaction (if you need to) in the Memo field. Perhaps a gift idea for Aunt Enid?

7. **Click Enter.**

   This command tells Quicken that you want to record the transfer transaction into your register.

Figure 4-6 shows the check register after transferring money from your checking account to your savings account so that you'll have money to purchase something nice for Aunt Enid's next birthday. Maybe that new Painter CD.

 Take a look at the Category field. Notice that Quicken uses brackets ([ ]) to identify the Category field entry as an account and not as an income or expense category.

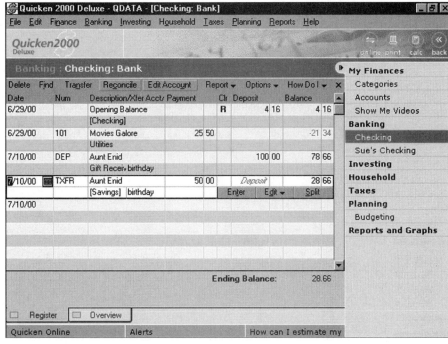

Figure 4-6:
The check
register
window
after you
enter the
transfer
transaction.

Working with the other half of the transfer

Here's the cool thing about transfer transactions. Quicken automatically
records the other half of the transfer for you. Figure 4-6 shows the $50 reduc-
tion in the checking account because of the transfer. Quicken uses this
information to record a $50 increase in the savings account. Automatically.
Biddabam. Biddaboom.

To see the other half of a transfer transaction, select the transfer transaction
by using the arrow keys or the mouse. Then click the Edit button and choose
Go To Transfer. Quicken displays the other account in a new register window
(see Figure 4-7).

Changing a transfer you've already entered

Predictably, this activity works just like changing a check or a deposit. First,
you select the transfer by using the arrow keys or by clicking the mouse.
Then you use the Tab and Shift+Tab keys to move the cursor to the field that
you want to change. Make your fix, click Enter, and then go to lunch.

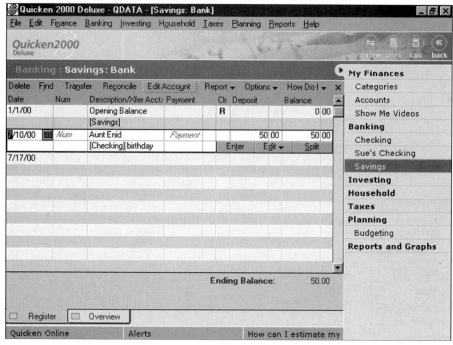

Splitting Transactions

Here's a sort of Quicken riddle for you: Suppose that you have a check that
pays more than one kind of expense. You trot down to the grocery store, for
example, and pick up $10 worth of junk food and junk beverages (which you
should categorize as a Groceries expense) and $10 worth of 10W-40 motor oil
(which you should categorize as an Auto expense). How do you categorize a
transaction like this? Well, I'll tell you. You use a *split category*.

Here's how a split category works. When you're ready to categorize the
check, you click the Split button, which appears in the Category drop-down
list box for the selected transaction. When you click this button, Quicken displays the Split Transaction window (see Figure 4-8).

Steps for splitting a check

Being a clever sort, you probably already know how the Split Transaction
window works. I'll go through the steps anyway. Suppose that you want to
categorize a $20 check that includes $10 for groceries and $10 for motor oil.

To categorize a check in the Split Transaction window, do the following:

1. **Enter the first category name in the first Category field.**

   Move the cursor to the Category field (if it isn't already there). Activate the drop-down list box by pressing Alt+↓ or by clicking the down arrow and then selecting the category name.

   (Despite what a dietitian may say, you can call the pork rinds, soda, and pretzels "Groceries.")

2. **Enter a memo description for the first categorized portion of the check.**

   Move the cursor to the first Memo field and then type whatever you want. (Maybe a description of the food you bought. Er, then again, maybe if you're buying real junk, you should just leave this blank.)

3. **Enter the amount spent for the first category.**

   Move the cursor to the first Amount field and then type, well, the amount. If the first category is what you're calling Groceries and you spent $10 on this, you type **10**.

4. **Repeat Steps 1, 2, and 3 for each spending category.**

   If you spent another $10 on motor oil, for example, move the cursor to the second Category field and enter the category you use to summarize Auto expenses. Optionally, move the cursor to the second Memo field and enter a memo description of the expenditure, such as **motor oil**. Move the cursor to the second Amount field and enter the amount of the expenditure, such as **10**.

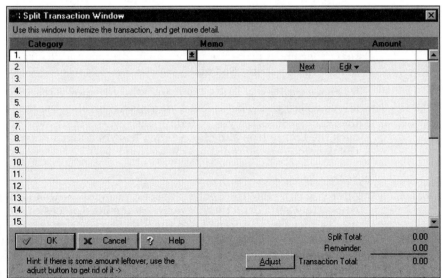

Figure 4-8: The Split Transaction window.

Figure 4-9 shows a Split Transaction window that is complete. A split transaction can have up to 30 pieces. Use the scroll bar and PgUp and PgDn keys to scroll through the list of split amounts.

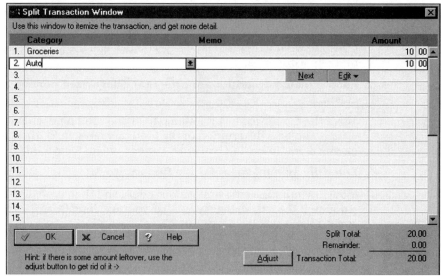

Figure 4-9:
The
completed
Split
Transaction
window.

5. **Verify that the Split Transaction window shows no uncategorized spending.**

   If you find extra spending, either add the category you need or delete the split transaction line that's uncategorized. To delete a split transaction line, move the cursor to one of the fields in the line, scream "Hi-Ya" loudly, click the Edit button, and choose Delete. (I learned the "Hi-Ya" business in tae kwon do. The only other thing I learned, by the way, was that those chest protectors don't really protect middle-aged men during full-contact sparring. So I quit.)

   If you want to insert a new line, move the selection cursor to the line above where you want to make your insertion, click the Edit button, and then choose Insert. If you're fed up and want to start over from scratch, click the Edit button and choose the Clear All command (which causes Quicken to erase all the split transaction lines).

6. **Click OK.**

   After you complete the Split Transaction window — that is, after you completely and correctly categorize all the little pieces of the transaction — click OK. Quicken closes the Split Transaction window. If you didn't enter an amount in the Payment column of the register before opening the Split Transaction window, Quicken displays a dialog box that asks whether the transaction is a payment or a deposit. You select an option button to make your choice known. To let you know that the transaction is one that you've split, however, the Category field shows the word –Split– when you select the split transaction. Take a peek at Figure 4-10 to see for yourself.

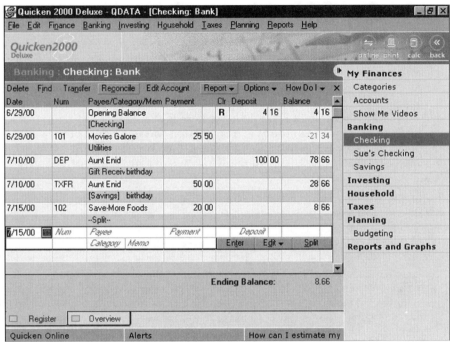

Figure 4-10:
The Register
window.
Can you find
the word
Split?

7. **Click Enter.**

   This command tells Quicken that you want to record the transaction in your register.

Editing and deleting split categories

You can delete or change any individual line of a split category. To do so, you first display the Split Transaction window by selecting the transaction and then clicking the check mark button, which appears in the Register window's Category field after you record the transaction. After Quicken dutifully displays the Split Transaction Window, you can edit any of the fields by selecting them and then typing over their contents. You can delete any line of the split category by clicking the Edit button and choosing Delete. (If you want to delete all the lines of the split category so you can start over, choose Clear All instead.)

If you want to unsplit the transaction so you can assign it to a single category, you need to use a little trick. Click the X button that appears in the Register window's Category field after you record the transaction.

Steps for splitting deposits and transfers

Wondering if you can split deposits and transfers? Well, you can. The steps for doing so work just like the steps for splitting categories for a check transaction. The basic trick — if you can call it a trick — is just to use the Split Transaction window to list each of the category names and amounts.

One other point I should make here is that you can mix and match categories and transfers in the Split Transaction window. Some of the splits, for example, can be categories and some can be transfer accounts. This type of transaction is quite common in a business setting (see Chapter 16 for more information).

Splitting hairs

Quicken assumes that any transaction amount you enter in the Register window should agree with the total of the individual split transaction amounts entered in the Split Transaction window.

If you're not sure what the split transaction amounts total is, your best bet is to NOT — I repeat, *NOT* — enter the amount on the Register window. Instead, enter the individual split transaction amounts in the Split Transaction window. When you leave the Split Transaction window, Quicken totals your individual split amounts and then prompts you to see if the total is a payment or a deposit. Then it plugs this total into either the Payment or the Deposit field.

If you've already entered either a payment amount or a deposit amount but you're not sure

that the split transaction amounts agree with what you entered, you can tell Quicken to adjust the Payment or Deposit amount on the Register window to whatever the individual split transaction amounts total. To do so, click the Split Transaction window Adjust button. Quicken then adds up the split transaction lines and plugs the total into the register. (This approach may best be called "I don't care if it is a round hole, I want to pound this square peg into it.")

By the way, Quicken shows any difference between the amount shown in the Register window and the individual split transaction amounts. It shows this difference as the last split transaction line so you can tell whether the individual splits agree with the payment or deposit amount shown in the register.

WARNING!

Sort of a voiding bug . . .

When you mark a transaction as void, Quicken does three things: It sticks the word VOID at the very start of the Payee field, it marks the transaction as cleared, and it erases the amount in the Payment or Deposit field. So far, so good. But if you happen to later fill in the Payment or Deposit field, and don't pay attention to the warning from Quicken that you're editing a reconciled transaction, Quicken uses the payment or deposit amount that you enter to adjust the account balance — even though Quicken still shows the transaction as void. I keep thinking the folks at Intuit will fix this, but they haven't — at least not yet. The bottom line is that you need to make sure that you don't edit transactions after you void them. Otherwise, you can all too easily foul up your account balance. I won't tell you about how I happened to learn this. . . .

Deleting and Voiding Transactions

You can delete and void register transactions by using the Edit button's Delete Transaction and Void Transaction commands. If you've looked at the Edit button, of course, you've probably already guessed as much.

Using either command is a snap. Just highlight the transaction you want to delete or void by using the arrow keys or by clicking the mouse. Then click the button and choose the command. And that's that.

Use the Void Transaction command any time you void a check. Quicken leaves voided transactions in the register but marks them as void and erases the Payment or Deposit amount. So by using the Void Transaction command, you keep a record of voided, or canceled, transactions.

Use the Delete Transaction command if you want to remove the transaction from your register.

The Big Register Phenomenon

If you start entering a bunch of checks, deposits, and transfers into your registers, you'll shortly find yourself with registers that contain hundreds and even thousands of transactions. You can still work with one of these big registers by using the tools and techniques I talk about in the preceding paragraphs. Nevertheless, let me give you some more help for dealing with . . . (drumroll, please) . . . the big register phenomenon.

Moving through a big register

You can use the PageUp and PageDown keys to page up and down through your register, a screenful of transactions at a time. Some people call this *scrolling.* You can call it whatever you want.

You can use the Home key to move to the first transaction in a register. Just move the cursor to the first (or Date) field in the selected transaction and press Ctrl+Home.

You can use the End key to move to the last transaction in a register. Bet you can guess how this works. Move the cursor to the last (or Category) field in the selected transaction and press Ctrl+End.

Of course, you can use the vertical scrollbar along the right edge of the Register window, too. Click the arrows at either end to select the next or previous transaction. Click either above or below the square scrollbar marker to page back and forth through the register. Or, if you've no qualms about dragging the mouse around, you can drag the scrollbar marker up and down the scrollbar.

Finding that darn transaction

Want to find that one check, deposit, or transfer? No problem. The Find command provides a handy way for doing just that. Here's what you do:

1. **Choose Edit⇨Find & Replace⇨Find or click the Find button in the Register window.**

   Quicken, with restrained but obvious enthusiasm, displays the Quicken Find window (see Figure 4-11). You use this dialog box to describe the transaction you want to find in as much detail as possible. (Notice, by the way, that you don't click the Edit button to get to this command; you click the menu bar's Edit menu.)

Figure 4-11:
The Quicken
Find
window.

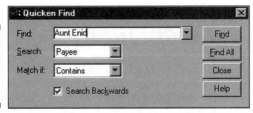

2. **Enter the piece of text or number that identifies the transaction you want to locate.**

   Move the cursor to the Find text box. Then type the text or number. By the way, the case of the text doesn't matter. If you type **aunt**, for example, Quicken finds AUNT or Aunt.

3. **Specify which pieces, or fields, of the register transaction you want Quicken to look at.**

   Move the cursor to the Search drop-down list box arrow, drop down the list box, and then select the field Quicken should look at during the search: Amount, Cleared Status (the Clr field), Memo, Date, Category/Class (whatever is in the Category field), Check Number (what's in the Num field), or Payee. Or get truly crazy and pick the All Fields list entry so that Quicken looks both high and low.

4. **Tell Quicken whether you're using a shotgun or a rifle.**

   You need to specify how closely what you stuck in the Find text box needs to match whatever you selected in the Search drop-down list box. To do so, open the Match If drop-down list box. Then select the appropriate matching rule:

   - **Contains:** Select this rule if the field or fields you're searching just need to use a piece of text. If you enter **Aunt** into the Find text box and use this matching rule to search Payee fields, Quicken finds transactions that use the following payee names: Aunt Enid, Aunt Enid and Uncle Joob, Uncle Harry and Aunt Edna, and — well, you get the idea.

   - **Exact:** Select this rule if the field you're searching needs to exactly match your Find text box entry. If you enter the Find text box entry as **Aunt**, for example, and you're searching Payee fields, Quicken looks for transactions where the Payee field shows Aunt — and nothing more or nothing less.

   - **Starts With:** Select this rule if the field you're searching for just needs to start with what you entered in the Find text box. For example, you enter **Aunt** in the Find text box and you're searching the Payee fields. Quicken looks for transactions where the Payee field starts with the word Aunt — such as Aunt Enid or Aunt Enid and Uncle Joob. (Uncle Joob and Aunt Enid wouldn't cut the mustard in this case, though.)

   - **Ends With:** Select this rule if the field you're searching for just needs to end with what you entered in the Find text box.

   - **Greater:** Select this rule if the field you're searching for needs to hold a value that exceeds the number you entered in the Find text box. This makes sense, right? Like you're looking for checks you wrote for more than $100?

- **Greater or Equal:** Select this rule if the field you're searching for needs to hold a value that either exceeds or equals the number you entered in the Find text box.

- **Less:** Select this rule if the field you're searching for needs to hold a value that is less than the number you entered in the Find text box.

- **Less or Equal:** Select this rule if the field you're searching for needs to hold a value that is less than or equal to the number you entered in the Find text box.

5. **Tell Quicken whether you want it to search forward or backward from the selected transaction.**

   Select the Search Backwards check box if you want to look backward starting from the selected transaction.

6. **Let the search begin.**

   You click either the Find or Find All button to begin the search. If you click Find, Quicken looks through the register and, if it can find one like you describe, it highlights the transaction. If you're thinking, "Well, that sounds straightforward enough," you're right. It is.

   If you click Find All, Quicken looks through the register and builds a list of all the transactions like the one you describe. Then it displays the list in an expanded version of the Find window (see Figure 4-12).

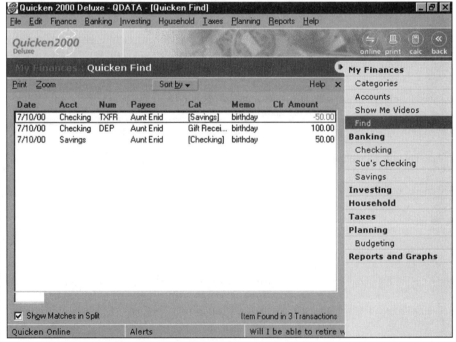

Figure 4-12: The Find window with a bunch of transactions that match the search criteria.

Quicken supplies another command that is similar to Find. The Edit menu's Find/Replace command lets you both locate and modify transactions that look like the one you describe. (To use the Find/Replace command, choose Edit⇨Find & Replace⇨Find/Replace.) For example, you may say that you want to locate any transaction showing Aunt Enid as the payee so you can replace payee fields showing Aunt Enid with Great Aunt Enid. The Find/Replace command works in a fashion very similar to the Find command except that you need to describe what you want to modify in the found transactions. After you complete the initial dialog box that Quicken displays when you choose the command, Quicken displays a window listing the transactions it has found. (This window looks like the one shown in Figure 4-13.) You mark — by clicking — the transactions you want to modify and then click the Replace button.

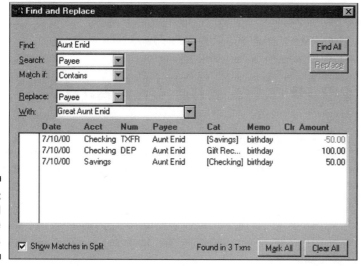

Figure 4-13:
The Find and Replace window.

You can't use the Find/Replace command to find and replace categories, by the way. But you can use another command: Recategorize. (To use the Recategorize command, choose the Edit⇨Find & Replace⇨Recategorize command.) For example, you may want to recategorize all your cable television payments as the Entertainment category (while earlier placing them as the Utilities category). When you choose the Recategorize command, Quicken displays the Recategorize window (shown in Figure 4-14). Enter the category you want to replace in the Search Category text box and the new replacement category in the Replace With text box. Next, click Find All to tell Quicken it should display a list of transactions that use the category you want to replace. Click the transactions you want to recategorize (to mark them) and then click the Replace button.

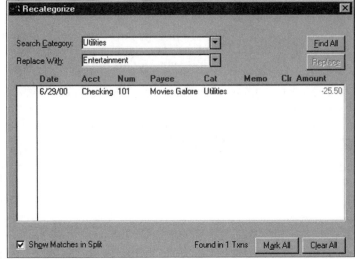

Figure 4-14:
The
Recategorize
window.

Pop-Up Calendars and Calculators

Can I tell you just a couple more things? (If not, skip this section. If so, read on.) Quicken provides a pop-up calendar anytime you move the selection cursor to a Date field. To get to the calendar, you just click the button that appears at the right end of the Date field. Quicken displays a calendar for the current month (see Figure 4-15). All you have to do is select the day you want as the date. (If you want to see a calendar for a different month, click the << and >> buttons.)

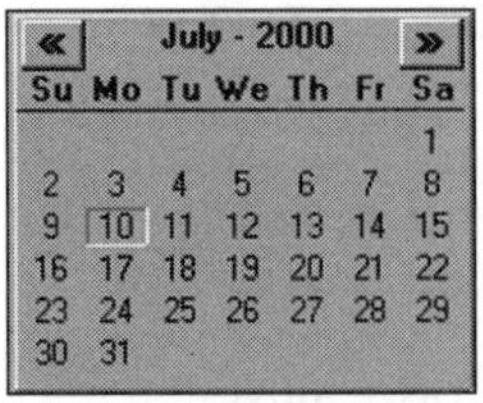

Figure 4-15:
The pop-up
calendar.

Quicken also provides a pop-up calculator anytime you move the selection cursor to an Amount field. To get to the calculator, you just click the button that appears at the right end of the Amount field. Quicken displays a calculator like the one shown in Figure 4-16. This baby works like a regular, handheld calculator. You just type the math you want to perform. Quicken displays the calculation result in the amount field.

Figure 4-16:
The pop-up
calculator.

Do the calculator keys make sense? Here's how they work. Use the / (slash) key for division. Use the X for multiplication. Use the – (minus) and the + (plus) keys for subtraction and addition. Use the . (period) to indicate the decimal point. Use the % key to indicate that the number you just typed is a percentage and should be converted to a decimal value. Use the = (equal sign) to calculate the amount and remove the pop-up calculator. You can use the <– to remove, or clear, the last digit you entered. You can use the CE key to clear the last number entered into the calculator, and you can use the C key to clear the amount text box.

Don't Forget QuickEntry

Over the years, Quicken has become more powerful. Every year — and I think this is a fair statement — the folks at Intuit think of more, cool new features to add to the product. In most every situation, all these extra features are really neat. But if you just want to quickly jump into the program and enter a handful of transactions — say it's a sunny Saturday morning and you'd rather be playing golf — all those extra whistles and bells can seem like nothing more than clutter. So, to deal with this situation, Quicken includes a separate program called QuickEntry. QuickEntry lets you quickly enter transactions into Quicken registers by using the same steps I describe in this chapter. If you start QuickEntry — which you do by double-clicking its shortcut icon on the Windows desktop — you see a window like the one shown in Figure 4-17.

This window is actually the same Register window you can get to from within Quicken. (Okay, it does look a little bare. But trust me. It's the same set of boxes you use to describe your payments, deposits, and transfers, and they appear in the exact same order.) You can enter transactions in the account named at the top of the window the same way you enter transactions in the regular Register window.

✔ You can't do all that much with the QuickEntry 2000 program — but often you'll be able to do everything you need.

✔ To switch to another account, choose Accounts⇨Bank Accounts or Accounts⇨Asset and Liability Accounts and choose the account you want to work with.

✔ To print the register shown in the QuickEntry window, click the Print button.

✔ If you want to move to Quicken and do some fancy stuff, click the Quicken Start button.

It really is that simple!

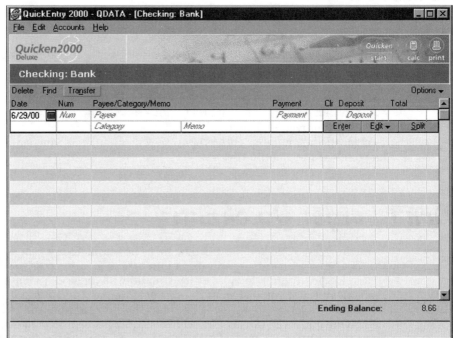

Figure 4-17: The QuickEntry window.

Chapter 5

Printing 101

● ●

In This Chapter

▶ Printing a check

▶ Fixing check form alignment problems

▶ Recovering from a mistake after you've printed the check

▶ Printing a register

● ●

I bet you can't guess what this chapter describes. Gee, you guessed it — how to print checks and reports.

Printing Checks

Printing checks in Quicken is, well, quick. All you basically need to do is enter the information you want to print on the check form and the number you want Quicken to use to identify the check. Sounds simple enough, doesn't it? It is, as you can read in the steps that follow.

To enter the information on a check form, follow these steps:

1. **Display the Write Checks window.**

   Choose Banking⇨Write Checks or press Ctrl+W. Figure 5-1 shows the Write Checks: Checking window. Note, by the way, that after you once display the Write Checks window, Quicken adds a Checks Feature tab to the set of tabs at the right edge of the Quicken program window.

2. **VERY IMPORTANT — select the account on which you want to write the check using the tabs at the bottom of the screen.**

   Figure 5-1 shows three tabs: Checking, Savings, and Sue's Checking.

3. **Enter the check date.**

   First, use the mouse or Tab key to move the cursor to the Date field. Then type the date that you're going to print the check (probably today's date). Remember to type the date in a MM/DD/YY format —

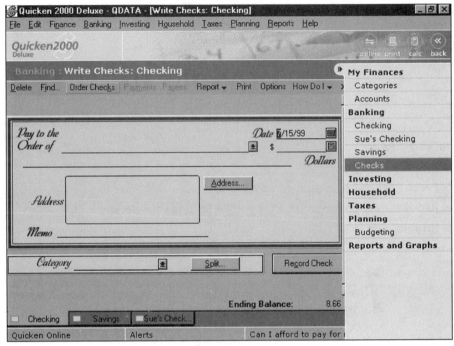

Figure 5-1:
The Write
Checks
window.

enter July 31, 2000, as **7/31/00**. You don't need to enter the year if the year number that Quicken retrieves from your computer's internal system clock is correct. You can adjust the date by a day using + and - from the numeric keypad. You can also click the button at the end of the Date field to display your friend, the pop-up calendar.

4. Enter the name of the person or business you're paying.

Move the cursor to the Pay to the Order of field and type away. For example, to write a check to me, type **Steve Nelson**. (Feel free to do so, by the way. If you send me a check, I'll even cash it as a sort of public service.) If you've written a check to the payee before, when you start to type the name, Quicken will recognize it and fill in the rest for you.

5. Enter the amount of the check.

Move the cursor to the $ text box and type the amount. (If you are sending a check to me, be sure to make the amount nominal — for sure, not more than $10 or $20. . .) When you press the Tab key, the cursor moves down to the next field, and Quicken writes the amount in words on the line under the payee name and before the word Dollars.

6. Enter the payee's address.

If you plan to mail the check in a window envelope, move the cursor to the Address field. Then enter the name and address of the person or business you're paying.

Here's a little address-entry trick: You can copy the payee name from the Pay to the Order of text box to the first line of the Address field. Click the mouse or select the first line of the address field. Then press the ' (apostrophe) key.

7. **Enter a memo description of the check (optional).**

   Move the cursor to the Memo field and enter a description (such as an account number or an invoice number) of why you are sending your money to this person or business. Or, if you're sending someone a check because you didn't have time to go out and buy a real gift, type **Happy Birthday** in the Memo field. It's the little things that make a difference.

8. **Enter the category.**

   Move the cursor to the Category field and type the category name for the expense you're paying with the check. If you don't remember the category name, scroll down the category list to find the category. Figure 5-2 shows the completed window for a check payable to Movies Galore, the local cable TV company.

   You can assign a check to more than a single category by using the Split Transaction window dialog box. Using the Split Transaction window with the Write Checks window works the same way as using the Split Transaction window with the Register window. (I describe using the Split Transaction window with the Register window in Chapter 4.) Okay. So why do I bring this up? You use the Split Transaction window when a check pays more than one type of expense or is transferred to more than one account.

   For example, if you're writing a check to pay your mortgage, with part of the check paying the actual mortgage and part of the check going into an escrow for property taxes, you can use the Split Transaction window to describe the transaction's individual components. To split a check amount so that the amount is assigned to multiple spending categories, click the Split button. Or press Ctrl+S. Either way, Quicken displays the Split Transaction window for you to indicate the categories and categorized amounts that make up the check total. If you have questions about how split transactions work, refer to Chapter 4.

9. **Click Record Check.**

   Quicken records the check. It displays the current account balance and the ending account balance, and it even adds a Checks to Print total at the bottom of the window. If you're working with a monitor that supports higher screen resolution, you'll also see a Checks to Print window that lists all the nitty-gritty about the checks you have to print (this doesn't appear in Figure 5-2 because I've set my monitor to a lower resolution). Shoot, when you're finished with one check, Quicken even scrolls the completed check off the screen and replaces it with a new blank check that you can use to pay your next bill. It doesn't get much better than this, does it?

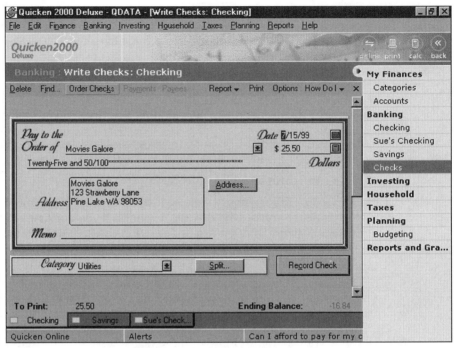

Figure 5-2:
A completed check.

What if you make a mistake entering a check?

Don't worry. If you haven't yet printed the check, fixing mistakes is easy. If you press the PgUp and PgDn keys with the Write Checks window displayed, Quicken pages you through the check transactions. This way, you can display any check that you wrote — but have not yet printed — in the Write Check window.

When you find the incorrect check, you can fix the mistake in two ways. If you incorrectly entered some bit of check information, move the cursor to the field with the incorrect data and just type over the data.

Or, if you're really mad or frustrated, you can delete the entire check by clicking the Delete button. (I should, 'fess up here and suggest that you delete the check if you accidentally entered a check to me, for example.)

Don't use this method to delete a check that you've already printed. To *void* a check that you've already printed, you must go into the Register window. To display the Register window, you can click the Feature tab for the account. Then find the check in the Register window, select the check, and void it by clicking the Edit button and choosing the drop-down menu's Void

Transaction command. You should also write something such as **VOID** in large letters across the face of the printed check.

Printing a check you've entered

For some reason, when I get to this part of the discussion, my pulse quickens. I don't mean this as a pun. It just feels terribly serious when I'm actually writing checks for real money. I get the same feeling whenever I mail someone cash — even if the amount is nominal.

I think the best way to lower my heart rate (and yours, if you're like me) is to just print the darn checks. To print the checks, do the following:

1. **Load the checks into your printer.**

   You do so the same way you load any other paper into your printer. If you have questions about it, refer to your printer documentation. (Sorry I can't help more on this, but with a million different printers on the market, I can't guess which one you have.)

2. **Choose File⇨Print Checks (or press Ctrl+P).**

   As long as the Write Checks window is the active window, Quicken displays the Select Checks to Print dialog box, as shown in Figure 5-3. At the top of the dialog box, Quicken shows how many checks you have to print and the total dollar amount for those checks.

3. **Enter the first check number.**

   Move the cursor to the First Check Number box and enter the number printed on the first check form you'll print. Figure 5-3 shows 1001, for example, so the first check form is numbered 1001. To quickly increase or decrease the check numbers, use + or – from the numeric keypad.

4. **Indicate which checks Quicken should print.**

   - Select the All Checks option button under Print if you want Quicken to print all the checks you've entered by using the Write Checks window, which is the usual case.

   - Select the Checks Dated Through option button under Print if you want to print all the checks through a certain date and then type that date in the text box.

   - Select the Selected Checks option button if you want to pick and choose which checks to print.

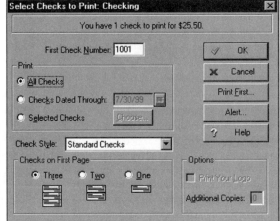

Figure 5-3:
The Select
Checks to
Print dialog
box.

5. **If you say that you want to select which checks to print, click the Choose button.**

   Quicken, with some annoyance, displays the Select Checks to Print window, as shown in Figure 5-4. Initially, Quicken marks all the checks dated on or earlier than the current date by placing a check mark in the Print column. If you don't want to print a check, either leave the Print field for that check clear (unchecked) or click the field to remove the check mark. When only the checks you want to print are marked to be printed, click the Close button to continue with this crazy little thing called check printing. Quicken, happy with your progress, redisplays the Select Checks to Print dialog box (refer to Figure 5-3).

6. **Indicate which Quicken check form you're using.**

   Move the cursor to the Check Style drop-down list box, click the arrow so that the list drops down, and then select the check form you purchased: standard, voucher, or wallet checks.

7. **Tell Quicken if you're printing a partial page.**

   If you're printing a partial page of forms on a laser printer, use the Checks on First Page option buttons to indicate the number of check forms on the partial page. Select the Three option button if you have three checks, the Two option button if you have two checks, or the One option button if you have one check.

8. **Indicate whether you want extra copies of the check form.**

   To do so, enter the number of copies you want in the Additional Copies text box. (This text box appears only if you are set up for the voucher check style.)

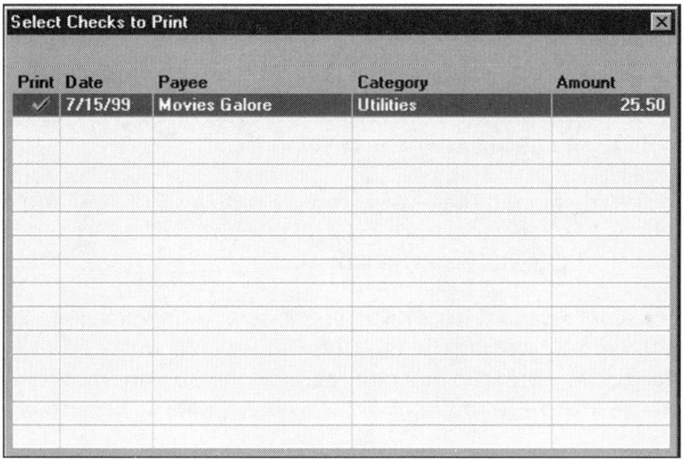

Select Checks to Print ☒

Print	Date	Payee	Category	Amount
✓	7/15/99	Movies Galore	Utilities	25.50

Figure 5-4:
The Select
Checks to
Print
window.

If you use Quicken for business to keep accounts payable files, make copies of checks to attach to the invoices that the checks pay. Then if a vendor calls later, starts hassling you, and asks which check paid an invoice, you can easily check your accounts payable files, quickly answer that question, and basically cover your derriere.

9. Click OK and let the games begin.

If you're using a partial starting page of forms, your printer may prompt you to manually feed the first page of forms. When it finishes, Quicken asks whether it printed your checks correctly (see Figure 5-5). If the check did print correctly, click OK. You're done. If the check didn't print correctly, enter the number of the first check that printed incorrectly and click OK; then repeat Steps 3 through 8.

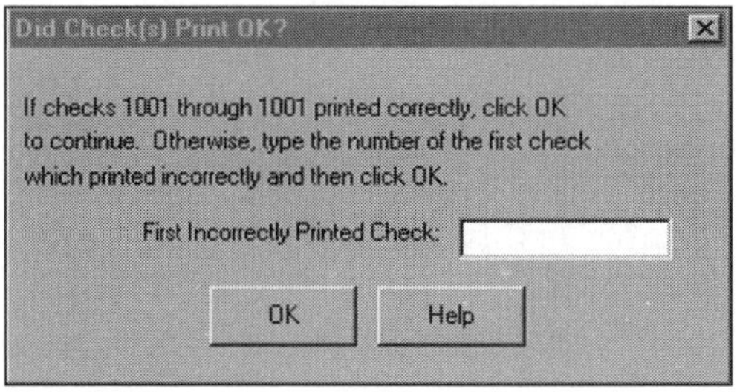

Did Check(s) Print OK? ☒

If checks 1001 through 1001 printed correctly, click OK
to continue. Otherwise, type the number of the first check
which printed incorrectly and then click OK.

First Incorrectly Printed Check: [＿＿＿＿＿]

[OK]   [Help]

Figure 5-5:
The Did
Check(s)
Print OK?
dialog box.

10. Sign the printed checks.

Then — and I guess you probably don't need my help here — put the checks in the mail.

What if I discover a mistake after I print the check?

This problem isn't as big as you may think.

If you've already mailed the check, you can't do a whole lot. You can try to get the check back (if the person you paid hasn't cashed it) and replace it with the correct check. (Good luck on this one.)

If the person has cashed the check, you can't get the check back. If you over-paid the person by writing the check for too much, you need to get the person to pay you the overpayment amount. If you underpaid the person, you need to write another check for the amount of the underpayment.

If you printed the check but haven't mailed it, void the printed check. Let's say, for example, that you've been using 1999 as the year because you just can't seem to get used to the new millennium. This operation is in two parts. First, write the word **VOID** in large letters — in ink — across the face of the check form. (Use a ballpoint pen if you're using multipart forms so that the second and third parts also show as VOID.) Second, display the register window, highlight the check, and then click the Edit button and choose the Void Transaction command. (This option marks the check as one that's been voided in the system, so Quicken doesn't use the voided check in calculating your account balance.)

A few words about check printing

Check printing is kind of complicated at first, isn't it?

For the record, I'm with you on this one. But you'll find that printing checks does get easier after the first few times.

Pretty soon, you'll be running instead of walking through the steps. Pretty soon, you'll just skate around things like check-form alignment problems. Pretty soon, in fact, you'll know all this stuff and never have to read "pretty soon" again.

Printing a Check Register

You can print a check register or a register for any other account, too. First, display the register window such as by clicking the Feature tab for the account. Then choose File⇨Print Register.

Oh where, oh where, do the unprinted checks go?

The register stores unprinted checks — those you've entered by using the Write Checks window but haven't yet printed. To identify them as unprinted checks, Quicken sets their check numbers as Print. If you choose the Finance⊅Reminders command, Quicken displays the Quicken Reminders window, listing the things you have to do, such as checks you have to print. Just click the Print Checks button; Quicken displays the Select Checks to Print dialog box, and you're off and running. What's more, after you tell Quicken to print the unprinted checks, Quicken prints the checks in your register that have Print in the check-number field.

All this information is of little practical value in most instances, but it results in several interesting possibilities. For example, you can enter the checks you want to print directly into the register — all you need to do is enter the check number as Print. (Notice that you can't enter an address anywhere in the register, so this process isn't practical if you want addresses printed on your checks.) You also can cause a check you've printed once to print again by changing its check number from, say, 007 to Print. I can't think of many good reasons why you would want to change a check number. The only one I can think of is that you accidentally printed a check on plain paper and want to reprint it on a real check form.

Quicken then displays the Print Register dialog box, as shown in Figure 5-6. To print a register, you follow these magic steps:

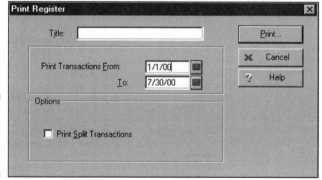

Figure 5-6:
The Print
Register
dialog box.

1. **Enter a register title (optional).**

   If you're the sort who likes to add your own special titles to things, move the cursor to the Title text box. Then type the report title or description that you want Quicken to print at the top of each and every page of the register.

2. Limit the range of dates (optional).

To print a register of something other than the current year-to-date transactions, use the Print Transactions From and To text boxes. This is pretty dang obvious, isn't it? You just move the cursor to the From and To text boxes and type the range of months the register should include.

3. Tell Quicken to print split transaction information (optional).

To print the split transaction information — categories, memos, and amounts — move the cursor to the Print Split Transaction check box. Then press the spacebar or select the check box.

4. Click Print.

Quicken displays the Print dialog box (see Figure 5-7). You don't have to fool around with this dialog box. If you want to print a register pronto, just click OK. Then again, if you're the sort of person who likes to fool around with this kind of stuff, carry on with the rest of these steps.

If you want to see the effect that the different register-printing text boxes and check boxes have, just experiment. You can't hurt anything or anybody.

The rest of these steps are optional. Do them if you feel like it.

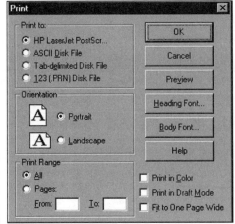

Figure 5-7:
The Print
dialog box.

5. Print the report to disk if you want (optional).

To print the report to disk as a text file, select one of the following Print To option buttons:

- ASCII Disk File if you want to create a text file, such as when you want to import the register into a word-processing program

- Tab-delimited Disk File, such as when you want to import the register into a database program (Oooh . . . Fancy . . .)

- 123 (.PRN) Disk File, such as when you want to import the register into Lotus 1-2-3 or any spreadsheet program that will open 1-2-3 files (which, basically, means any spreadsheet program)

If you do indicate that you want a disk file, after you click the Print button to start the ol' printing process, Quicken displays the Create Disk File dialog box as shown in Figure 5-8. This dialog box asks for the file-name that Quicken should create as part of printing the file to disk and the location where you want to store the file. Just enter the filename you want into — you guessed it — the File Name text box. (Use a valid DOS filename, of course.) Use the Save In box to indicate where you want to store the file. Or don't do anything, and Quicken creates the file in the active Quicken directory — probably C:\QUICKENW. And what do you do with the disk file? You're on your own here. . . .

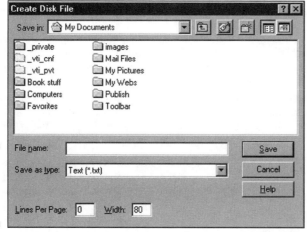

Figure 5-8:
The Create
Disk File
dialog box.

6. **Tell Quicken which pages to print (optional).**

   Use the Print Range option buttons and text boxes to limit the pages Quicken prints (refer to Figure 5-7). How? Select the Pages option button and then type the range of page numbers you want to print. That's simple enough, right?

7. **Color your world (optional).**

   If you have a color printer and want to print your register in color, select the Print in Color check box on the Print dialog box (refer to Figure 5-7).

8. **Trade speed for quality (optional).**

   Or you can select the Print in Draft Mode check box to tell Quicken it should print faster and spend less time worrying about the quality of the printing job (see Figure 5-7). In other words, you can use this check box to trade print speed for print quality. Life is full of trade-offs, isn't it?

9. **Tell Quicken to scrunch the information so it fits across the page (optional).**

   Use the Fit to One Page Wide check box to tell Quicken that you want its register information to fit across the width of the page (refer to Figure 5-7).

10. **Click OK.**

   Now click OK one last time. Quicken finally prints the register. I'm not going to show a printed copy of the register here. All it is, really, is just a printed copy of the same account detail information you see in the register window.

Should you save a printed copy of your register?

Here's a question for you: Should you save a printed copy of your register? I don't know. The case for printing a copy of your register and then having it handy in case, well, just in case, is this: If your computer does go haywire and you need to re-enter your transactions or you need a hardcopy record of your transactions and for some reason don't have access to Quicken, having a printed register will make things much easier for you. You know what though? I think that most people, if they religiously back up their Quicken data files (something I describe in Chapter 9) don't really need to print copies of their registers.

Now I should say that if you're someone who likes to keep meticulous records of your income and spending and you always double-check to make sure that you haven't left the iron on or even plugged in whenever you leave your house, you could print a copy of the register. And what I would suggest is that you print a copy of the register at the very end of the year and then file this report away with your tax return.

By the way, I've been using Quicken since 1988 and have never needed a printed copy of my register. I've made frequent use of other reports. But never have I needed a hard, paper copy of the register. Anytime I have had a question, I've simply looked through the online version of my current register or archived files from previous years.

Chapter 6

Online and In Charge

*B*anks are moving toward offering electronic banking services in a big, big way. This exciting area is a step toward providing a pretty impressive variety of online services to the general consumer. (That means you and me.) So this chapter talks about the Quicken electronic banking services: Online Account Access and Online Bill Payment.

What Are Online Account Access and Online Bill Payment?

I'm going to start with the basics — a definition of these two services.

Online services means that you can connect your computer to your bank's computer electronically through your average phone line and Internet connection. You may think that doing so sounds scary, but Online Account Access and Online Bill Payment provide some very neat benefits:

✔ With Online Bill Payment, you can tell your bank to make payments to specific individuals or businesses. In other words, rather than providing all of this information in the usual way (on checks), you just send the same information — the payees' names, their addresses, the amounts, and so forth. And then the bank writes the checks. You can also tell the bank to make automatic recurring payments for bills that you pay on a regular basis, such as a rent or mortgage payment. You can use Online Bill Payment at any bank.

✔ With Online Account Access, you can get transaction information — such as information about which checks and deposits cleared your account and what bank service fees you've been charged — from the bank's computer. You can also transfer money between accounts — such as from your savings account to your checking account and even from your checking account to your credit card account (to pay a credit card bill). In order to use Quicken for Online Account Access, your bank must support the Quicken Online Account Access service.

Wise Whys and Wherefores

Neither Online Account Access nor Online Bill Payment are difficult to use. And despite the nightmares that people with delusional paranoia may develop about electronic banking, the service is safe, secure, and very solid. Nevertheless, before you, too, jump onto the Online Account Access and Bill Payment bandwagon, you should probably consider a few points:

✔ As I noted a paragraph or so ago, if you want to use the Online Account Access feature, your bank must be a part of the Quicken Online Account Access program. (See the next section for directions on how to find out whether your bank qualifies.)

✔ In order to sign up for and use Online Account Access or Online Bill Payment services, you need an Internet connection.

✔ You should be fairly comfortable with Quicken, especially with account transactions and transferring money between accounts. (Therefore, if you're new to Quicken, you should at least record a handful of checks, make some deposits, and reconcile your account before venturing into Online Account Access.)

✔ Make sure that your records are completely up-to-date and reconciled with the last statements you've received from the bank.

One other consideration — you've probably been waiting for me to bring this one up — this stuff ain't free. I can't tell you how much these two services will cost because your bank sets the charges. A good guess is $5 to $10 a month — and that adds up over the course of a year. But in choosing to use Online Account Access or Online Bill Payment, do consider all the hidden costs of the normal way of banking and paying bills. Gasoline, time, and postage can all add up, and these almost-hidden costs may make the costs of the online services appear more reasonable. (Besides, you won't have to deal with all that nasty glue on your tongue from licking envelopes.)

Banking with Online Account Access and Online Bill Payment

To begin using either the Online Account Access or the Online Bill Payment service, you have to sign up. If you want to use Online Account Access, you sign up with your bank. Just call your local branch and ask someone whether the bank supports Online Account Access. (If your bank doesn't support Online Account Access, you can still sign up with Intuit for Online Bill Payment.)

To set up Quicken to use Online Account Access or Online Bill Payment services, choose the Banking⇨Online Banking Setup command. When you do, Quicken starts a wizard and displays a dialog box asking if you want to set up an existing account for online services or if you want to create a new account. Figure 6-1 shows this dialog box.

Select the account you want to set up for online services and click Next. Quicken displays the Online Setup window for your bank. This window has three hyperlinks. Click the Tell Me More hyperlink to learn about which services your bank offers and how much they cost. If you decide to take the plunge, click the Enroll hyperlink to fill out your bank's application form online. After you've applied (and you may have to wait to receive a welcome packet in the mail with all of the necessary information), click the Set Up Quicken hyperlink to set up Quicken to work with your online account.

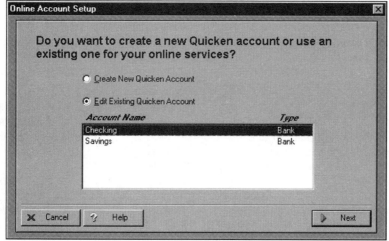

Figure 6-1:
The first dialog box of the Online Account Setup wizard.

Let me say a couple more quick things about setting up for Online Account Access or Online Bill Payment. Your bank or the Quicken folks may, as part of the application process, send you a letter asking for more information, a

Finding an online bank — online

You can also find out which banks support Online Account Access by using your Internet connection. To do so, choose the Finance➪Online Financial Institutions List command. When you choose this command, Quicken starts your web browser and then opens a page that lists the banks that allow you to bank online. (Appendix B talks in a bit more detail about Quicken and its Internet connectivity, but note that you need an Internet connection to use Online Account Access and Online Bill Payment.)

canceled check, or a signature. (If they do, of course, be sure to respond.) Then again, they may not. And then, a couple of weeks after you make your initial application, you'll receive a welcome letter in the mail. The letter indicates that you're now about to either bank online or pay bills online, and it explains what you need to do within Quicken to begin doing all this. (I talk about the welcome letter and what you do with it in the next part of the chapter.)

Honest Steve's evaluation of online services

I'm pretty much a cynic when it comes to new bells and whistles — or at least the kinds of bells and whistles that software companies like to add to the mature versions of their products. And I hate making financial record keeping more complicated. I like things simple. But all that said, I must tell you that I think Online Bill Payment and, in particular, Online Account Access are really, really slick.

If you're already using Quicken to keep your financial records, you get to pay your bills and reconcile your bank accounts for basically no extra work. Well, okay, you have to click your mouse an extra time. And initially, you need to provide addresses and account numbers for your payees (which takes about five minutes). So you do have to do a little extra work at the beginning. But Online Account Access saves you lots of time and hassle.

The only catch — and this is a big one for some Quicken users — is that to use Online Account Access, your bank needs to have its act together. (Note that if your bank doesn't support Online Account Access with Quicken, you can still use Online Bill Payment.)

Now, all that said, I want to close with a caveat. Online Account Access isn't worth it if it means you end up banking at some poorly run bank. I, er, well, yeah, you see, I've been there. And it isn't pretty. To make a long, sorry story short, a long time ago I had the experience of moving my banking from a well-run bank that didn't have Online Account Access to a poorly managed bank that did. Online Account Access is not — I repeat, is not — such a cool tool that you'll be happy banking at First National Idiots.

Setting up your Quicken accounts

After you receive the necessary information from your bank (such as the bank's routing number and your online PIN), you're ready to prepare your Quicken accounts for Online Account Access and Online Bill Payment.

1. **Choose the Banking⇨Online Banking Setup.**

2. **Select the account you want to set up and click Next.**

3. **Click the Set Up Quicken hyperlink.**

   Quicken connects to the Internet and updates the financial institution information.

4. **When Quicken displays the Edit Bank Account dialog box, click the Enable Online Account Access check box and/or the Enable Online Payment check box and click Next.**

   Quicken displays the dialog box shown in Figure 6-2.

5. **Enter your bank's routing number in the Routing Number text box.**

   You can get the routing number, by the way, from the welcome letter.

6. **Click Next again; enter your bank account number and specify which type of account you're adding or editing, as shown in Figure 6-3.**

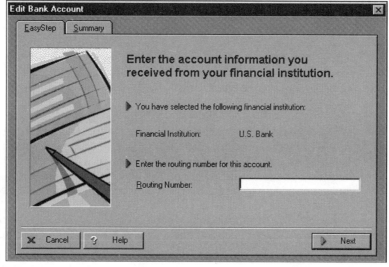

Figure 6-2:
The
EasyStep
tab of the
Edit Bank
Account
dialog box.

This step makes sense, right? You know what your account number is. And to specify the type of bank account, just select an entry like "checking" from the Account Type drop-down list box.

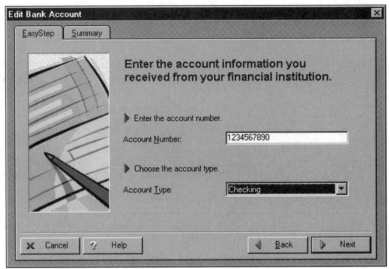

Figure 6-3:
You use this
tab of the
Edit Bank
Account
dialog box
to provide
your
account
number and
account
type.

7. **Click Next yet again; enter your customer identification number, which, almost as sure as the sun rises in the east, is your Social Security number.**

   My editor likes it if I follow the numbered steps with little blurbs of text. I can't really think of anything important to say about your Social Security number, however. So I want to tell you that if you're an average baby boomer or Generation X wage earner and you could have invested the money you pay in Social Security taxes, you would have ended up with $1,000,000 and an annual retirement income of roughly $60,000. If you are this average person, you'll actually get about $8,000 a year of Social Security. Great deal, huh?

8. **Click Next twice and then click Done.**

   You just finished the hardest part of the Online Account Access and Online Bill Payment thing. A lightning icon should now appear next to the account in the Type column of the Account List window. This icon signifies that you successfully set up the account for online services. And you're now ready to begin enjoying your newfound financial freedom.

I guess this point is probably obvious, but you need to repeat the preceding setup process for every account that you want to use for Online Account Access and/or Online Bill Payment.

A bank where only the telephones have long lines

Using Online Account Access and Online Bill Payment is extremely easy. You pay bills in pretty much the usual manner. You make account transfers in the same manner. And then you reconcile transactions with a mouse click.

Paying bills

You have three ways to record online payments. If you're comfortable using the Write Checks window, you write a check in the usual way. You enter the payee name, an amount, probably a category, and so forth. Just make sure that you mark the Online Payment check box (see Figure 6-4).

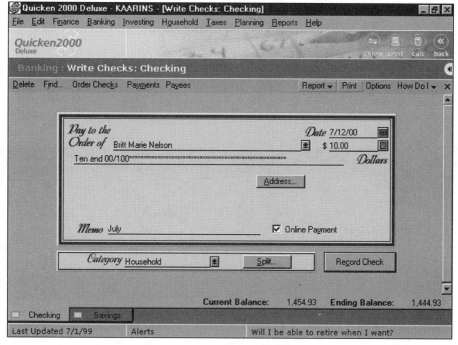

Figure 6-4:
You record online payments with the Write Checks window by marking the Online Payment check box.

If you have questions about how the Write Checks window works, take a peek at Chapter 5. Chapter 5 describes — among other things — how you use the Write Checks window to describe checks you want to print. You use the same basic procedure to describe online payments that you want to make.

If you're more comfortable using the register window to record payments, you can make online payments with that, too. Just specify the payment number as Send, as shown in Figure 6-5.

If you have questions about how the register works, you may want to refer to Chapter 4. Chapter 4 describes — in some detail, I might add — how the Quicken register works.

You can also use the Payments tab in the Online Center to record an online payment. If you take a close look at Figure 6-7, you can see this tab. Just fill out the blanks on this tab like you fill out a check in the Write Checks window. No sweat.

By the way, I should mention that the first time you make an online payment to someone, Quicken asks for some information about where the person lives or where the business is located, what account number Quicken can use to identify you and your payment to the person or business, and so forth (see Figure 6-6).

After you record a payment, you send it to the bank. To do so, display the Online Center by choosing the Banking⇨Online Banking command. When Quicken displays the Online Center window (see Figure 6-7), click the Update/Send button.

When you click the Update/Send button, Quicken connects to your Internet Service Provider and then, through the Internet, to your bank's computer. As part of making this connection, you need to provide a personal identification number, or PIN, as shown in Figure 6-8. When Quicken finishes sending your

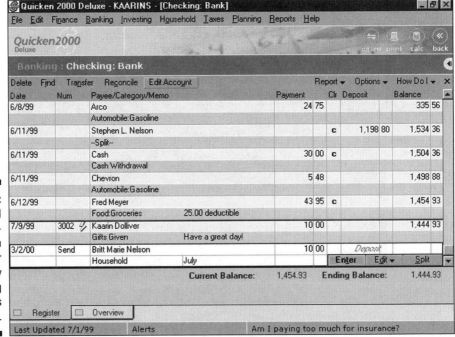

Figure 6-5:
You record online pay-ments with the register window by specifying the Num as Send.

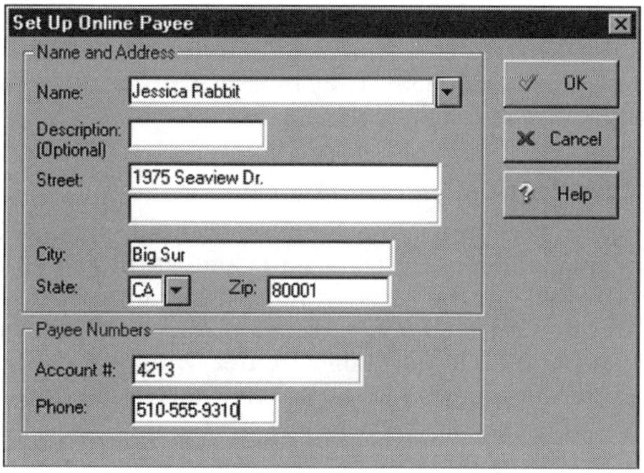

Figure 6-6:
The first
time you
record an
online pay-
ment, you
need to
provide the
name,
address,
and account
number.

bank your payment instructions, it displays the Online Transmission
Summary dialog box that, basically, just says you've connected to the bank's
computer and sent it some payment instructions. At this point, you're done.

Note: The first time that you use Online Account Access, Quicken asks you to
change your personal identification number, or PIN.

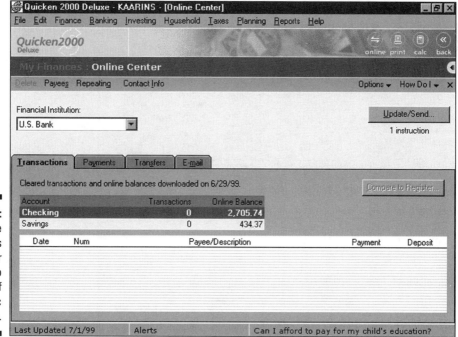

Figure 6-7:
The Online
Center is
your
window into
the world of
electronic
finance.

I need to make an important point here. You must send your payment instructions to the bank several days in advance of the time the bill needs to be paid. For obvious reasons, the bank needs a day or two to process the bill. And then the check has to go through U.S. Mail. . . .

Transferring money between accounts

As you may expect, you record Online Account Access transfers in the same way you record regular transfers. Or at least in almost the same way. For online transfers, you can use the register in the normal way, but you need to specify that the transaction is an online transfer. You can record an account transfer on the Transfers tab in the Online Center window (see Figure 6-9). Just enter the transfer information in the boxes Quicken provides.

You can also do this task by entering the online transfer code, **Oxfr**, into the Num field. Or you can activate the Num drop-down list box and select the Online transfer entry.

As with online payments, after you describe the online transfer that you want to make, you need to make an online connection. To do so, click the Update/Send button and then, when prompted, provide your PIN and click Send. When Quicken finishes sending your bank your account transfer instructions, you're done.

If you have a credit card with a bank that supports Online Account Access and if you also set up the credit card for the Online Account Access (following the same procedure that I describe earlier in this chapter), you can pay

Figure 6-8:
You desig-
nate your
personal
identifica-
tion number
in the
Instructions
to Send
dialog box.

And so what's the deal with CheckFree?

Intuit (the maker of Quicken) used to highly tout CheckFree, which closely resembles Online Bill Payment. Although Quicken users can still use CheckFree, Intuit encourages new users to use Online Bill Payment. Translation: Quicken strongly supports Online Bill Payment, and it integrates that feature into the program more smoothly than it does CheckFree. Nevertheless, you can still use the CheckFree service. To do so, you use the Banking⇨Banking Activities⇨Set Up CheckFree command.

your credit card bill by transferring money from a bank account to your credit card account. You probably already thought of this if you have a credit card account. But I thought I'd mention it anyway. (For more information about credit card accounts, refer to Chapter 11.)

Updating your Quicken accounts

One major advantage of Online Account Access is that you can get the most up-to-date information regarding your accounts. Let me explain. When you click the Online Center window's Update/Send button, the bank automatically sends current transactions to your computer. They are not loaded immediately

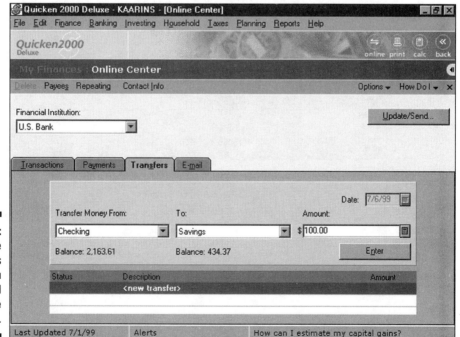

Figure 6-9:
The
Transfers
tab lets you
record
online
transfers.

into your Quicken registers. Quicken gives you a chance to examine them before they go into your records. To update a Quicken account, click the Transactions tab of the Online Center window and select an account from the list box at the upper-left corner of the window tab. When you do, the new transactions for that account appear in the lower half of the tab window. (Figure 6-10 shows this window.)

To add the transaction that you've downloaded from the bank to your account register, click the Compare to Register button. Quicken then displays the appropriate register in the top half of the window and the list of new transactions in the bottom half, as in Figure 6-11. You can accept each new transaction one at a time by clicking it and then clicking Accept. If you're the daring sort, you can click Accept All, and Quicken places all the new transactions in your register. Click Done to close the window.

Communicating online with the bank

Quicken also provides a means of sending and receiving e-mail from your bank. Click the E-mail tab of the Online Center window, and you'll see something similar to Figure 6-12.

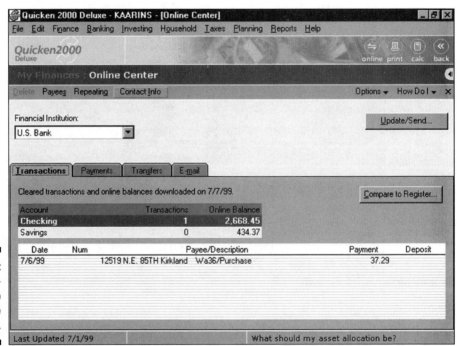

Figure 6-10:
The Trans-
actions tab
of the Online
Center.

Are you still with me?

Okay, I'm going to take a little breather here — just to make sure that you understand what's going on. When you boil everything down to its essence, online payments are really just payment instructions you send your bank. And when you make an online transfer, you are effectively just calling the bank and saying, "Please transfer money from my one account to that other account."

This makes sense, right? You're really just giving instructions to the bank. And then the bank (or

actually the bank's computer) goes off and does whatever you've told it to do. It's pretty simple.

Is Online Account Access anything to get all excited about? Is it really as slick as some people think? I think so. Sure, it's not cheap. But once you get going, you get away from that business of finding your checkbook, signing checks, finding stamps, and then, on occasion, running down to the post office to drop off some overdue bill.

Quicken sends and receives e-mail with any transaction when you click the Update/Send button and then lists any messages that are received in the text box on the E-mail tab. In order to read a message, you just highlight it (by clicking it) and then click Read. Click Close when you finish, and Quicken returns you to the Online Center window. If you don't want to save the message, click it to highlight it and click Delete to remove it from the list.

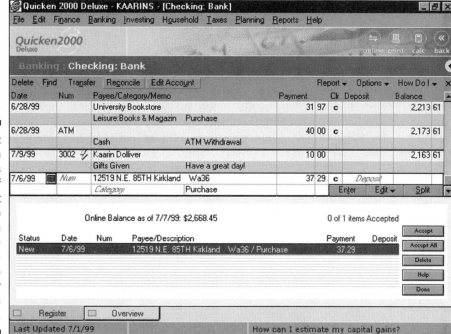

Figure 6-11:
Quicken displays this version of the account register so you can compare the new transactions to your Quicken register.

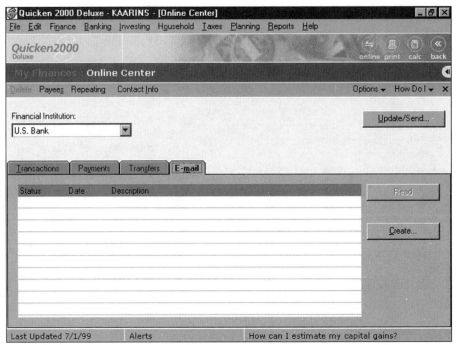

Figure 6-12:
The E-mail
tab of the
Online
Center.

If you want to send your bank a message, click Create. If you have a general question about the bank's online services or an online account, click the E-mail about an Online Account button and select the online account from the Account drop-down list box. If you want to send a message regarding a specific online payment, click the E-mail about an Online Payment button and select the online account and payment. Click OK. Quicken opens a dialog box similar to the one shown in Figure 6-13.

Quicken automatically fills in the date and the To text box. Fill in the other text boxes by clicking them and then typing the necessary information. Open the Regarding Account drop-down list box by clicking the down arrow, and then choose the appropriate account.

After you complete your message, click OK. Quicken records your message and forwards it to the bank the next time that you click Update/Send.

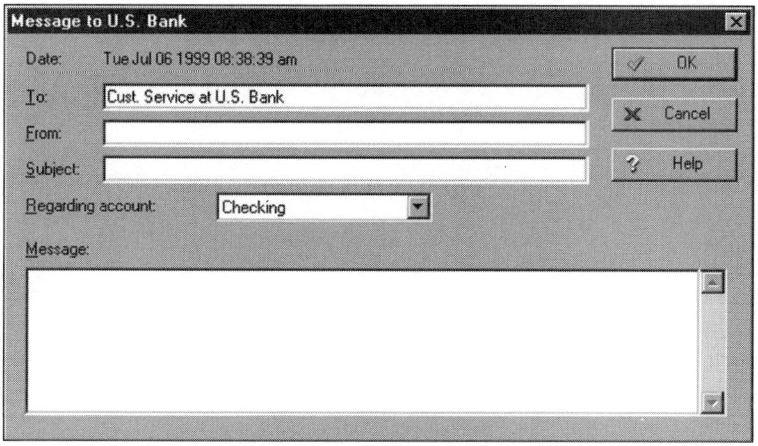

Figure 6-13:
Creating an
e-mail
message.

Chapter 7

Reports, Charts, and Other Cool Tools

. . . .

In This Chapter

▶ Printing Quicken reports

▶ Using the Reports menu commands

▶ QuickZooming report totals

▶ Sharing information with a spreadsheet

▶ Editing and rearranging report information

▶ Creating a chart

▶ Using QuickReports and Snapshots

. . . .

*Q*uicken enables you to summarize, slice, and dice register and account information in a variety of ways. This chapter describes how to easily use reports and produce graphs. This stuff is much easier to understand if you know how to print a register first (a trick I describe at the end of Chapter 5).

Creating and Printing Reports

After you know how to print checks and registers, all other printing in Quicken is easy, easy, easy.

Printing the facts, and nothing but the facts

The transactions you enter in the Register window and the checks you enter in the Write Checks window determine the information in a report. To print a report, just choose the Reports menu and tell Quicken which report you want to print (see Figure 7-1).

Quicken produces a bunch of different reports. To make sense of what may otherwise become mass confusion, Quicken arranges all its reports into five groups: Own & Owe reports, Spending reports, Investing reports, Taxes reports, and Business reports.

To see the reports in one of these groups, select the report group from the Reports menu. If you read the fast-paced and exciting Appendix A, you know that those little triangles to the right of menu command names tell you that another menu follows.

Figure 7-2 shows the Business group of reports. Pretty exciting stuff so far, don't you think?

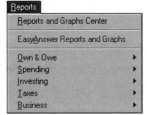

Figure 7-1:
The Reports
menu.

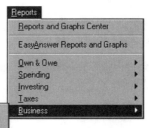

Figure 7-2:
The
Business
group of
reports.

To create a Business report (or any other report, for that matter) on the fly, choose the report from the appropriate menu. For example, to create the Business Cash Flow Report, choose Reports⇨Business⇨Cash Flow Report. After you create a report, you can change the report date or date range using the boxes at the top of the report.

To find out what type of information a report includes before you create the report, or to preview a report, choose Reports⇨Reports and Graphs Center. This displays the Reports and Graphs Center shown in Figure 7-3. Select a report group by clicking a tab on the left side and then select the report you want to create. You can change the report date or date range using the boxes provided. Click View Sample to preview the report first, or click Create Now to create the report.

If you don't enter a new range of dates, Quicken assumes that you want to include transactions from the start of the current calendar year through the present date.

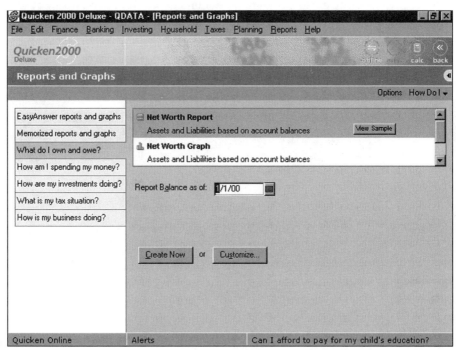

Figure 7-3:
The Reports and Graphs Center.

Notice that a report that shows account balances — such as the Account Balances Report, the Net Worth Report, the Balance Sheet Report, or the Portfolio Value Report — doesn't need a range of dates because the report shows account balances as of a specific date. In these cases, if you don't enter a date, Quicken assumes that you want account balances for the current system date from your computer's internal clock.

Figure 7-4 shows an on-screen version of the Cash Flow Report from the Business group.

You can't see the entire on-screen version of a report unless your report is very small (or your screen is monstrously large). Use PageUp and PageDown to scroll up and down and use Tab and Shift+Tab to move left and right. Or if you're a mouse lover, you can click and drag various pieces of the scrollbars.

To print your report, click the Print button in the upper-right corner. Quicken displays the Print dialog box (see Figure 7-5).

To accept the given specifications — which is almost always fine — just click OK. You'll never guess what happens next: Quicken prints the report!

When you're ready — but not before — remove the on-screen version of the report by closing the report document window. (You do so by clicking the Close button.)

Figure 7-4:
An on-screen version of the Cash Flow Report.

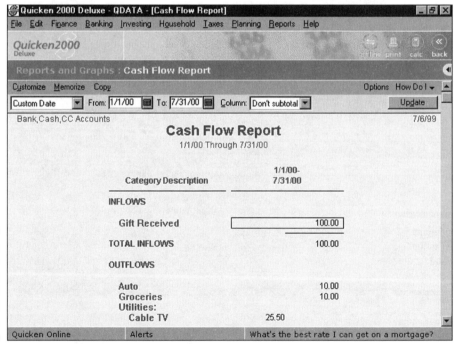

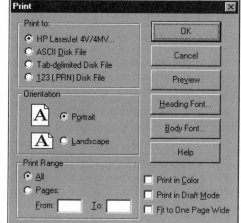

Figure 7-5:
The Print
dialog box.

Print dialog box settings

I almost forgot. The Print To option buttons let you tell Quicken where it should send the report it produces: to the printer or to a disk file. The check boxes let you control aspects of printing, and the Print Range option buttons and text boxes let you print a specific portion of the report.

I describe how these things work in Chapter 5, so I won't repeat the discussion. If you want the scoop, refer to the section about printing a check register.

Reviewing standard reports

Most of the time, you want to select one of the reports listed in the Home, Business, or Investment reports menu.

Tables 7-1 to 7-5 describe Quicken's reports by group. (Some of these babies won't make sense unless you understand how to collect the information that goes into the report, as I describe in Chapters 12 and 13 and in Part IV.)

Table 7-1	Quicken Own & Owe Reports
Report	*Description*
Net Worth	Lists all accounts, their balances, and the difference between the sum of the asset accounts and the sum of the liabilities accounts, which the report identifies as your net worth.
Account Balances	Lists all accounts and their balances.

(continued)

Table 7-1	Quicken Own & Owe Reports *(continued)*
Report	*Description*
Cash Flow	Summarizes the money that flows into and out of an account by income and expense categories and by transfers. Cash is king, dude, so this report only includes transactions that you record in your bank, cash, and credit card accounts.
Cash Flow Comparison	Lets you compare category totals from two periods. You can use this report to compare January's activity with February's activity, for example. Remember: Because you are comparing two periods, you need to enter two transaction date ranges.
Transaction	Lets you list transactions in multiple accounts chronologically.
Itemized Categories	Lists transactions by category.
Banking Summary	Summarizes spending totals by category.
Income/Expense Comparison	Summarizes spending totals by category for two time periods.
Budget	Summarizes income and expense categories and compares actual category totals for the year to budgeted category amounts. This report includes only transactions that you record in your bank, cash, and credit card accounts. (For this report to work, of course, you need to have a budget set up.)
Monthly Budget	Summarizes income and expense categories and compares actual category totals for a month to monthly budgeted category amounts. This report includes only transactions that you record in your bank, cash, and credit card accounts. (For this report to work, of course, you need to have a budget set up.)
Missing Checks	Lists all the checks you've written and flags any gaps in the check number sequence. This report helps you identify missing checks.

Table 7-2	Quicken Investing Reports
Report	*Description*
Capital Gains	Lists all the realized gains on individual investments you hold. (A capital gain occurs when an investment is worth more than you paid for it. When you sell the investment, you realize the gain.)
Investment Performance	A power-user report. This report calculates the internal rates of return delivered by each of the individual investments in your portfolio.
Portfolio Value	Lists the current value of all securities in your investment accounts.
Investment Income	Summarizes income and expense categories for the transactions you record in your investment accounts.
Investment Transactions	Lists recorded transactions for all your investment accounts.

Table 7-3	Quicken Taxes Reports
Report	*Description*
Tax Summary	Lists all transactions you've described as falling into tax-related categories.
Capital Gains	Lists all the realized gains on individual investments you hold. (A capital gain occurs when an investment is worth more than you paid for it. When you sell the investment, you realize the gain.)
Tax Schedule	Lists all transactions you've entered as tax-related and subtotals them by line item.

Table 7-4	Quicken Business Reports
Report	*Description*
P&L Statement	Summarizes income and expense category totals. This report includes transactions from all your accounts. It also helps you answer the business question, "Am I compensated fairly for the hassle and the risk?"
P&L Comparison	Lets you compare profit and loss by category for two periods. You can use this report to compare January's profit with February's profit, for example.
Job/Project	Summarizes income and expense category totals with each class's information displayed in a separate column. You must be using *classes,* an advanced Quicken feature, for this report to make any sense.
Accounts Payable	Summarizes unprinted checks by payee for all your bank accounts.
Accounts Receivable	Summarizes uncleared transactions for all other asset accounts.
Payroll	Summarizes income and expense categories that begin with the word *payroll.* If you do things correctly, you can use this report to prepare quarterly and annual payroll tax reports. (See Chapter 15 for the rest of the story.)
Balance Sheet	Lists all accounts, their balances, and the difference between the sum of your asset accounts and the sum of your liabilities accounts, which the report identifies as your equity. This report is almost identical to the Net Worth report in the Own & Owe group.
Missing Checks	Lists all the checks you've written and flags any gaps in the check number sequence. This report helps you identify missing checks and is identical to the Missing Checks report in the Spending group.
Cash Flow	Summarizes the money received by and paid out of an account by income and expense categories and by transfers. This report includes only transactions you record in your bank, cash, and credit card accounts.
Cash Flow Comparison	Lets you compare category totals from two periods. You can use this report to compare January's activity with February's activity, for example. (Because you are comparing two periods, you must enter two transaction date ranges.) This report is identical to the Cash Flow Comparison report in the Spending group.

Finding the report you want

Okay, if you've just read or even skimmed the reports I describe in Tables 7-1 to 7-5, you're probably a little overwhelmed. Quicken produces a bunch of different reports. How do you know which one provides the answers you want? What are you supposed to do? Sift your way through a couple dozen of these babies?

Thankfully, the answer is no. Quicken also provides something called EasyAnswer reports. In effect, EasyAnswer reports let you identify the question that you want a report to answer. After you identify the question, Quicken produces the appropriate report. Here's how this all works:

1. **Choose Reports⇨EasyAnswer Reports and Graphs.**

   Quicken displays the EasyAnswer Reports and Graphs tab (see Figure 7-6).

2. **Indicate your question.**

   To tell Quicken what your question is, click one of the questions and then use the drop-down list boxes that accompany each question to further refine your question. For example, the "Where did I spend my money?" question lets you pick the period of time you're asking about: Last Year, Last Month, Current Year, Month to Date, and so forth.

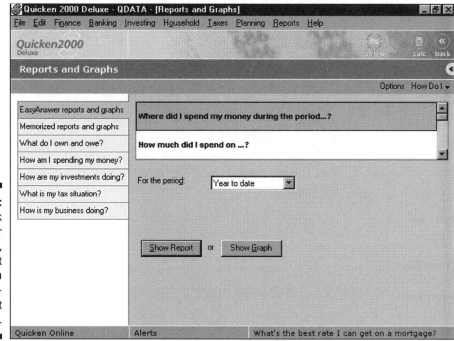

Figure 7-6:
Ask
EasyAnswer
a question,
and it
directs you
to the cor-
rect report
or graph.

3. Click Show Report.

Quicken produces a report that answers your questions. If you ask the question, "Where did I spend my money last year?" for example, Quicken produces a cash flow report that summarizes the previous year's income and expenses by category.

Going to the printing dog and pony show

You can do some neat things with the reports you create. I won't spend a bunch of time talking about these things, but I do want to give you a quick rundown of some of the most valuable tricks.

Got a question about a number? Just zoom it

If you don't understand where a number in a report came from, point to it with the mouse. As you point to numbers, Quicken changes the mouse pointer to a magnifying glass marked with a *Z*. Double-click the mouse, and Quicken displays a list of all the transactions that make up that number.

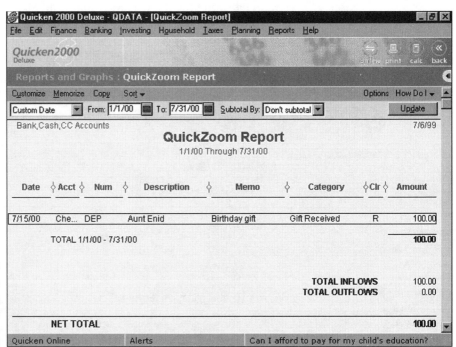

Figure 7-7:
The
QuickZoom
Report.

This feature, called *QuickZoom,* is extremely handy for understanding the figures that appear on your reports. If you double-click the Gift Received number in the report (refer to Figure 7-4), for example, Quicken displays the QuickZoom Report shown in Figure 7-7.

Ah, yes. Now you remember Aunt Enid's thoughtful gift. You have to send her that thank-you note.

Sharing report data with spreadsheets

If you use a Windows spreadsheet such as Microsoft Excel, 1-2-3 for Windows, or Quattro Pro for Windows, you can copy the stuff that shows in a report window to the Clipboard. Select the information and then click the Copy button. Start your spreadsheet program and choose Edit⇨Paste to paste the stuff from the Clipboard into your spreadsheet. This process really isn't very hard, so go ahead and try it. You may need to use this feature if you want to use a spreadsheet to analyze the report data.

Editing and rearranging reports

You may notice that when Quicken displays the report window, it also displays a row of buttons, including (left to right) Customize, Memorize, Copy, Options, and How Do I (refer to Figure 7-7). Below are the date boxes and the Column box. Earlier in the chapter, I talk about what some of these buttons do. So in the interest of fair play, I'll briefly discuss what the other buttons do. (Not all these buttons are available in every report document window. I don't know why, really. Maybe it's just to keep you guessing.)

You really don't need to worry about these other buttons. Read through the discussion that follows only if you're feeling comfortable, relaxed, and truly mellow. Okay?

Customizing

The Customize button works pretty much the same no matter which report shows in the document window.

When you click this button, Quicken displays a dialog box that lets you enter the report title and specify the range of dates the report should cover by using text boxes. It also lets you choose from a variety of other options, too, such as which accounts to use, which transactions to use, and how the report's information should be arranged.

Customizing your reports

If you want to extract some financial tidbit, you can usually get what you want from one of the reports listed on the Reports menu, especially if you use the EasyAnswers feature to find the right report!

I should tell you something: Quicken is remarkably sophisticated in its reporting. You can customize any report you see in the Reports menu.

To customize these reports, click the Customize button to get to the nuts and bolts of your selected report.

I'm not going to describe the Customization process. I feel kind of bad about this because a few people are probably out there who, late one night, will decide that they want to know how to filter, sort, and customize. Of course, there are

also people who will decide late some night that they want to know how to replace the transmission on a 1971 Triumph Spitfire. And I'm not describing that here, either.

If you really want to customize your reports, just noodle around. You can't hurt anything.

If you do play around with these items, you can save any custom report specifications that you create. To do so, click the Memorize button at the top of the report window. Quicken displays a dialog box that asks you to supply a name for your customized report. (You can also provide a default report date range.) After you name the customized report, Quicken lists it whenever you choose Reports⇨Memorized Reports and Graphs.

Memorizing

Say you get into this customization thing. If you do, you should know that you can save your customized reports by clicking the Memorize button. When you click Memorize, Quicken displays the Memorize Report dialog box shown in Figure 7-8. Mostly, Quicken displays this dialog box so you can give your creation a name. If you want, you can also specify whether Quicken should always use some special date range for the report.

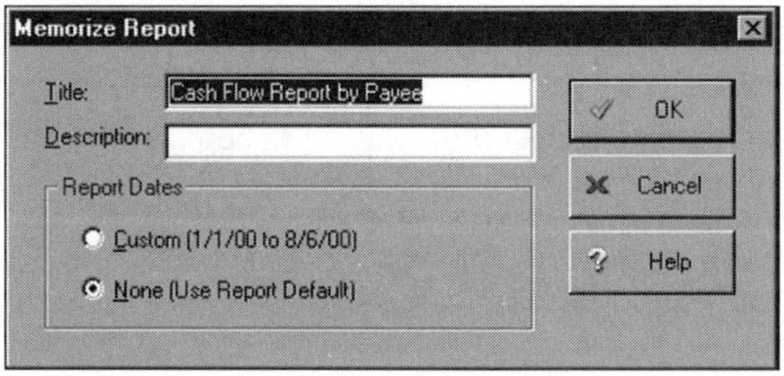

Figure 7-8:
The
Memorize
Report
dialog box.

By the way, after you create a memorized report, you can reproduce it by choosing Reports⇨Memorized Reports and Graphs and then selecting the memorized report name.

What's the Options button for?

Most of the document windows that Quicken displays — the report window is just one example — also display an Options button. When you choose this button, Quicken displays a dialog box with a bunch of boxes and buttons that let you change the way the window looks or works.

If I were a really great writer — the John Grisham of computer books, for example — I might be able to whip up a riveting discussion of how the Report Options dialog box works. I'm going to do both you and my publisher a favor, however, by making a suggestion. Just play with these option settings if you're interested. You'll find it more fun and a better learning experience.

Column subtotaling

The Columns button displays a list that looks suspiciously like the one shown in Figure 7-9. Using this list menu, you can tell Quicken you want to subtotal amounts by some criteria. Just select the criteria and click Update.

Figure 7-9:
The
Columns
drop-down
list box.

Charts Only Look Tricky

I love charts. I know that sounds goofy. But *data graphics* — as the snobs and academics call it — open up wonderful opportunities for communicating. And Quicken charts are really easy to use.

To produce a Quicken chart, choose the Reports menu and select a graph from one of the submenus or choose Reports⇨Reports and Graphs Center, click a group tab, select a graph, and click Create Now.

Use the date boxes at the top of the graph to tell Quicken which days or months of account information you want the graph to summarize.

Finally, click the Customize button to display the Customize Graph dialog box. There you can pick and choose which accounts, categories, and classes you want the graph to include and tell Quicken whether you want the graph to show subcategories.

Figure 7-10 shows a picture of a bar graph of monthly income and expense figures and a pie chart that breaks down monthly spending. They're kind of cool, but you'll have much more fun looking at your own data in a picture. By the way, you can use QuickZoom on a chart to see a report that describes the data being plotted.

The other graph types work basically the same way. The Budget Variance Graph depicts your actual and planned spending and income in bar charts. The Net Worth Graph shows your total assets, total liabilities, and net worth by month in a bar graph. The Investment Graph displays a bar graph showing total portfolio and individual securities values by month. (If you're not working with Quicken investments, of course, this last description sounds like gibberish. Peruse Chapters 12 and 13 first.)

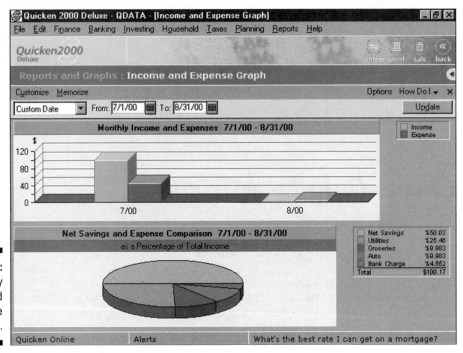

Figure 7-10:
The Monthly
Income and
Expense
Graph.

You can memorize customized graphs the same way you memorize customized reports. Just click the Memorize button at the top of the Graph window. Then, when Quicken prompts you, give the graph a name. To later reuse the graph, choose Reports➪Memorized Reports and Graphs, select the memorized graph from the menu that Quicken displays, and click OK.

QuickReports: Last but Not Least

Before I forget, I need to tell you about one other variant of the Quicken reporting feature: QuickReports. Ah, yes, QuickReports. Here's the deal. Quicken supplies a quick-and-dirty report called, cleverly enough, a QuickReport. If you're working with the register, you can produce a quick report that summarizes things such as the checks written to a particular payee or the transactions assigned to a specific income or expense category. To produce a QuickReport, first move the cursor to the field you want to summarize in the report. Then click the Report button at the top of the register window. Choose the report you want from the Report menu that drops down. The report shown in Figure 7-11, for example, is a QuickReport summarizing payments received from Aunt Enid.

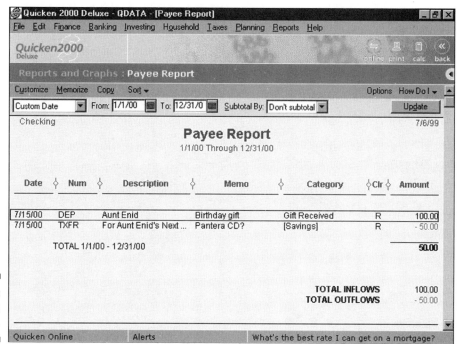

Figure 7-11:
Here's a
QuickReport.

Chapter 8

A Matter of Balance

1 want to start this chapter with an important point: Balancing a bank account in Quicken is easy and quick.

I'm not just trying to get you pumped up about an otherwise painfully boring topic. I don't think balancing a bank account is any more exciting than you do. (At the Nelson house, we never answer the "What should we do tonight?" question by saying, "Hey, let's balance an account.")

My point is this: Because bank account balancing can be tedious and boring, use Quicken to speed up the drudgery.

Selecting the Account You Want to Balance

This step is easy. And you probably already know how to do it, too.

Choose Finance⇨Account List or press Ctrl+A. Quicken displays the Account List window (see Figure 8-1).

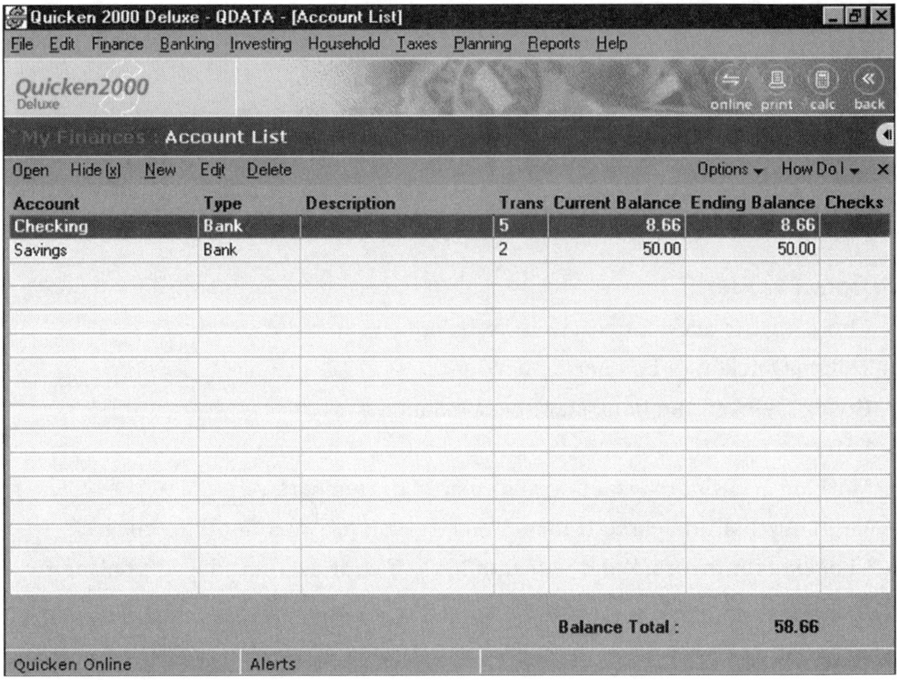

Figure 8-1:
The
Account List
window.

Next, double-click the account that you want to balance. Quicken displays the register window, which lists information about the account.

Balancing a Bank Account

As I said, balancing a bank account is remarkably easy. In fact, I'll go so far as to say that if you have any problems, they'll stem from . . . well, sloppy record-keeping that preceded your use of Quicken.

Telling Quicken, "Hey, man, I want to balance this account"

To tell Quicken that you want to *balance,* or *reconcile,* your account records with the bank's records, click the Reconcile button. Quicken displays the Reconcile Bank Statement dialog box, as shown in Figure 8-2.

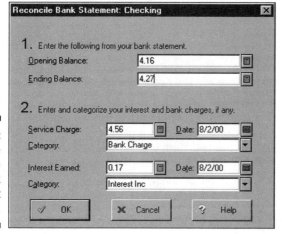

Figure 8-2:
The
Reconcile
Bank
Statement
dialog box.

Giving Quicken the bank's information

As you probably know, in a reconciliation, you compare your records of a bank account with the bank's records of the same account. You should be able to explain any difference between the two accounts — usually by pointing to checks that you've written but that haven't cleared. (Sometimes deposits fall into the same category; you've recorded and mailed a deposit, but the bank hasn't yet credited your account.)

The first step, then, is to supply Quicken with the bank's account information. This information comes from your monthly statement. Supply Quicken with the figures it needs as follows:

1. **Verify the Opening Balance.**

   Quicken displays a figure in the Opening Balance text box. If this figure isn't correct, replace it with the correct figure. To do so, move the cursor to the text box and type over the given figure. (If you're reconciling your account for the first time, Quicken gets this opening balance figure from your starting account balance. If you've reconciled before, Quicken uses the Ending Balance that you specified the last time you reconciled as the Opening Balance.)

2. **Enter the Ending Balance.**

   Move the cursor to the Ending Balance text box and enter the ending, or closing, balance shown on your bank statement.

3. **Enter the bank's service charge.**

   If your bank statement shows a service charge and you haven't already entered it, move the cursor to the Service Charge text box and type the amount (for example, type $4.56 as **4.56**).

4. **Enter a transaction date for the service charge transaction.**

   Quicken supplies its best guess for the date. If you're reconciling for the first time, Quicken uses the current system date from your computer's clock. If you have reconciled the account before, Quicken picks a date one month later from the last time you reconciled the account. If the date Quicken picks isn't correct, enter the correct one.

   Remember that you can adjust a date one day at a time by using either the + or - key.

5. **Assign the bank's service charge to a category.**

   Quicken helps you out by displaying the Bank Charge category in the first <u>C</u>ategory text box — the one beneath the Service Charge text box. If you want to use a different category, click the down arrow in the Category text box to open the Category drop-down list box; then select a category by scrolling down the list and pressing Enter.

6. **Enter the account's interest income.**

   If the account earned interest for the month and you haven't already entered this figure, type an amount in the Interest Earned text box (for example, type $.17 as **.17**).

7. **Enter a transaction date for the interest income transaction.**

   You already know how to enter dates. I won't bore you by explaining it again (but see Step 4 if you're having trouble).

8. **Assign the interest to a category.**

   Quicken comes to the rescue again by displaying Interest Inc in the second Category text box. To select a different category from the Category drop-down list box, open the drop-down list box by clicking the down arrow; then select the category and press Enter.

9. **Tell Quicken that the reconciliation is complete.**

   To do so, just click OK. Quicken displays the Reconcile window, which I describe in the next section.

Explaining the difference between your records and the bank's

Next, Quicken compares your register's account balance with the bank statement's ending account balance. Then it builds a list of checks and deposits that your register shows but that haven't yet *cleared* (haven't been recorded by the bank). Figure 8-3 shows the window that Quicken displays to provide you with this information.

As Figure 8-3 shows, the Reconcile Bank Statement window is basically just two lists — one of account withdrawals and one of account deposits. The window also displays some extra information at the bottom of the screen: the Cleared Balance (which is your account balance including only those transactions that you or Quicken have marked as cleared), the Statement Ending Balance, and the Difference between these two figures.

If you don't like the order in which withdrawals and deposits are arranged, you can change it. Click the View button and choose Sort by Date, and Quicken reorders the transactions by date.

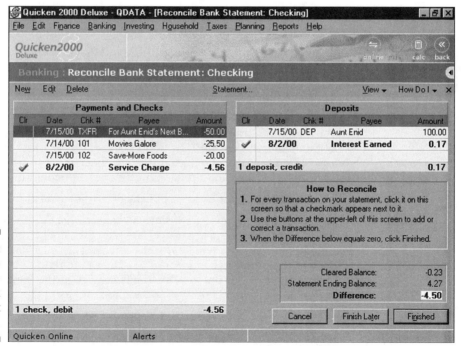

Figure 8-3:
The
Reconcile
Bank
Statement
window.

Marking cleared checks and deposits

You need to tell Quicken which deposits and checks have cleared at the bank. (Refer to your bank statement for this information.)

1. **Identify the first deposit that has cleared.**

   You know how to do so, I'm sure. Just leaf through the bank statement and find the first deposit listed.

2. **Mark the first cleared deposit as cleared.**

   Scroll through the transactions listed in the right column of the Reconcile Bank Statement window, find the deposit, and then mark it as cleared by clicking it. Quicken places a check mark in front of the deposit and updates the cleared statement balance.

3. **Record any cleared but missing deposits.**

   If you can't find a deposit, you haven't entered it into the Quicken register yet. I can only guess why you haven't entered it. Maybe you just forgot. In any event, return to the Quicken register by clicking the Edit button and then enter the deposit in the register in the usual way — but enter a **c** (for "cleared") in the Clr column. This mark identifies the deposit as one that's already cleared at the bank. To return to the Reconcile Bank Statement window, click the Reconcile button.

4. **Repeat Steps 1, 2, and 3 for all deposits listed on the bank statement.**

5. **Identify the first check or other withdrawal that has cleared.**

   No sweat, right? Just find the first check or withdrawal listed on the bank statement.

6. **Mark the first cleared check or other withdrawal as cleared.**

   Scroll through the transactions listed in the left column of the Reconcile Bank Statement window, find the first check, and select it to mark it as having cleared the bank. Quicken inserts a check mark to label this transaction as cleared and updates the cleared statement balance.

7. **Record any missing but cleared checks or withdrawals.**

   If you can't find a check or withdrawal — guess what? — you haven't entered it in the Quicken register yet. Display the Quicken register by clicking the Edit button. Then enter the check or withdrawal in the register. Be sure to enter a **c** (for "cleared") in the Clr column to identify this check or withdrawal as one that's already cleared at the bank. To return to the Reconcile Bank Account window, click the Reconcile button.

8. **Repeat Steps 5, 6, and 7 for withdrawals listed on the bank statement.**

By the way, these steps don't take very long. It takes me about two minutes to reconcile my account each month. And I'm not joking or exaggerating. By two minutes, I really mean two minutes.

Making sure that the difference equals zero

After you mark all the cleared checks and deposits, the difference between the cleared balance for the account and the bank statement's ending balance should equal zero. Notice that I said, "should," not "will." Figure 8-4 shows a Reconcile Bank Statement window in which everything is hunky-dory and life is grand.

If the difference does equal zero, you're done. Just click the Finished button to tell Quicken that you're done. Quicken displays a congratulatory message telling you how proud it is of you, and then it asks whether you want to print a Reconciliation report.

As part of the finishing-up process, Quicken changes all the cs to Rs. There's no great magic in this transformation. Quicken makes the changes to identify the transactions that have already been reconciled.

Can't decide whether to print the Reconciliation report? Unless you're a business bookkeeper or an accountant reconciling a bank account for someone else — your employer or a client, for example — you don't need to print the Reconciliation report. All printing does is prove that you reconciled the account. (Basically, this proof is the reason you should print the report if you *are* a bookkeeper or an accountant — the person for whom you're reconciling the account will know that you did your job and has a piece of paper to come back to later if she has questions.)

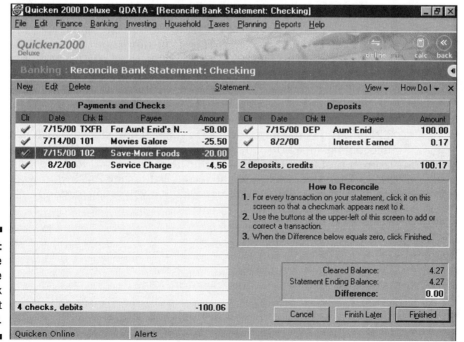

Figure 8-4:
The Reconcile Bank Statement window.

If the difference doesn't equal zero, you have a problem. If you click Finished, Quicken provides some cursory explanations as to why your account doesn't balance (via a dialog box similar to that shown in Figure 8-5). This box tells you that you can force the two amounts to agree by clicking the Adjust button.

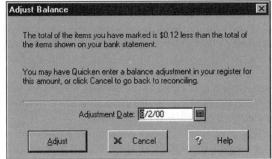

Figure 8-5:
The Adjust
Balance
dialog box.

Adjust Balance

The total of the items you have marked is $0.12 less than the total of the items shown on your bank statement.

You may have Quicken enter a balance adjustment in your register for this amount, or click Cancel to go back to reconciling.

Adjustment Date: 8/2/00

Adjust   ✕ Cancel   ? Help

Forcing the two amounts to agree isn't a very good idea. To do so, Quicken adds a cleared and reconciled transaction equal to the difference. (I talk about this transaction a little later in the chapter.)

If you want to reconcile later without saving your unfinished work, click Cancel in the Reconcile Bank Statement window, and then click Yes when Quicken asks you if you really want to quit without saving your work. The next time you click Reconcile, you will have to start over from scratch.

If you can't get your account to reconcile but want to save your work, click Finish Later. Quicken leaves your reconciliation work basically half done. The transactions that you marked as cleared still show a c in the Clr field. And you still have an explainable difference between the bank statement and your register.

Either way, postponing a reconciliation and not choosing to adjust the bank account balance is usually the best approach. It enables you to locate and correct problems. (I give you some ideas about how to do so in the next section.) Then you can restart the reconciliation and finish your work. (You restart a reconciliation the same way that you originate one.)

Ten Things You Should Do If Your Account Doesn't Balance

I have some suggestions for reconciling an account that's causing you problems. If you're sitting in front of your computer wringing your hands, try the following tips.

Make sure that you're working with the right account

Sounds dumb, doesn't it? If you have a bunch of different bank accounts, however, ending up in the wrong account is pretty darned easy. So go ahead and confirm, for example, that you're trying to reconcile your checking account at Mammoth International Bank, using the Mammoth International checking account statement.

Look for transactions that the bank has recorded but you haven't

Go through your bank statement and make sure that you have recorded every transaction that your bank has recorded. Cash machine withdrawals, special fees or service charges (such as for checks or your safety deposit box), automatic withdrawals, direct deposits, and so on are easily overlooked.

If the difference is positive — that is, the bank thinks you have less money than you think you should — you may be missing a withdrawal transaction. If the difference is negative, you may be missing a deposit transaction.

Look for reversed transactions

Here's a tricky one. If you accidentally enter a transaction backwards — a deposit as a withdrawal or a withdrawal as a deposit — your account won't balance. And the error can be difficult to find. The Reconcile Bank Statement window shows all the correct transactions, but a transaction amount appears positive when it should be negative or negative when it should be positive. The check you wrote to Mrs. Travis for your son's piano lessons appears as a positive number instead of a negative number, for example.

Look for a transaction that's equal to half the difference

One handy way to find the transaction that you entered backwards — *if* you only have one — is to look for a transaction that's equal to half the irreconcilable difference. For example, if the difference is $200, you may have entered a $100 deposit as a withdrawal or a $100 withdrawal as a check.

I don't want to beat a dead horse, but the sign (that is, positive or negative) of the difference should help you find the problem. If the difference is positive — the bank thinks you have less money than your register indicates — you may have mistakenly entered a withdrawal as a deposit. If the difference is negative — the bank thinks you have more money than your register says — you may be missing a deposit transaction.

Look for a transaction that's equal to the difference

While I'm on the subject of explaining the difference by looking at individual transactions, let me make an obvious point. If the difference between the bank's records and yours equals one of the transactions listed in your register, you may have incorrectly marked the transaction as cleared or incorrectly left the transaction marked as uncleared.

I don't know. Maybe that was too obvious.

Check for transposed numbers

Transposed numbers occur when you flip-flop two digits in a number. For example, you enter $45.89 as **$48.59**.

These turkeys always cause accountants and bookkeepers headaches. If you look at the numbers, detecting an error is often difficult because the digits are the same. For example, when comparing a check amount of $45.89 in your register with a check for $48.59 shown on your bank statement, both check amounts show the same digits: 4, 5, 8, and 9. They just show them in different orders.

Transposed numbers are tough to find, but here's a trick you can try. Divide the difference shown on the Reconcile Bank Statement window by nine. If the result is an even number of dollars or cents, you may have a transposed number somewhere.

Have someone else look over your work

This idea may seem pretty obvious, but I am amazed at how often a second pair of eyes can find something that you've been overlooking.

If you're using Quicken at home, ask your spouse. If you're using Quicken at work, ask the owner or one of your co-workers (preferably that one person who always seems to have way too much free time).

Look out for multiple errors

By the way, if you find an error by using this laundry list and still can't balance your account, you should start checking at the top of the list again. You may, for example, discover — after you find a transposed number — that you entered another transaction backwards or incorrectly cleared or uncleared a transaction.

Try again next month (and maybe the month after that)

If the difference isn't huge in relation to the size of your bank account, you may want to wait until next month and attempt to reconcile your account again.

Before my carefree attitude puts you in a panic, consider the following example. You reconcile your account in January, and the difference is $24.02. Then you reconcile the account in February, and the difference is $24.02. Then you reconcile the account in March, and, surprise, surprise, the difference is still $24.02.

What's going on here? Well, your starting account balance was probably off by $24.02. (The more months you try to reconcile your account and find that you're always mysteriously $24.02 off, the more likely it is that this type of error is to blame.)

After the second or third month, I think it's pretty reasonable to tell Quicken that it should enter an adjusting transaction for $24.02 so that your account balances. (In my opinion, this is the only circumstance that merits your adjusting an account to match the bank's figure.)

By the way, if you've successfully reconciled your account with Quicken before, your work may not be at fault. The mistake could be (drum roll, please) the bank's! And in this case, you should do something else. . . .

Get in your car, drive to the bank, and beg for help

As an alternative to the preceding idea — which supposes that the bank's statement is correct and that your records are incorrect — I propose this idea: Ask the bank to help you reconcile the account. (Check whether they charge for this service first, of course.) Hint that you think the mistake is probably theirs. Smile a great deal. And one other thing — be sure to ask about whatever product they're currently advertising in the lobby. (This behavior encourages them to think that you're interested in that 180-month certificate of deposit, and they'll be extra nice to you.)

In general, the bank's record-keeping is usually pretty darned good. I've never had a problem as a business banking client or as an individual. (I've also been lucky enough to deal with big, well-run banks.)

Nevertheless, your bank may have made a mistake, so ask the people there to help you. (***Note:*** Be sure to have them explain any transactions that you discover only by seeing them on your bank statement.)

Chapter 9

Housekeeping for Quicken

. . . .

In This Chapter

▶ Formatting your floppy disks

▶ Backing up your Quicken data

▶ Knowing when and how often to back up your data

▶ Knowing what to do if you lose your Quicken data

▶ Creating and working with more than one set of Quicken data

▶ Setting up a new file password

▶ Changing a file password

. . . .

*O*kay, you don't have to worry about chasing dust bunnies in Quicken, but you do have to take care of little housekeeping tasks. This chapter describes these chores and how to do them right, with minimal hassle.

Formatting Floppy Disks

You need someplace safe to store the financial information you collect with Quicken — someplace in addition to your computer's hard disk. No, I'm not talking about under your mattress or that secret place in the attic. I'm talking about floppy disks. So, you need to know how to format a floppy disk.

A floppy disk needs to be formatted before you can store information on it. You can buy preformatted floppy disks. (The package says "Formatted Disks.") You also can buy unformatted floppy disks.

Density is a little trickier because you can use both low- and high-density disks in a high-density drive. If you don't know the density of your drive, I suggest that you find the paperwork you got when you (or whoever) bought the computer. The paperwork should tell you whether the drive is high-density (by using the code HD or by giving you the amount of storage space that you have — 1.44MB on a 3½-inch floppy). You can also scrounge around to see whether you've been using low-density or high-density floppy disks. High-density floppy disks often have the letters HD printed on them. Low-density disks often either have the letters DD printed on them or sometimes give the amount of storage space — 720K on a 3½-inch floppy. They may even have the words Double Sided printed on them.

Anyway, after you figure out the density and size thing, you're ready to format the disk. Just follow these steps:

1. **Stuff a floppy disk of the right size and density into the correct floppy disk drive.**

   Start Windows Explorer and then right-click the floppy drive icon. To start Windows Explorer in a flash, right-click the Start button and choose Explore.

2. **Right-click the floppy disk icon and choose the For_mat command from the menu that Windows displays.**

   Hopefully you know that when you start Windows Explorer it displays a little tree diagram of all your computer in the left pane of the Explorer window. One branch of the tree shows an icon for your floppy disk. This icon is the thing you want to right-click so Windows displays the short-cuts menu. When you choose the Format command from the shortcuts menu, Windows Explorer displays the Format dialog box (as shown in Figure 9-1).

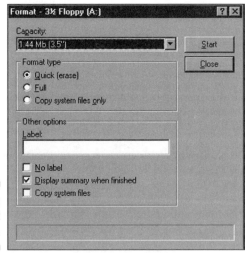

Figure 9-1:
The Format
dialog box.

3. **Use the Capacity drop-down list box to indicate the floppy disk density.**

4. **If you're formatting a new disk (and not just recycling an old, already formatted one), click the Full option button.**

5. **Click Start.**

   Windows Explorer goes off and formats the disk. Next, you see a message that tells you the format is complete (see Figure 9-2).

   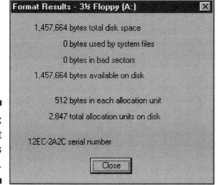

   If Windows Explorer reports that your disk has bad sectors, throw the disk away and use a different one. Disks are so cheap that it just doesn't make sense to risk storing important information on a faulty one.

6. **Click Close.**

7. **Remove the Format dialog box by clicking Close.**

8. **Exit Windows Explorer by clicking its Close button.**

Figure 9-2:
The Format
Results
dialog box.

```
Format Results - 3½ Floppy (A:)          [X]

    1,457,664 bytes total disk space

         0 bytes used by system files

         0 bytes in bad sectors

    1,457,664 bytes available on disk

         512 bytes in each allocation unit

       2,847 total allocation units on disk

  12EC-2A2C serial number

              [  Close  ]
```

This formatting business involves more than I describe here. If you want more information and you're adventurous, flip open the Windows user guide that came with your computer and look up the Format command in the index. If you're not adventurous, you should probably be buying preformatted floppy disks.

Backing Up Is Hard to Do

You should back up the files that Quicken uses to store your financial records. But you need to know how to back up before you can back up.

Backing up the quick and dirty way

You're busy. You don't have time to fool around. You just want to do a passable job backing up files. Sound like your situation? Then follow these steps:

1. **Insert a blank, formatted floppy disk into your floppy drive.**

   If you have two floppy drives, the top one is drive A and the bottom one is drive B. I'm going out on a limb here and assuming that you're using the ol' drive A.

2. **Verify that the file you want to back up is active.**

   Display the register window and make sure that it displays one of the accounts in the file you want to back up. You can do so by clicking the register's QuickTab. (If you don't remember setting up multiple files, don't worry. You probably have only one file — the usual case.)

3. **Start the backup operation.**

   Choose File⇨Backup from the menu bar. Quicken asks you if you're ready to start backing up to your disk. Click Yes to display the Select Backup Drive dialog box, as shown in Figure 9-3.

Figure 9-3:
The Select
Backup
Drive dialog
box.

4. **Identify the backup floppy drive.**

   If necessary, open the Backup Drive drop-down list box and select the letter of the floppy drive you stuffed a disk into. If you've followed my sage advice, this is drive A.

5. **Select the Select From List option button only if the file you're currently working on isn't the file you want to back up (optional).**

(If you want to back up the current file you're working on, you can skip to Step 7.)

Okay, here's the deal. In Quicken, you can have more than one set of financial records, and each set of records gets stored in its own file. If you've been following along in this book, however, you probably have only one set of financial records so far. (In fact, I'd bet my neighbor's dog's life on it.) But if, by chance, you've used File⇨New to create an entirely new file, you need to indicate which file you want to back up.

6. **Tell Quicken which file you want to back up — only if you have done Step 5.**

After you select the Select From List option button and click OK, or press Enter, Quicken displays the Select a Quicken Data File to Back Up dialog box (shown in Figure 9-4) for you to select the file that should be backed up. Just select the file so that it appears in the File Name text box. Figure 9-4 displays two files: QDATA.QDF, which Quicken creates when you install it, and BUSINESS.QDF, which I created to illustrate this step.

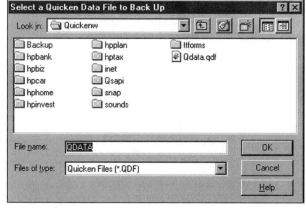

Figure 9-4:
The Select a
Quicken
Data File to
Back Up
dialog box.

7. **Click OK.**

You see a message on-screen that says, "Aye, Cap'n, I'm working just as fast as I can" (or something to that effect). Then you see a message that says the backup is complete. Don't worry. You'll never see a message that says, "She's starting to break up, Cap'n. She can't take warp 9 much longer." You will see a warning message if the file you want to back up is too large. In this case, you'll need to either shrink the file, use a different disk, or use multiple disks.

Deciding when to back up

Sure, I can give you some tricky, technical examples of fancy backup strategies, but they have no point here. You want to know the basics, right? So here's what I do to back up my files. I back up every month after I reconcile. Then I stick the floppy disk in my briefcase, so if something terrible happens at home, I don't lose both my computer and the backup disk with the data.

I admit that my strategy has a few problems, however. For example, because I'm backing up only once a month, I may have to reenter as much as a month's worth of data if the computer crashes toward the end of the month. In my case, I wouldn't lose all that much work. However, if you have really heavy transaction volumes — if you write hundreds of checks a month, for example — you may want to back up more frequently than this, such as once a week. If you use the same disk or set of disks to back up your Quicken file, Quicken will warn you before it replaces the old file with the new one. You can go ahead and let Quicken do this, as long as you're sure that you won't want to access the old file anymore.

A second problem with my strategy is only remotely possible but is still worth mentioning. If something bad does happen to the Quicken files stored on my computer's hard disk *and* the files stored on the backup floppy disk, I'm up the proverbial creek without a paddle. I should also note that a floppy disk is far more likely to fail than a hard drive. If this worst-case scenario actually occurs, I'll need to start over from scratch from the beginning of the year. To prevent this scenario from happening, some people — those who are religiously careful — make more than one backup copy of their Quicken files.

By the way, Quicken periodically prompts you to back up when you try to exit. (You'll see a message that basically says, "Friend, backing up is a darn good idea.") You can, of course, choose to ignore this message. Or you can take Quicken's advice and do the backup thing as I describe earlier in this chapter.

You know what else? Here's a secret feature of Quicken: Quicken adds a subdirectory to the Quicken directory named Backup. And it'll stick a backup copy of your files in this directory every few days. (Sorry to be vague on this point, but it's hard to be specific and concrete when it comes to undocumented features.) More on this later, in the section titled "Losing your Quicken data when you haven't backed up."

Losing your Quicken data after you have backed up

What happens if you lose all your Quicken data? First of all, I encourage you to feel smug. Get a cup of coffee. Lean back in your chair. Gloat for a couple of minutes. You, my friend, will have no problem.

After you've sufficiently gloated, carefully do the following to reinstate your Quicken data on the computer:

1. **Get your backup floppy disk.**

   Find the backup disk you created and carefully insert it into one of your disk drives. (If you can't find the backup disk, forget what I said about feeling smug — stop gloating and skip to the next section.)

2. **Start Quicken.**

   You already know how to do this, right? By the way, if the disaster that caused you to lose your data also trashed other parts of your computer, you may need to reinstall Quicken. Shoot. I suppose it's possible that you may even need to reinstall Windows.

3. **Choose File⇨Restore Backup File from the menu.**

   Quicken displays the Select Restore Drive dialog box. Select the floppy drive that holds your backed up Quicken file and click OK. Quicken displays the Restore Quicken File dialog box, shown in Figure 9-5.

   Quicken looks at the floppy disk in drive A and displays a list of the files stored on the floppy disk, as shown in Figure 9-5. (If you have only one Quicken file on the disk — the usual case — only one file is listed.) If your computer has another floppy disk in it and this other floppy disk has the backup copy of the file, use the Look In drop-down list box to select the other floppy drive.

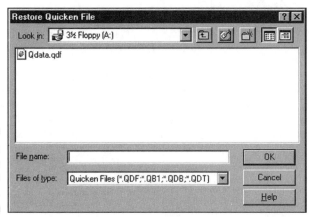

Figure 9-5:
The Restore Quicken File dialog box.

4. **Select the file you want to restore and click OK.**

   Use the arrow keys or the mouse to select the file that you want to restore.

   If the file you select is the one Quicken used last, the program displays a message asking if it's okay to overwrite, or replace, the file with the one stored on the floppy disk.

   When you restore a file, you replace the current, in-memory version of the file with the backup version stored on the floppy disk. Don't restore a file for fun. Don't restore a file for entertainment. Restore a file only if the current version is trashed and you want to start over by using the version stored on the backup floppy disk.

5. **Click OK.**

   Quicken replaces the file it's currently using with the one from the backup floppy disk. After it finishes, Quicken displays a message telling you that it has restored the file. You're almost done.

6. **Update the account registers as necessary.**

   Using the register windows for each of the accounts in a file, reenter each of the transactions you recorded since you created the backup. Be sure that you update your accounts, because you've almost certainly entered transactions since the last time you backed up.

   Just to be on the safe side, you should back up the file after you complete this process. Using a new floppy disk is probably a good idea, too. I have heard that lightning never strikes the same place twice, but I'm not sure that the old saying is true. If you have hard disk problems or another recurring problem, whatever fouled up your file this time may rear its ugly head again — and soon.

Losing your Quicken data when you haven't backed up

What do you do if you haven't backed up your files in a while and you lose all the data in your Quicken files? Okay. Stay calm. All may not be lost.

First, you can try restoring the files from the Quicken backup directory. To do so, you follow the same file restoration steps I cover in the preceding section, with one minor exception. When you get to the Select Restore Drive dialog box, you select your C drive. Then use the Look In box to indicate that you want to see the backup files in the BACKUP folder of the QUICKENW folder.

At this point, you'll probably see a list of files with names similar to the file you lost. If the file you lost had the name QDATA, for example, you may see files named QDATA1 and QDATA2. Select the newest file, which is the one with the "1" suffix, as in QDATA1; then click OK. Quicken uses the file to restore the current file. As alluded to earlier, this may just work. And if it does, you should feel very lucky. Very lucky indeed.

Okay. So suppose that you've tried the approach described in the preceding paragraph, and it didn't work. What next?

You have to reenter all the transactions for the entire year. Yeah. I know. It's a bummer. This method isn't quick, and it isn't pretty, but it works.

If you have copies of the registers, of course, you can use these as your infor-mation source to reenter the information in your files. If you don't have copies of the registers, you need to use your bank statements and any of the other paper financial records you have.

If, for some unfortunate reason, the only copy you have of your Quicken data seems to have become corrupted, you can have Quicken rebuild the file. To do so, choose File➪File Operations➪Validate and enter the name of the file you want rebuilt in the File Name text box. You typically do this, however, only when instructed by Quicken or Intuit technical support people.

Working with Files, Files, and More Files

As part of setting up Quicken, you create what Quicken calls a *file:* a place where Quicken stores all your accounts (bank accounts, credit card accounts, investment accounts, and so on).

You can have more than one Quicken file at any time. Most people won't want to do this. But, for example, you can use different files to keep your personal financial records separate from business financial records.

In the old days, Quicken referred to personal account and business account files as *account groups.* I mention this fact for the benefit of those readers who are history buffs and, therefore, love to fill their heads with boring bits of technology trivia.

Using multiple files does have a little drawback, however. You can't easily record, in one fell swoop, account transfer transactions between accounts in different files. You need to record the transaction twice — once in the *source account,* the file where the transaction originates, and again in the *destination account,* the file where you are transferring the transaction.

If the two accounts involved in a transfer are in the same file, just enter the account name in the Category text box. Quicken then records the transfer in the other account for you.

Setting up a new file

To set up a new file so that you can create accounts in it, follow these steps:

1. **Choose File⇨New from the menu bar.**

   Quicken displays the Creating new file: Are you sure? dialog box, as shown in Figure 9-6.

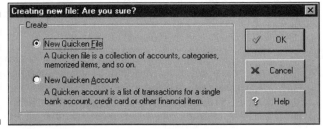

Figure 9-6:
The Creating new file: Are you sure? dialog box.

2. **Select the New Quicken File option button and then click OK or press Enter.**

   Quicken displays the Create Quicken File dialog box, as shown in Figure 9-7.

Figure 9-7:
The Create Quicken File dialog box.

3. **Enter a name for the Quicken file.**

   Position the cursor on the File Name text box and type some meaningful combination of letters and numbers. You don't need to enter a file extension because Quicken supplies the correct file extension, QDF, for you.

   Note: You can use the symbol characters on your keyboard, but doing so gets a little tricky. If you must use symbol characters in the filename, refer to the user documentation for Quicken.

4. **Use the default file location.**

   Accept Quicken's suggestion to store the file in the QUICKENW directory — I can think of no good reason to put it in another file location.

5. **Click OK.**

   Quicken displays the Create New Account dialog box, as shown in Figure 9-8.

6. **Select one of the appropriate account option buttons.**

   You need to set up at least one account for the new file, so click the appropriate account button.

7. **Describe the account.**

   When Quicken displays a Checking Account Setup dialog box, such as the one in Figure 9-9, click the Summary tab. Fill out the text boxes to collect the starting account balance information for the new account. (If you need help filling out this dialog box, refer to Chapter 2.)

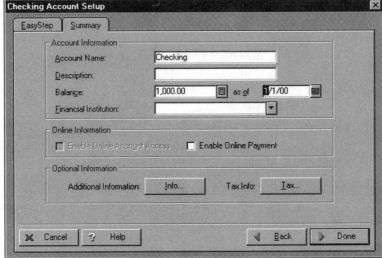

Figure 9-9:
The
Checking
Account
Setup dialog
box with the
Summary
tab
showing.

Flip-flopping between files

You can only work with one file at a time. So, after you create a second file, you need to know how to flip-flop between your files. If you're recording business stuff, for example, you want to be using the business file. However, what if a transaction comes in that clearly is meant for your personal file and you want to enter it there immediately? Flip-flopping allows you to get from one file to another in no time.

For people who just have to be in the know . . .

What Quicken refers to as a file is really a set of data and index files with the same filename, such as HOME, but different file extensions, such as ABD, QDF, QEL, and QSD. So when Quicken refers to the HOME file, it really is referring to the set of files that includes HOME.ABD, HOME.QDF, HOME.QEL, and HOME.QSD.

In most cases, you never need to know the distinction between the files in the set, but the knowledge may come in handy someday. For example, if you happen to stumble onto the Quicken directory, knowing about the set of HOME files keeps you from panicking when you see all the multiple copies of the HOME file. Or, on a more serious note, if you use a third-party backup utility, you need to know which of these files contains data that should be backed up.

Flip-flopping is easy: Just choose File⇨Open. Quicken displays the Open Quicken File dialog box. Pick the file you want from the File Name text box and then click OK. Zap! You are in the new file.

If you really want to switch to another file with lightning speed, you can select the name of the other file directly from the bottom of the File menu, where Quicken lists the last four files you used.

When files get too big for their own good

You can enter a large number of transactions in a Quicken file; in fact, you can record tens of thousands of transactions in a single account or file. Wowsers!

In spite of these huge numbers, I can think of some good reasons to work with smaller files, if you can. For example, you can fit only about 5,000 transactions on a double-density 3½-inch disk. So working with files of a manageable size means that you can more easily back them up on a floppy disk. Also, fewer transactions means Quicken runs faster because more memory is available for Windows. (Windows likes lots of memory — the same way that some people like lots of ice cream.)

If your files have gotten too big for their own good, you can knock them down to size by creating a new file that contains only the current year's transactions. You end up with a copy of the big file that you won't use anymore and a smaller, shrunken file with just the current year's transactions. Working with a smaller file probably means that Quicken will run faster. (The memory thing comes into play again.) And smaller files should make backing up easier because you can probably keep your files small enough to fit on a single, double-density floppy disk.

Call me a Nervous Nellie — or a Nervous Nelson — but because shrinking a file involves wholesale change, I'd really feel more comfortable helping you through this process if you first back up the file you're about to shrink. I don't think that you need to be anxious about anything, but just in case something does go wrong during the shrinking process, I know that you would like to have a backup copy of the file to fall back on.

To shrink a Quicken file, follow these steps:

1. **Choose File⇨File Operations⇨Year-End Copy from the menu bar.**

   Quicken displays a portrait of Barry Nelson, the first actor to portray James Bond. No, not really — I just wanted to see if you were awake. Actually, Quicken displays the Year-End Copy dialog box, as shown in Figure 9-10.

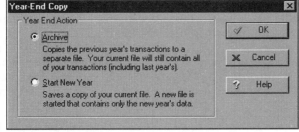

Figure 9-10:
The Year-
End Copy
dialog box.

2. **Select the Start New Year option button.**

   You know how this works — just click the mouse.

3. **Click OK.**

   Quicken displays the Start New Year dialog box, as shown in Figure 9-11.

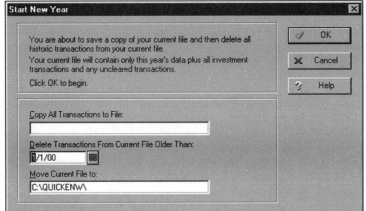

Figure 9-11:
The Start
New Year
dialog box.

4. **Enter a name in the Copy All Transactions to File text box.**

   Name the old-transactions file that Quicken creates. (Quicken stores all
   your old transactions in this file.) For example, if you have a file named
   Dummies, you may want to name the archive filed for 1999 *Dummies99*.
   At this point, the old-transactions file you're creating is an exact copy of
   the original file.

5. Specify a cutoff date.

Using the Delete Transactions From Current File Older Than text box, enter a cutoff date. Quicken deletes all cleared transactions with dates that fall before this cutoff date from the current Quicken file. (Remember, this file is the one you work with and want to shrink.) I chose January 1, 2000, as the cutoff date in Figure 9-11 so that I could create a new file for all 2000 transactions. (*Note:* Quicken doesn't delete uncleared transactions, and it doesn't delete investment transactions.)

6. Move the current file (optional).

You do this step only if you want to change the location of the current file from the current Quicken directory to another directory. Type the path name of the new directory in the Move Current File to text box. If this optional step sounds confusing or complicated, don't worry about it because you have no good reason to change the directory right now anyway.

7. Click OK.

Quicken creates an old-transactions file with the filename you gave it in the Start New Year dialog box. Quicken also deletes all the old transactions from the current file so that your current file contains only the transactions that are dated after the cutoff date.

Quicken then displays the message box, shown in Figure 9-12, that tells you the file was successfully copied. Select the Old File option button if you want to use the old-transactions file. Select the File for New Year option button if you want to use the current file you've just shrunk. Click OK after you make your choice.

Figure 9-12:
The File
Copied
Successfully
dialog box.

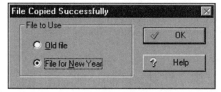

If you want to see the old-transactions file again, you can select it from the dialog box of the File⇨Open command. You should *not* enter any new transactions in the old-transactions file, however, because these new transactions will change the old file's ending account balance without changing the current file's beginning account balance.

Using and Abusing Passwords

I have mixed feelings about passwords. Theoretically, they let you lock up your Quicken data so that your rebellious teenagers (if you're using Quicken at home) or the night janitors (if you're using Quicken in a business) can't come in and print checks, process automatic payments, and just generally mess things up.

Using passwords sounds pretty good, of course. But before you set up a password and then start relying on it to protect your information, let me remind you that a Quicken password only prevents someone from accessing your data with Quicken. Using a password does not prevent someone from fooling around with your computer itself. If the night janitors — or, heaven forbid, your teenagers — are the nefarious types, they can erase your files with Windows or scramble them with another program, such as a spreadsheet or word-processing program. And they may even be able get in and manipulate the data with another checkbook or accounting program.

Passwords come with one other little annoying problem, too. Darn it, you have to remember them.

For these reasons, I think that passwords are best left to computer systems that use them on a global basis to control access to all programs and to computer systems that can track all users (you, your teenagers, the night janitors, and anyone else) by name. Your PC doesn't fall into this category.

Setting up a file password

You still want a password? Okay, with much trepidation, I give you the following steps for setting up a password for a Quicken file:

1. **Select the file you want to protect with a password.**

   If the file you want to password-protect is not the active file, choose File⇨Open from the menu and then either double-click the file you want or select it and click OK.

2. **Choose File⇨Passwords from the menu bar.**

   Quicken displays the — you guessed it — Passwords submenu, which lists two commands: File and Transaction.

3. **Choose the File command.**

   Quicken displays the Set Up Password dialog box, as shown in Figure 9-13.

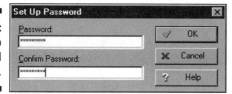

Figure 9-13:
The Set Up
Password
dialog box.

4. **Enter the password into the Password text box.**

   You can use up to 16 characters. Quicken doesn't differentiate between lowercase and uppercase characters, by the way, so Washington, wASHINGTON, and WASHINGTON are all the same from its point of view. Quicken doesn't display the actual characters you type; it displays asterisks instead. If you type **Dog**, for example, it displays ***. (Passwords require strict secrecy, you see.)

5. **Enter the password you want to use again — only this time into the Confirm Password text box — and click OK.**

   Congratulations! You're done.

Assigning a password to a file doesn't prevent you from doing anything with the file that you would normally do. However, the next time you try to use this file — after you start Quicken or when you try to select the file by using the File⇨Open command — Quicken will ask you for the file's password. You need to supply the password to gain access to the file.

Changing a file password

After you set up a file password, you're not stuck with it forever. You can either change the password or remove it by choosing File⇨Passwords⇨File.

If you've already set up a password, however, Quicken doesn't display the Set Up Password dialog box, shown in Figure 9-13. Instead, Quicken displays a Change Password dialog box that asks for the password you're now using and the new password you want to use in the future (see Figure 9-14). Type the current password in the Old Password text box and the new password in the New Password and Confirm Password text boxes. Then press Enter or click OK. From now on, you need to use the new password to gain access to the file. If you don't want to use a password anymore, just leave the New Password and Confirm Password text boxes blank.

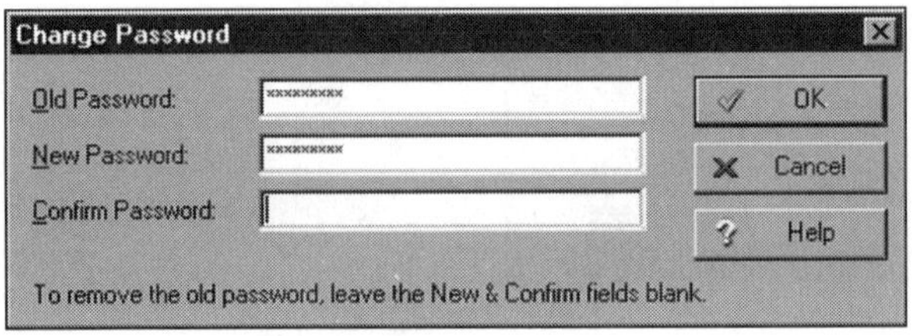

Figure 9-14:
The Change
Password
dialog box.

Change Password	☒
Old Password:	xxxxxxxx	✓ OK
New Password:	xxxxxxxx	✗ Cancel
Confirm Password:		? Help

To remove the old password, leave the New & Confirm fields blank.

So what are transaction passwords?

After you choose File⇨Passwords from the menu bar, you can create a file password or a transaction password by choosing File or Transaction from the Passwords submenu. In general, you use a *file password* to protect the access into a Quicken file.

A *transaction password* works like a file password except that the user has to enter the transaction password if he or she tries to enter a transaction that is dated before a specified date. You specify the date, called the *cutoff date,* when you set up the transaction password.

Maybe it's just me, but transaction passwords don't make much sense. I guess the logic is that you use a transaction password to prevent

some idiot from fouling up last year's or last month's transactions. It seems to me, though, that you can take a couple of easier approaches.

You can create and safely store backup copies of the Quicken file for last year or last month. Or you can keep the idiots from fooling around with your Quicken files. Jeepers, if somebody can't understand an instruction such as, "Use the current date," do you really want them mucking about in your books?

Chapter 10

Compound Interest Magic and Other Mysteries

*T*he folks at Intuit have added several nifty little calculators (most are dialog boxes) to recent versions of Quicken. I strongly encourage you to use these tools. At the very least, the calculators should make your work easier. And if you invest a little time, you should gain some enormously valuable perspectives on your financial affairs.

What's more, the most recent version of Quicken Deluxe includes a handful of more powerful financial planning wizards that I want you to know about. I won't walk you through the steps of using these wizards. But I do want to preview them in the same way that a restaurant critic tells you what you should and shouldn't order at some nice restaurant. You know what I mean. "Darling, you absolutely must try the foie gras, but do stay away from the chocolate mousse. It's abominable. . . ."

Noodling Around with Your Investments

My favorite Quicken calculator is the Investment Savings Calculator. I guess I just like to forecast portfolio future values and other similar stuff.

Using the Investment Savings Calculator

Suppose that you want to know how much you'll accumulate if you save $2,000 a year for 35 years, using a stock mutual fund that you anticipate will earn 10 percent annually. Use the Investment Savings Calculator to estimate how much you should ultimately accumulate. To use it:

1. **Choose Planning⇨Financial Calculators⇨Savings.**

   Quicken displays the Investment Savings Calculator dialog box (see Figure 10-1).

2. **Enter what you've already accumulated as your Opening Savings Balance.**

   Move the cursor to the Opening Savings Balance text box and then type the amount of your current investments. If this amount is zero, for example, type **0**.

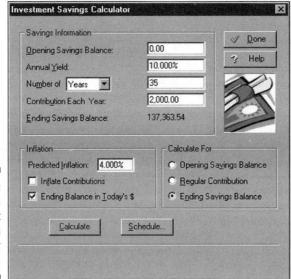

Figure 10-1:
The
Investment
Savings
Calculator
dialog box.

3. **Enter the Annual Yield that you expect your investments to earn.**

   Move the cursor to the Annual Yield text box and type the percent. If you plan to invest in the stock market and expect your savings to match the market's usual return of about 10 percent, for example, type **10** (don't type **.10**).

4. **Indicate how long you plan to let your investments earn income.**

   Move the cursor to the Number Of drop-down list box and select the time period appropriate to your investment planning. (Usually, you will select Years, as Figure 10-1 shows.) Then move the cursor to the Number Of text box and indicate how long (enter the number of time periods) you want to maintain these investments. For example, if you select Years in the drop-down list box and you plan to let your investments grow for 35 years, you enter **35**.

5. **Enter the amount you plan to add to your investments every period.**

   Move the cursor to the Contribution Each text box and enter the amount you plan to add. (Figure 10-1 shows how to calculate an IRA's future value assuming a $2,000 annual contribution.)

6. **Enter the anticipated inflation rate.**

   Move the cursor to the Predicted Inflation text box and enter the inflation rate. By the way, over the twentieth century, the inflation rate has averaged just over 3 percent.

7. **Indicate whether you plan to increase your annual contribution as a result of inflation.**

   Select the Inflate Contributions check box if you plan to annually increase — by the annual inflation rate — the amount you add to your investment portfolio. Don't select the check box if you don't want to inflate the payments.

After you enter all the information, the Ending Savings Balance field shows how much you'll accumulate in present-day, uninflated dollars: $137,363.54. Hmmm. Nice.

If you want to know the amount you'll accumulate in future-day, inflated dollars, deselect the Ending Balance in Today's $ check box.

To get more information on the annual deposits, balances, and so on, click the Schedule button, which appears at the bottom of the Investment Savings Calculator dialog box. Quicken whips up a quick little report showing the annual deposits and ending balance for each year you plan to add into the savings. Try it. You may like it.

Trying to become a millionaire

So you want to be a millionaire some day.

To learn how to realize this childhood dream, use the Calculate For option buttons, which appear on the Investment Savings Calculator dialog box. With these buttons, you click the financial variable (Opening Savings Balance, Regular Contribution, or Ending Savings Balance) you want to calculate. For example, to determine the annual amount you need to contribute to your investment so that your portfolio reaches $1,000,000, here's what you do:

1. **Select the Regular Contribution option button.**

2. **Select the Inflate Contributions check box.**

3. **Deselect the Ending Balance in Today's $ check box.**

4. **Enter all the other input variables.**

   Remember to set the Ending Savings Balance text box to **1000000** (the Ending Savings Balance field becomes a text box after you select the Regular Contribution option).

The Investment Savings Calculator computes how much you need to save annually to hit your $1,000,000 target.

Starting from scratch, it'll take 35 years of roughly $2,500-a-year payments to reach $1,000,000.00, as shown in Figure 10-2. (All those zeros look rather nice, don't they?) Note that this calculation assumes a 10-percent annual yield.

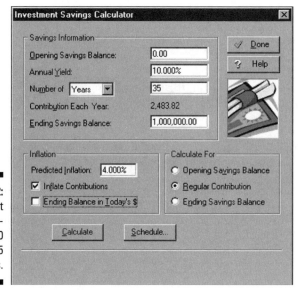

Figure 10-2:
The secret to your success: $2,500 a year for 35 years.

"Jeepers, creepers," you say. "This seems too darn good to be true, Steve."

Well, unfortunately, the calculation is a little misleading. With 4 percent inflation, your million bucks will be worth *only* $253,415.55 in current-day dollars. (To confirm this present value calculation, select the Ending Savings Balance option button and then the Ending Balance in Today's $ check box.)

A timing assumption you should know

The Investment Savings Calculator assumes that you will add to your portfolio at the end of the period — what financial planners call an *ordinary annuity*.

I have to tell you that one of my pet ideas is that it really is possible for most people to become a millionaire. There are just three tricks to doing so. First, make sure that you use tax-advantaged investments like 401(k) plans and IRAs. Second, invest this money into a stock mutual fund like the Vanguard Total Stock Market Portfolio to make sure that over time your returns average out to the average. Three, use your computer to make smarter financial decisions because by doing this, you can rather easily free up an extra $50, $100, even $200 a month. I wrote an entire book about this subject called *The Millionaire Kit* (published by Times Books), but you can get a pretty good overview of how all this works by reading Chapter 19.

The Often Unbearable Burden of Debt

To help you better manage your debts, Quicken provides a neat Loan Calculator that computes loan payments and balances.

Using the Loan Calculator to figure payments

Suppose that one afternoon, you're wondering what the mortgage payment is on one of those monstrous houses: tens of thousands of square feet, acres of grounds, cottages for the domestic help, and so on. You get the picture — something that's a really vulgar display of wealth.

To calculate what you would pay on a 30-year, $5,000,000 mortgage if the money costs 7 percent, use the Loan Calculator:

1. **Choose Planning⇨Financial Calculators⇨Loan.**

   Quicken displays the Loan Calculator dialog box (see Figure 10-3 for a picture of this handy tool).

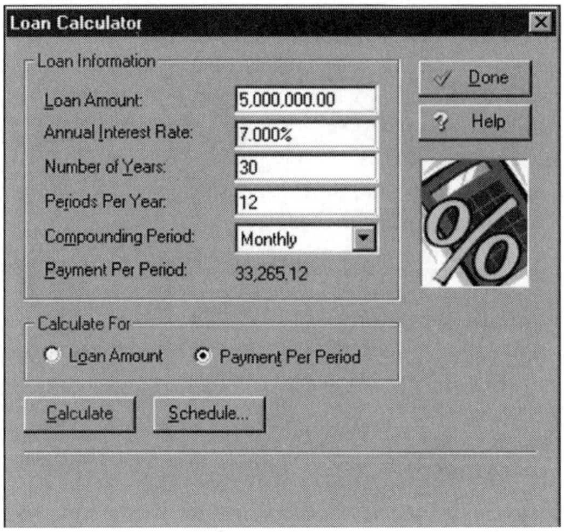

Figure 10-3:
The Loan
Calculator
dialog box.

2. **Enter the loan amount.**

   Move the cursor to the Loan Amount text box and enter the amount of
   the loan. (If you're checking the lifestyle of the ostentatious and vulgar,
   type **5,000,000**.)

3. **Enter the annual interest rate.**

   Move the cursor to the Annual Interest Rate text box and enter the interest rate percent. If a loan charges 7 percent interest, for example, type **7**.

4. **Enter the number of years you want to take to repay the loan.**

   Move the cursor to the Number of Years text box and enter the number
   of years you plan to make payments.

5. **Indicate how many loan payments you plan to make a year.**

   Move the cursor to the Periods Per Year text box and enter the number
   of loan payments you plan to make in a year. If you want to make
   monthly payments, for example, type **12**.

Quicken calculates the loan payment and displays the amount in the Payment
Per Period field. Hey, wait. $33,265. That doesn't seem so bad, does it? I mean,
you could almost make an annual — oh, never mind. That's a monthly payment, isn't it? Yikes!

I guess if you have to ask how much the mortgage payment is, you really
can't afford it.

To get more information on the loan payments, interest and principal portions of payments, and outstanding loan balances, click the Schedule button,
which appears on the face of the Loan Calculator dialog box. Quicken whips
up a quick loan amortization schedule showing all this stuff.

Calculating loan balances

To calculate the loan principal amount, select the Loan Amount option button under Calculate For. Then enter all the other variables.

For example, those $33,265-a-month payments for the monster mansion seem a little ridiculous. So calculate how much you can borrow if you make $1,000-a-month payments over 30 years and the annual interest rate is 7.25 percent:

1. **Select the Loan Amount option button.**

2. **Type** 7.25 **in the Annual Interest Rate text box.**

3. **Type** 30 **in the Number of Years text box.**

4. **Type** 12 **in the Periods Per Year text box.**

5. **Type** 1000 **in the Payment Per Period text box.**

The Loan Calculator computes a loan amount of $146,589, as shown in Figure 10-4.

The Refinance Calculator

You won't read about the Refinance Calculator here — but not because I'm lazy. Believe it or not, I enjoy writing about things that help you make better financial decisions. The Refinance Calculator merely calculates the difference in mortgage payments if you make lower payments; then it tells you how long it would take with these lower payments to pay back the refinancing costs you incur.

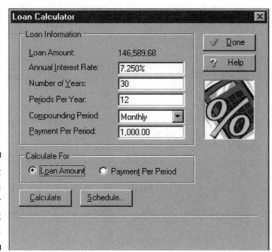

Figure 10-4:
The Loan
Calculator
dialog box
again.

For example, if you save $50 a month because you refinance and it costs $500 to refinance, the Refinance Calculator tells you that it would take ten months of $50-a-month savings to recoup your $500.

You know what? Although you may want to know how long it would take to recoup the refinance costs, that information doesn't tell you whether refinancing is a good idea. Deciding whether to refinance is very, very complicated. You can't just look at your next few payments, like the Refinance Calculator does. You also need to look at the total interest you would pay with the old mortgage and the new mortgage.

I can't think of any good reason to use the Refinance Calculator; it just doesn't do what it purports to do.

So that I don't leave you hanging, however, let me give you two general rules to help you make smarter refinancing decisions:

- ✔ First, if you want to save interest costs, don't use refinancing as a way to stretch out your borrowing. That is, if you refinance, make sure that you make payments large enough to pay off the new mortgage by the same time you would have paid off the old mortgage. In other words, if you have 23 years left on your old mortgage, don't go out and get a 30-year mortgage. Find a lender who will let you pay off the new mortgage in 23 years.

- ✔ Here's a second trick, if you can find a willing lender. Ask the lender to calculate the *annual percentage rate* (APR) on the new mortgage, assuming that you'll pay off the mortgage by the same time you would have paid off the old mortgage. (An APR includes all the loan's costs — interest, points, miscellaneous fees, and so on — and calculates an implicit interest rate.) If the APR on the new loan is lower than the current loan's interest rate, refinancing would probably save you money.

Let me issue one caveat. When you base your refinancing decision on the comparison between the new loan's APR and the current loan's interest rate, you assume that you'll live in your current house until the mortgage is paid.

I hope this information helps. As I said, mortgage refinancing decisions are tough if you truly want to save money.

The Retirement Calculator

I think that this section is the most important one in this book. No joke. Your financial future is much too consequential to go for easy laughs or cheap shots.

The dilemma in a nutshell

By the time the 30-something and 40-something crowd reaches retirement, Social Security coverage almost certainly will be scaled back. As you may know, the current recipients are getting everything they paid in as well as much of what we pay in.

If you currently receive Social Security, please don't feel defensive or betrayed. I think your generation overcame challenges far more important (World War I, the Great Depression, World War II, the Cold War, the end of segregation, and so on) than the problem of inadequate Social Security funding we young ones face.

I know this sentiment sounds corny, but I think you've made the world a better place. I hope my generation does the same.

But the problem isn't just Social Security. More and more often, employer-provided pension plans are *defined contribution plans,* which add specific amounts to your pension (such as 2 percent of your salary), rather than *defined benefit plans,* which promise specific pension amounts (such as $1,000 a month). As a result, although you know that someone will throw a few grand into your account every so often, you don't know how much you'll have when you retire.

I urge you to think ahead about your financial requirements. Fortunately, the Quicken Retirement Calculator can help you.

I'll get off my soapbox now. Thank you.

The truth about Social Security

The American Institute of Certified Public Accountants recently prepared a nonpartisan white paper about Social Security. If you're really interested, visit the Institute's web site at /www.aicpa.org/. But let me give you a couple of pieces of information you may find useful. First of all, if Congress does nothing, the AICPA figures that the best guess of what happens is that the trust fund runs out of money in roughly 40 years, which means that, if nothing is done, at that point benefits will have to be cut back to 75 percent of their current level. For example, someone who would have gotten $800 a month will only get $600. Okay, that's not good. But as long as you're not depending solely on Social Security, it isn't quite a financial meltdown either. Here's a second thing you may find interesting: It actually wouldn't be that tough to fix the whole thing. A little tinkering here (invest some money in the stock market) and a little fiddling there (fix the way the inflation adjustment is made), and you could basically fix everything. Or at least you could if you made these changes today.

More about timing

The Retirement Calculator assumes that you or your employer will add to your retirement savings at the end of the year — what financial planners call an *ordinary annuity.* If you or your employer adds to your retirement savings at the beginning of the year, you earn an extra year of interest. As a result, your after-tax income will be more than Quicken shows.

Retirement planning calculations

Imagine that you decide to jump into your employer's 401(k) thing (a type of profit-sharing plan), which allows you to plop about $3,000 into a retirement account that you think will earn about 9 percent annually.

Fortunately, you don't need to be a rocket scientist to figure this stuff out. You can just use the Retirement Calculator:

1. **Choose Planning➪Financial Calculators➪Retirement.**

   Quicken displays the Retirement Calculator dialog box, as shown in Figure 10-5.

2. **Enter what you've already saved as your current savings.**

   Move the cursor to the Current Savings text box and type your current retirement savings (for example, if you have some Individual Retirement Account money or you've accumulated a balance in an employer-sponsored 401(k) account). Don't worry if you don't have anything saved — most people don't.

3. **Enter the annual yield that you expect your retirement savings to earn.**

   Move the cursor to the Annual Yield text box and type the percent. In the little example shown in Figure 10-5, I say the annual yield is 9 percent. This is, I'll remind you, about the average return that the stock market produces over long periods of time. And yes, I do know that over the last few years the market has almost tripled this percentage. But I urge you not to expect the party to continue through the rest of your saving years. I certainly don't.

4. **Enter the annual amount added to your retirement savings.**

   Move the cursor to the Annual Contribution text box and enter the amount that you or your employer will add to your retirement savings at the end of each year. In the example, I say that I plan to add $3,000 (refer to Figure 10-5).

5. Enter your current age.

Move the cursor to the Current Age text box and enter a number. You're on your own here, but let me suggest that this is a time to be honest.

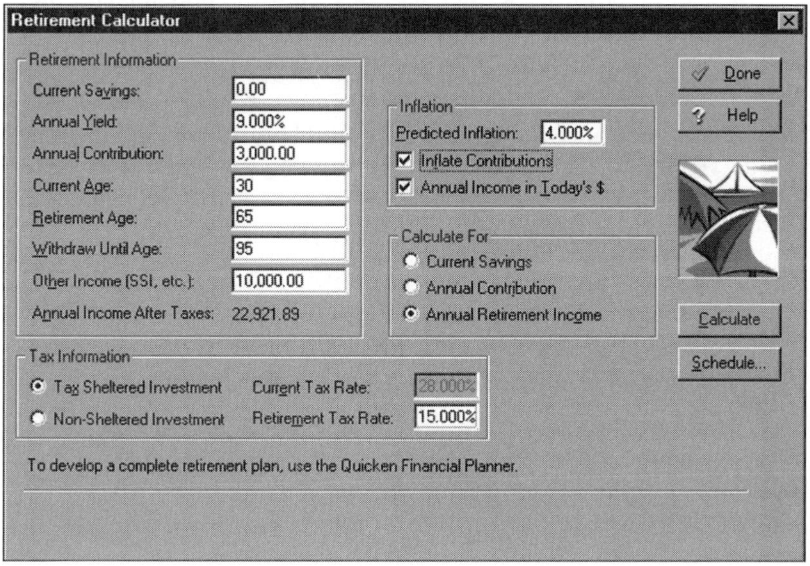

Figure 10-5:
The
Retirement
Calculator
dialog box.

6. Enter your retirement age.

Move the cursor to the Retirement Age text box and enter a number. Again, purely a personal matter. (Figure 10-5 shows this age as 65, but you should retire when you want.)

7. Enter the age to which you want to continue withdrawals.

Move the cursor to the Withdraw Until Age field and enter a number. I don't want to beat around the bush here. This number is how old you think you'll be when you die. I don't like the idea any better than you do. Let me say, though, that ideally you want to run out of steam — there, that's a safe metaphor — before you run out of money. So go ahead and make this age something pretty old — like 95 (sorry, Grandma).

8. Enter any other income you'll receive — such as Social Security.

Move the cursor to the Other Income (SSI, and so on) text box and type a value (Figure 10-5 shows $10,000). Note that this income is in current-day, or uninflated, dollars. By the way, you can request an estimate of your future Social Security benefits by visiting the Social Security Administration's web site at www.ssa.gov or by contacting your local Social Security Administration office. Also, note that if you haven't received it already, the Social Security Administration is actually supposed to be sending every worker an estimate of his or her future benefits.

9. **Indicate whether you plan to save retirement money in a tax-sheltered investment.**

Select the Tax Sheltered Investment option button if your retirement savings earns untaxed money. Select the Non-Sheltered Investment option button if the money is taxed. *Tax-sheltered investments* are things such as Individual Retirement Accounts, annuities, and employer-sponsored 401(k)s and *403(b)s* (a 403(b) is kind of a profit-sharing plan for a non-profit agency).

As a practical matter, tax-sheltered investments are the only way to ride. By deferring income taxes on your earnings, you earn interest on the money you otherwise would have paid as income taxes.

10. **Enter your current marginal tax rate, if needed.**

If you're investing in taxable stuff, move the cursor to the Current Tax Rate text box. Then enter the combined federal and state income tax rate that you pay on your last dollars of income.

11. **Enter your anticipated retirement tax rate.**

Move the cursor to the Retirement Tax Rate text box, then . . . hey, wait a minute. Who knows what the rates will be next year, let alone when you retire? I think that you should enter **0**, but remember that the Annual Income After Taxes is really your pretax income (just as your current salary is really your pretax income).

12. **Enter the anticipated inflation rate.**

Move the cursor to the Predicted Inflation text box and enter the inflation rate. By the way, in recent history, the inflation rate has averaged just above 3 percent (see Figure 10-5).

13. **Indicate whether the annual additions will increase.**

Select the Inflate Contributions check box if the additions will increase annually by the inflation rate. (Because your salary and 401(k) contributions will presumably inflate if there's inflation, Figure 10-5 shows the Inflate Contributions check box selected.)

After you enter all the information, take a peek at the Annual Income After Taxes field (Figure 10-5, for example, shows $22,921.89). Not bad. Not bad at all. If you want to see the after-tax income in future-day, inflated dollars, deselect the Annual Income in Today's $ check box.

To get more information on the annual deposits, balances, income, and so on, select the Schedule button, which appears on the face of the Retirement Calculator dialog box. Quicken whips up a quick little report showing the annual deposits, income, and ending retirement account balances for each year you plan to add to and withdraw from your retirement savings.

If you're now bummed out about retirement

First, don't feel depressed. At least you know *now* if your golden years seem a little tarnished. After all, you acquired Quicken to help you sort out your finances. Now you can use Quicken and your newly gained knowledge to help improve your financial lot.

Basically, retirement planning depends on just three things:

> ✔ The number of years that the retirement savings will accrue interest
>
> ✔ The real yield (that is, adjusted for inflation) you earn — in other words, the annual yield minus the predicted inflation
>
> ✔ The yearly payments

Anything you do to increase one of these variables increases your retirement income.

If you invest, for example, in something that delivers higher real yields, such as the stock market, you should see a big difference (of course, you usually bear more risk). Or, if you wait an extra year or two to retire, you wind up making more annual payments and earning more interest. Finally, if you boost the yearly payments (for example, by participating in an employer-sponsored 401(k) or 403(b) plan, where your employer matches a portion of your contribution, you'll see a huge change.

Noodle around with the variables. See what happens. You may be surprised.

Retirement roulette

Use the Calculate For option buttons to determine a retirement income variable. You can calculate current savings, annual contribution, or, as I describe earlier, the annual after-tax income.

To calculate the yearly payment required to produce a specific level of retirement income, for example, select the Annual Contribution option button. Then enter all the other variables — including the desired after-tax income. The Retirement Calculator figures how much you need to save to hit your target retirement income.

Cost of College

Ouch. I have a couple of daughters, so I know how you feel. Man, oh man, do I know how you feel.

The College Calculator

Suppose that you have a child who may attend college in 13 years. And you haven't started to save yet. If the local university costs $10,000 a year and you can earn 9 percent annually, how much should you save?

The College Calculator works like the Retirement Calculator:

1. **Choose Planning⇨Financial Calculators⇨College.**

   Quicken displays the College Calculator dialog box, as shown in Figure 10-6.

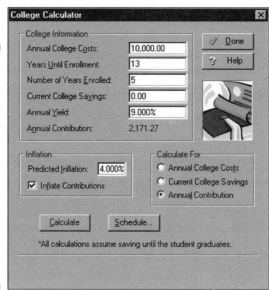

Figure 10-6: Use the College Calculator dialog box to determine whether you will have to take out a second mortgage to pay for Junior's college education.

2. **Enter the annual college costs.**

   Move the cursor to the Annual College Costs text box. Then enter the current annual costs at a school Junior may attend. Figure 10-6 shows this amount as $10,000.

3. **Enter the number of years until enrollment.**

Move the cursor to the Years Until Enrollment text box and enter a number. For example, if Junior will start college in 13 years, type **13**.

4. Enter the number of years enrolled.

Move the cursor to the Number of Years Enrolled text box and enter a number. Assuming that Junior doesn't fool around, type **4** or **5**.

5. Enter the amount of the current college savings.

Move the cursor to the Current College Savings field and enter an amount. Figure 10-6 shows this amount as $0.00.

6. Enter the annual yield that you expect the college savings to earn.

Move the cursor to the Annual Yield text box and type the percent. Figure 10-6 shows the yield as 9 percent.

7. Enter the inflation rate anticipated in college tuition.

Move the cursor to the Predicted Inflation text box and type the inflation rate percent. Figure 10-6 shows this rate as 4 percent.

8. Indicate whether you plan to increase your annual contribution as a result of inflation.

Select the Inflate Contributions check box if you plan to annually increase — by the annual inflation rate — the amount you save. Figure 10-6 shows this check box selected.

After you enter all the information, the Annual Contribution field shows how much you need to save each year until the child graduates from college.

Just to beat this thing to death, Figure 10-6 shows that the lucky student will attend five years at a college that currently costs $10,000 a year and that you expect to earn 9 percent annually and anticipate 4 percent annual inflation. Given these cold hard facts, you need to start saving $2,171.27 every year.

To get more information on the annual deposits, tuition, and balance, click the Schedule button, which appears on the face of the College Calculator dialog box. Quicken whips up a quick little report showing the annual deposits, tuition, and ending college savings account balances for each year you'll add to, and Junior withdraws from, the college savings money.

If you're now bummed out about college costs

Look at the positive side: You now understand the size of the problem and the solution.

College planning depends on four things:

- ✔ College costs
- ✔ The number of years that the savings earns interest
- ✔ The *real yield* (that is, adjusted for inflation) you earn — in other words, the annual yield minus the predicted inflation
- ✔ The yearly payments

I don't mean to sound like a simpleton, but you can successfully save for a college education in three basic ways:

- ✔ Reduce the costs (find a less-expensive school)
- ✔ Invest in things that deliver higher yields
- ✔ Boost the yearly payments

Use the Calculate For option buttons to compute a specific financial variable. Select the variable you want to calculate and then input the other values. The College Calculator computes the flagged variable.

Income Tax Expenses

The folks at Quicken added a very cool calculator to Quicken after Intuit, the maker of Quicken, bought the company that makes TurboTax: a Tax Planner. Okay — you two guys in the back row. Stop sniggering. I'm serious. I think it's really neat. Not because I like income tax planning and preparation. No, I think it's neat because this little tool makes it possible to estimate with a fair degree of accuracy one of the most complicated expenses of our little lives: federal income taxes.

Tax Planner calculator

The Tax Planner works pretty much like the other financial planning calculators. Here's the straight scoop:

1. **Choose <u>T</u>axes➪Tax <u>P</u>lanner.**

   Quicken displays the Tax Planner calculator, as shown in Figure 10-7.

2. **Indicate your filing status.**

   Move the cursor to the Status field and click the down arrow. Then, when Quicken displays a list of possible filing statuses, pick the one you think you'll use this year: Single, Married filing separate, Married filing jointly, and so on.

3. **Indicate the tax year.**

Move the cursor to the Year field and click the down arrow. After Quicken displays a pop-up box listing 1998 and 1999, select one of those years.

4. **Enter the wages and salaries you and your lovely or handsome spouse expect.**

Move the cursor to the Wages and Salaries-Self field and type what you think you'll make this year. If your filing status isn't single, move the cursor to the Wages and Salaries-Spouse field and type what you think your spouse will make this year.

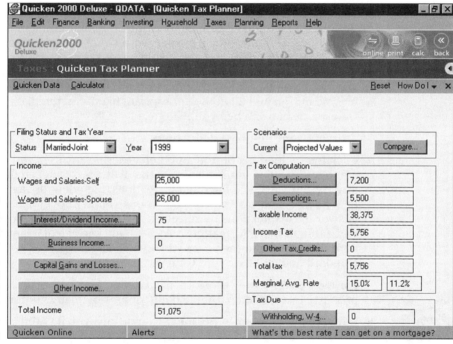

Figure 10-7:
The Tax
Planner
calculator.
Friends, it
doesn't get
any better
than this.

5. **Indicate approximately how much other taxable income you'll have.**

Quick as you can, click the Interest/Dividend Income, Business Income, Capital Gains and Losses, and Other Income buttons and fill in the pop-up worksheets that Quicken displays. (In each case, the Quicken pop-up worksheets prompt you for a handful of inputs.) If some income thingamajig doesn't apply, just leave it blank. Figure 10-8 shows the Interest/Dividend Income pop-up worksheet. This makes sense, right? You enter your taxable interest income into the first input field. You enter your taxable dividend income into the second field. When you're done, click OK. Quicken calculates the total and then plugs this value back into the Tax Planner calculator.

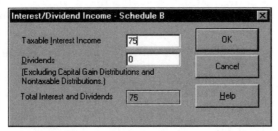

Figure 10-8:
The
Interest/
Dividend
Income
pop-up
worksheet
thingy.

6. Indicate whether you'll have any adjustments to your gross income.

I know that this step sounds too technical, but you really only have to deal with a handful of these adjustments: IRA, SEP/IRA, and Keogh deductions; alimony; moving expenses; a couple of adjustments for self-employed types (half their self-employment tax and a chunk of their health insurance premiums); and any penalty on early withdrawals of savings. If you have one or more of these, click the Adjustments to Income button and fill in the appropriate blanks on the dialog box Quicken displays. When you're done, click OK.

7. Estimate your itemized deductions.

Click the Deductions button and then describe any itemized deductions you have by filling in the blanks on the dialog box Quicken displays. You also need to answer a handful of questions, including "Is taxpayer a dependent?" and "Are you or your spouse blind or over age 65?" You answer these questions by selecting or deselecting check boxes. After you enter all this information, click OK. Quicken calculates your standard deduction and then uses whatever is larger for your return: your standard deduction or your total itemized deductions.

For most people, only three itemized deductions — mortgage interest, property taxes, and charitable deductions — actually matter.

8. Indicate the number of personal exemptions you'll claim.

You know the drill by now, right? Click the Exemptions button and then use the dialog box that Quicken displays to indicate the number of personal exemptions you get. When you're done, click OK. The basic rule is that you get one exemption for everybody in your family (you, your spouse if you're filing jointly, and your dependents) as long as they live at your house. I should mention, however, that things get tricky if you have shirt-tail relatives living at your house, if your kids live away from home or are married, or if some of the kids in the house have divorced parents. If you have questions because one of these situations sounds vaguely familiar, get the IRS return preparation instructions and read the part about who is and is not a dependent.

9. Indicate whether you owe any other taxes or have tax credits you can use to reduce your taxes.

Click the Other Tax, Credits button and fill in the blanks on the dialog box that Quicken displays. When you finish, click OK. By the way, if you and your spouse get all your income from salaries and a handful of investments, you probably don't need to worry about this "other taxes and credits" business.

10. **Enter any estimated taxes or federal income withholding you've paid.**

Click the Withholding, W-4 button and fill in the blanks on the dialog box that Quicken displays. When you finish, click OK. If you make estimated tax payments — and you know if you do — click the Est. Tax Pmts button and fill in the blanks on the dialog box that Quicken displays. All you are doing here is indicating how much you and your spouse have already had withheld and how much you'll have withheld from your future paychecks.

When you complete these ten steps, you not only see what your total income taxes are, but also whether you need to increase your payments. (Look at the Remaining Tax Due field in the lower-right corner of the screen to see whether you're coming up short.)

If you want to print the tax planner information, click the Print button. If you want to erase all your inputs and start over, click the Reset button. After you finish using the calculator, click the Close button.

Another Tax Planner trick

You can try a Tax Planner trick. Rather than enter the data into text boxes (as I describe here), you can tell the Tax Planner to grab taxable income and tax-deduction information from your registers. Doing so is pretty straightforward, as long as you're diligently using tax-related categories to track these income and expense amounts and — this is important — you've indicated the tax schedule line on which category totals should be reported.

Really, You Must Try the Foie Gras

In the preceding pages of this chapter, I've talked about the personal financial planning tools that are most useful. Before we wrap up our discussion, however, let me quickly mention that Quicken provides some other interesting and, for some people, useful financial planning tools.

If you open the Planning menu or noodle around on the Planning Center window, specifically, you'll notice links to financial planning wizards under the headings Retirement, College, Home Purchase, Debt Reduction, and Other Goals. These wizards walk you through the steps to planning for big, important events. Like retirement. Or college. In my opinion, these are all special interest tools. Most people won't be interested in taking the time to use the wizards. (The Retirement Planner, for example, takes about half an hour.) But if you're really serious or worried or compulsive about one of these topics, well, it just might be worth your time to explore a bit.

And now let me sneak in one other snidbit. If you choose the Planning⇨ Professional Planning Resources command, Quicken opens a Quicken.com web site that talks about personal financial planners. Go ahead and look at this stuff. But, well, can I be blunt? I think you need to be very careful about getting personal financial advice from a so-called personal financial advisor. Some advisors are very skilled. For example, I think anyone who's got the personal finance specialist (PFS) designation is a good bet. This person is a certified public accountant, which means he is either a college graduate or business school graduate who's passed a grueling three-day test and spent time working with a publicly licensed CPA in a sort of apprenticeship, and this person has also met a bunch of other knowledge and experience require-ments. I also think a tax attorney who specializes in estate tax planning usually provides pretty good advice. I don't think, however, that someone who's gone through a company-sponsored training program or one of these night school correspondence programs — even one that leads to a profes-sional designation — is automatically good. Okay, some are. I grant you that. But I would urge you to be very cautious about taking advice from someone who earns a commission by selling your financial products and services. Be careful. It's a jungle out there.

Part III
Home Finances

The 5th Wave   By Rich Tennant

"IT SAYS HERE IF I SUBSCRIBE TO THIS MAGAZINE, THEY'LL SEND ME A FREE DESK-TOP CALCULATOR. DESKTOP CALCULATOR?!! WHOOAA— WHERE HAVE I BEEN?!!"

In this part . . .

Are you going to be using Quicken for your personal financial stuff? If so, you should know that this program offers more than just the checkbook-on-a-computer business that I describe in the preceding part. Quicken can help you manage and monitor things such as credit cards, home mortgages, and investments. If this stuff sounds interesting, keep reading.

Chapter 11

Credit Cards (And Debit Cards, Too)

*Y*ou can use Quicken to track your credit cards in much the same way you use Quicken to keep a checkbook. Tracking credit cards uses a nearly identical process — with a few wrinkles.

First, however, I need to discuss whether you should even bother.

Why Bother — Then Again, Why Not?

I don't use Quicken to track my credit card purchases because I always pay my credit card balance in full every month. (Don't feel bad if you don't — it's like a natural law that CPAs like me must do this.) Therefore, I don't have an open credit card balance to track. What's more, when I pay the monthly credit card bill, I can easily use the Split Transaction Window to describe my spending categories: $3.53 on food for lunch, $52.64 for a car repair, and $217.54 for books (a dangerous and ultimately destructive personal weakness).

If you're in the same boat — meaning you use a credit card but you don't carry a balance — you don't need anything special to track your credit card purchases and, of course, you don't need to use Quicken to tell you your account balance because it's always zeroed out at the end of the month.

Of course, if you do carry a credit card balance — and about 50 percent of people do — you can set up a Quicken credit card account and use it for tracking credit card purchases. If you just need to keep track of how much you charge during the month (even if you are going to pay the balance in full), you must also set up a credit card account and use it.

I should make one other point: In order to track not just what you charge — by using spending categories — but also *where* you charge it — by using the Payee field — you must set up a credit card account and use it.

My father-in-law uses a Quicken credit card account for this purpose. Although he doesn't carry a balance (or so he tells me), he does like to know how much he spends at the International House of Pancakes, Kmart, and the truck stop. He could use the Split Transaction window to record spending on things such as breakfast, clothing, and gasoline when he pays his credit card balance at the end of the month. But the Split Transaction window doesn't have a field to record where he said, "Charge it."

How to Set Up a Credit Card Account

If you want to track credit card spending and balances with Quicken, you must set up a special credit card account. (In comparison, you use bank accounts to track things such as the money that flows into and out of a checking account.)

Adding a credit card account

To set up a credit card account, you follow roughly the same steps as you do to set up a bank account. Here's what you do:

1. **Choose Fi_nance⇨_Account List.**

   Quicken displays the Account List window, as shown in Figure 11-1.

2. **Click the _New button on the Account List window.**

   Quicken displays the Create New Account dialog box, shown in Figure 11-2.

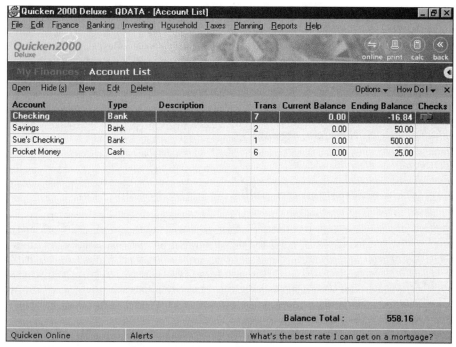

Figure 11-1:
The
Account List
window.

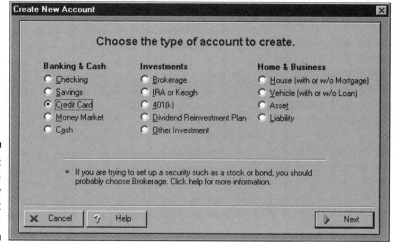

Figure 11-2:
The Create
New
Account
dialog box.

3. **Select the Credit Card option button and click Next to display the Credit Card Account Setup dialog box (see Figure 11-3).**

4. **After Quicken displays the dialog box, click the Summary tab to move directly to the tab where all the action occurs.**

   (If you've been working with Quicken a bit, you don't need the extra handholding that Quicken provides when you click the Next button to move through the other tabs.)

5. **Name the account.**

   Why not? Move the cursor to the Account Name text box and type a name.

6. **Provide a description for the account (optional).**

   Usually, naming an account is enough. With a name, an account is easy enough to identify when you see it listed in places such as the Account window. If a name isn't enough, however — usually because you've set up a bunch of different accounts — you can use the Description text box to further describe and identify the account. How this works is probably darn obvious to you, but because I have an obsessive-compulsive personality, I need to say that you move the cursor to the Description text box and type something.

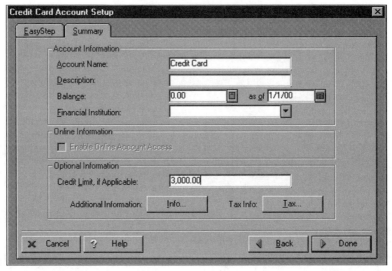

Figure 11-3:
The Credit
Card
Account
Setup dialog
box.

7. Enter the balance you owed at the end of the last credit card billing period after making your payment.

Move the cursor to the Balance text box and type the balance value by using the number keys.

8. Enter the date on which you will start keeping records for the credit card account.

You should probably choose the date that you made your payment. Move the cursor to the As Of text box and type a two-digit number for the month, a two-digit number for the day of the month, and a two-digit number for the year.

9. Indicate whether you'll use the Quicken Online Account Access feature.

If you are using the Quicken Online Account Access feature (which allows you to get a list of your credit card charges on disk or by modem), indicate this by selecting the Enable Online Account Access check box. Then, from the Financial Institution drop-down list box, click next to the name of the bank that issued your credit card. (I ramble on about online banking later in the chapter.)

10. Type in the amount of your credit limit (optional).

If you want, indicate the amount of your credit card limit by moving the cursor to the Credit Limit, If Applicable text box and then typing in whatever number the credit card company has arbitrarily decided is a reasonable balance for you to shoulder.

11. Collect some additional information about the credit card (optional).

You can collect and store additional information about the credit card accounts you set up. To do so, click the Info button. Then, when Quicken displays the Additional Account Information dialog box, use its text boxes to store whatever information you want: the credit card company's name, your credit card account number (just in case you lose the credit card), the interest rate the credit card charges, and so forth.

Ignore the Tax button. It doesn't apply to credit card accounts.

12. Click Done.

If you enabled Online Account Access, Quicken displays the Select Financial Institution window. See later in this chapter and Chapter 6 for more information about the whole online banking thingamajig.

If you decided to do the online banking stuff, you have to finish that first, but when you're done (or if you never started in the first place) Quicken redisplays the Account List window (refer to Figure 11-1). But this time, the window lists an additional account — the credit card account you just created.

Selecting a credit card account so that you can use it

To tell Quicken you want to work with an account, you use the Account List window — the same window you saw in Figure 11-1. Go figure.

Choose Finance⇨Account List or click the credit card account's Feature tab if it shows up with the QuickTabs along the right edge of the window. After you display the window, select the account you want to use by double-clicking it. Quicken selects the account and displays the register window for that account so that you can begin recording transactions (which I describe in the next section).

How to Enter Credit Card Transactions

After you select a credit card account, Quicken displays a special version of the register window, as shown in Figure 11-4.

Touring the credit card register

The credit card register works like the regular register window that you use for a bank account. You enter transactions into the rows of the register. After you record a charge, Quicken updates the credit card balance and the remaining credit limit (if you entered the optional credit limit info when you set up the account).

You can use the same techniques and commands as you do for your regular ol' bank account register. I talk about these in earlier chapters, so I won't regurgitate those discussions here.

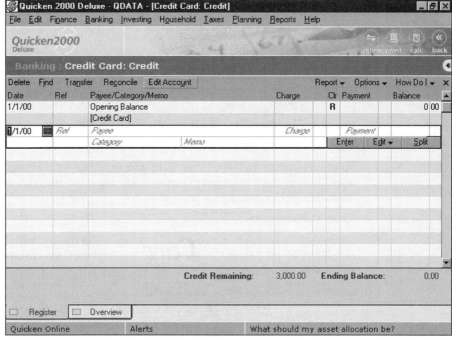

Figure 11-4: The credit card version of the Quicken register.

Recording a credit card charge

Recording a credit card charge is similar to recording a check or bank account withdrawal. For the sake of illustration, suppose that you charge $30.47 for dinner at your favorite Mexican restaurant. Here's how you record this charge:

1. **Enter the charge date.**

   Move the cursor to the Date field (if it isn't already there) and type the date using the MM/DD format. For example, enter July 15, 2000 as **7/15**. You usually don't have to type the year because Quicken retrieves the current year number from the little clock inside your computer. Or, if you want, get crazy — click the box that remotely resembles a calendar at the end of the field and Quicken displays a pop-up calendar (see Chapter 4 for more information) from which you can select the appropriate month and day.

Don't bother with the Ref field. Quicken supplies it so you can record the credit card reference number — a bit of data that's usually about 20 characters long. You, my friend, have better things to do with your time, however. So just skip the field.

2. **Record the name of the business you paid with a credit card.**

   Move the cursor to the Payee field and type the name of the person or business you paid. If the restaurant is Mommasita's Cantina, for example, type **Mommasita's Cantina** into the Payee field.

3. **Enter the charge amount.**

   Move the cursor to the Charge field and type the total charge amount — **30.47** in this example. Don't type a dollar sign, but do type the period to indicate the decimal place and cents.

4. **Enter the category.**

   Move the cursor to the Category field, open the drop-down list box, and select the appropriate category. You may categorize a restaurant charge as Dining, for example.

5. **Enter a memo description (optional).**

   Move the cursor to the Memo field and type the specific reason you're charging the item, such as a special date with your spouse or an important business meeting.

6. **Record the charge.**

   Click the Enter button. Quicken beeps and then calculates both the new credit card balance and the remaining credit limit. Quicken then moves the cursor to the next slot in the register.

Figure 11-5 shows the charge at Mommasita's Cantina. Good food and reasonable prices — you can't ask for much more than that.

Changing charges you've already entered

Use the arrow keys or click the mouse to highlight the charge that you want to change. Use Tab and Shift+Tab or the mouse to move the cursor to the field that contains the misinformation you want to fix. You can then fix the entry and record the transaction. That's easy enough, isn't it?

Paying credit card bills

If you're tracking the credit card account balance with a credit card account like the one I'm describing here, Quicken provides two ways for you to pay a credit card bill.

Note: If you're not using a credit card account, you record the check you send to pay a credit card bill in the same way you record any other check. And that means you don't have to read anything I'm about to say. Shoot, you shouldn't even be reading this chapter.

A most bodacious way to pay a credit card bill

This method is pretty simple, so don't blink your eyes because you may miss the action.

Look at your credit card statement. Decide how much you want to pay. Select the bank account on which you'll write the check. Then write the check and record it in the bank account register — but as a transfer to the credit card account.

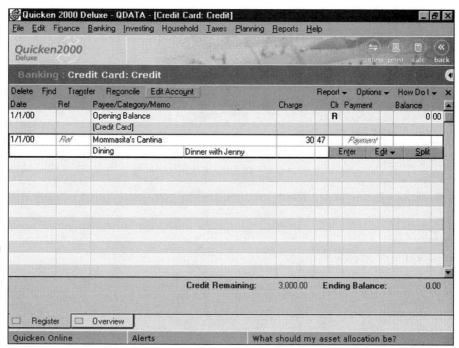

Figure 11-5:
The charge at Mommasita's Cantina.

You're done. If you have questions, take a peek at the check transaction shown in Figure 11-6. It pays $100 of the credit card balance. The only trick — if you want to call it that — is that the credit card account is specified as the account to which the money is transferred. (You can see the other account by right-clicking on the transaction and selecting Go To Transfer, or you can click on the other Accounts tab of course.)

If you look at the credit card account register now, you see that this check reduces the credit card balance by $100.

A less bodacious way to pay a credit card bill

You can also tell Quicken that you want to pay some portion of the credit card bill as part of reconciling the credit card's account balance.

I think that this method is slightly more difficult. But if you want to reconcile your credit card account, think about using this second method. If you are reconciling a credit card statement and paying some portion of the credit balance at the same time, you may find this method more convenient. Who knows?

I describe how to reconcile a credit card account in the very next section.

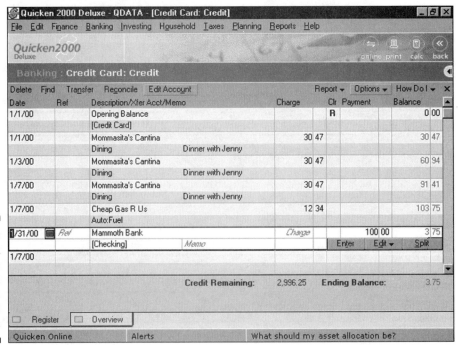

Figure 11-6: A check transaction that pays a portion of a credit card balance.

Reconciling That Crazy Account

You know that trick in which you compare your checking account records with your bank's records of your checking account? The one in which you calculate the difference between what you think is your account balance and what the bank thinks is your balance? And this difference is supposed to equal the total of the transactions floating around out there in the system? You can use this same trick on your credit card account.

Reconciling your credit card account, neat and straight up

To reconcile a credit card account, first get your credit card statement. Next, display the credit card account in a register window.

What the nasty credit card company says

To tell Quicken what that nasty credit card company says, follow these steps, and put on some music if you can't seem to get the rhythm thing right:

1. **Click the Reconcile button.**

   Quicken displays the Credit Card Statement Information dialog box, as shown in Figure 11-7.

2. **Enter the charges and cash advances that your statement shows.**

   Move the cursor to the Charges, Cash Advances text box and then type the number.

3. **Enter the payment and credits that your statement shows.**

   You know the drill: Move the cursor to the Payments, Credits text box and type the number.

4. **Enter the new balance shown on the credit card statement.**

   Now I bet this is a surprise. Go ahead and type the figure in the Ending Balance text box — even if you just can't believe you charged that much.

5. **Enter the monthly interest charge by using the Finance Charges text box.**

   Pause for a moment of silence here if this topic makes you sad, sad, sad.

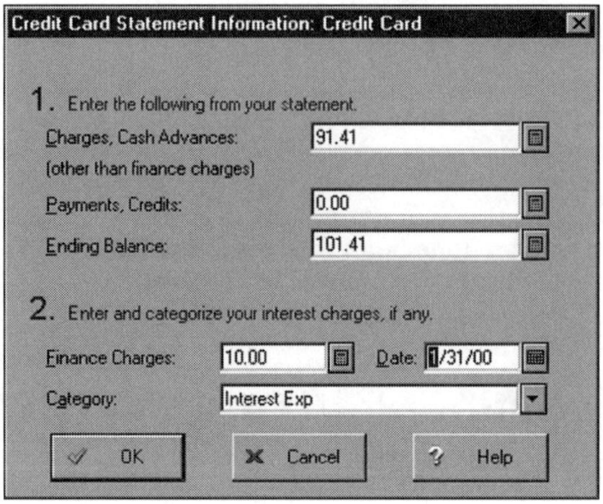

Figure 11-7:
The Credit
Card
Statement
Information
dialog box.

6. **Assign the monthly interest to the appropriate spending category, such as Interest Exp.**

   Move the cursor to the Category text box and type the category name. (Are you getting bored yet? I know, move and type . . . move and type . . . all I ever seem to say is move and type.) Remember that you can click the little down arrow at the end of the text box to see a list of categories to select from.

7. **Click OK.**

   Quicken displays the Reconcile Credit Statement window (see Figure 11-8). Use this window to tell Quicken which credit card charges and payments appear on your statement. (This step is akin to looking at a bank statement and noting which checks and deposits have cleared the bank.)

Ouch! Did I really spend that much?

After you give Quicken an overview of your credit card situation, you can note which charges have cleared and which charges have not.

If you're comfortable whipping through a bank reconciliation, you can probably do this reconciliation with your eyes closed. If you need some help, leave your eyes open so you can read these steps:

1. **Find the first charge listed on the credit card statement.**

2. **Mark the charge as cleared.**

   Charges are listed in the left list box. Hmmm. It's not really any of my business, but maybe someone's eating at Mommasita's a bit too often?

Scroll through the transactions listed in the Charges window until you find the charge and then click it. Or select the charge by using the arrow keys and then press the spacebar. Quicken adds the check mark symbol in front of the list entry in the Clr column to mark this charge as cleared and then updates the cleared statement balance.

3. Enter any missing charges.

If you can't find a charge, you probably didn't enter it in the Quicken register yet. Open the credit card account register by clicking its tab and then enter the charge into the register in the usual way — except enter a **c** (the letter *c*) into the Clr column by clicking the Clr field. By doing so, you identify the charge as one that's already cleared. After you finish, click the Return to Reconcile button to return to the Reconcile Credit Statement window.

4. Repeat Steps 1, 2, and 3 for charges listed on the credit card statement.

Or until you're blue in the face.

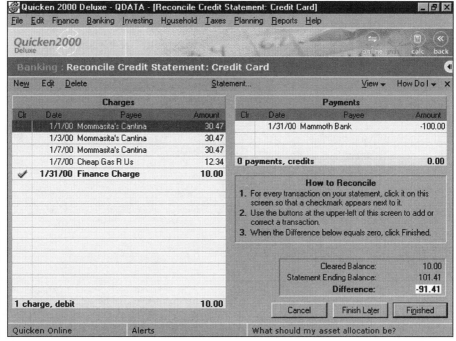

Figure 11-8:
The
Reconcile
Credit
Statement
window.

5. Find the first payment or credit listed on the credit card statement.

The payments and credits appear in the right list box. Figure 11-9 has only one of these: the $100 payment to the credit card company, Mammoth Bank. But it hadn't cleared the bank by the statement date, so it shows up in the window, but I haven't marked it.

6. Mark the payment or credit as cleared.

Scroll through the transactions listed on the Payment window until you find the first payment or credit and then click it. Or select the credit and then press the spacebar. Quicken adds the check mark symbol in front of the list entry to mark the payment or credit as cleared and then updates the cleared statement balance.

7. Enter any missing payments or credits.

If you can't find the payment or credit — you probably know what I'm going to say — it means you haven't entered it into the Quicken register yet. Open the credit card account register by clicking its tab and then enter the payment or credit into the register in the usual way, but put a **c** in the Clr column. When you finish, click the Return to Reconcile button to return to the Reconcile Credit Statement window.

8. Repeat Steps 5, 6, and 7 for payments or credits listed on the credit card statement.

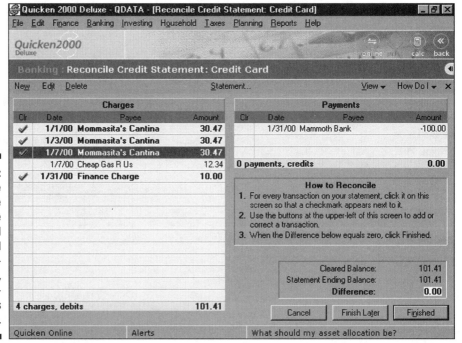

Figure 11-9: When the difference between the cleared balance and the statement is zero, the reconciliation is complete.

If you record a transaction wrong, do this

As you're looking through the credit card statement, you may discover that you incorrectly recorded a transaction. If this happens, display the Credit Card register so that you can make the necessary fixes.

Oh, that explains the difference

After you mark all the cleared charges and payments, the difference between the cleared balance for the credit card and the statement's ending balance should be zero.

Figure 11-9 shows how this looks. By the way, reconciling with fictitious data is darned easy.

If you're ready to finish

If the difference does equal zero, you're cool. You're golden. You're done. (Sort of makes you sound like fried chicken, doesn't it?)

All you need to do is click Finished to tell Quicken that you're done. Quicken asks you if you want to make a credit card payment. Jump ahead a couple of paragraphs for help doing just that.

If the difference doesn't equal zero, you have a problem. If you clicked Finished in spite of the problem, Quicken displays a message that has some cursory explanation as to why your account doesn't balance. This message also tells you that you can force the two amounts to agree by pressing Enter.

Forcing the two amounts to agree isn't a very good idea, though. To make the balances agree, Quicken adds a cleared transaction equal to the difference. (Quicken asks for a category if you choose the adjustment route.)

Despite the ease of making adjustments, you should still correct the error responsible for the difference.

Chapter 8 provides some ideas for trying to figure out why a bank account that should balance doesn't. You can apply the same list of tips to credit card reconciliations if you're in a bad way.

If you want to postpone the inevitable

You can postpone reconciling the account by clicking the Finish Later button. When you click this button, you abandon your reconciliation work. Transactions that you mark as cleared still show the c in the Clr text box. You still have an inexplicable difference between the credit card statement and your register. Even so, postponing a reconciliation is usually better than forcing the cleared balance to equal the credit card statement balance. By postponing a reconciliation, you can hopefully find the problem or problems and fix them. Then you can restart the reconciliation and finish your work. (You restart a credit card reconciliation in the same way that you originally start one.)

Paying the bill as part of the reconciliation

After you finish the reconciliation, Quicken politely asks if you want to pay the bill. Figure 11-10 shows the Make Credit Card Payment dialog box, which is the tool that Quicken uses to collect the necessary data.

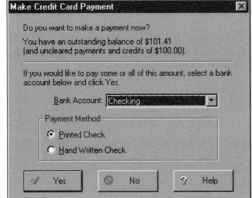

Figure 11-10:
The Make
Credit Card
Payment
dialog box.

You can probably figure out how to use this baby yourself, but hey, I'm on a roll, so here are the steps:

1. **Enter the bank account on which you'll write the check.**

   Open the Bank Account drop-down list box and select the account. Notice that the screen tells you what your register shows as the credit card balance, not what your credit card statement shows. I thought this was a nice touch.

2. **Indicate whether you'll print a check with Quicken or write one by hand.**

   Select the Printed Check option button if you want to print a check with Quicken. Select the Hand Written Check button if you'll write a check by hand.

3. **Click Yes.**

   If you told Quicken that you want to print a check, Quicken displays the Write Checks window so that you can tell Quicken to print a check. (See Chapter 5 for information on doing so.) If you told Quicken that you want to write a check, Quicken displays the register window in which you can add the missing information to complete the transaction. (See Chapter 4 for information.) Quicken assumes that you want to pay the entire credit card balance.

   If you don't want to pay the entire credit card balance, you can edit the check amount that Quicken suggests after Quicken displays the Write Checks window or the register window.

4. **Enter the check into the Write Checks window or the register window.**

   Describe the check as one that you will either print with Quicken or write by hand.

As I say earlier in this chapter, this method usually isn't the easiest way to pay a credit card bill. But, hey, you're an adult. You make your own choices.

When you finish, Quicken redisplays the Register window. You may notice that as you mark credit card transactions as cleared, Quicken puts a c in the Clr column of the credit card register. When you finish reconciling the credit card account, Quicken changes all these cs to rs. None of what Quicken does here is magical. Quicken just makes this change to identify the transactions that have already been through the reconciliation process. (The c shows that a transaction has been marked as cleared. The r shows that a transaction has been reconciled.)

So What about Debit Cards?

Debit cards, when you get right down to it, aren't really credit cards at all. They're more like bank accounts. Rather than withdrawing money by writing a check, you withdraw money by using a debit charge.

Although a debit card looks (at least to your friends and the merchants you shop with) like a credit card, you should treat it like a bank account.

In a nutshell, here's what you need to do:

✔ Set up a checking account with the starting balance equal to the deposit that you make with the debit card company. Note, however, that you only need to do so if your debit card uses a new, separate account. If your debit card just taps an existing account, you don't need to take this step.

✔ When you buy something by using your debit card, record the transaction just as you would record a regular check.

✔ When you replenish the debit balance by sending more money to the debit card company, record the transaction just as you would record a regular deposit.

If these steps sound pretty simple, they are. In fact, I'd go so far as to say that if you've been plugging along, doing just fine with a checking account, you'll find that keeping track of a debit card is as easy as eating a bag of potato chips.

The Online Banking Hoopla

As I mention in Chapter 6, Quicken supports online banking. If you have your credit card with a credit card company — probably a bank — that is set up to handle Quicken online banking, you can grab your credit card statement directly from the credit card company. If you have a checking account at the bank that issued the credit card, you can also pay your credit card bill simply by transferring money from your checking account to your credit card. (This feature is actually pretty slick, I have to say.)

The big hoopla concerning this feature — at least as it relates to credit cards — is that you don't have to enter the credit card transactions into a register. Rather, you retrieve them by using a modem.

Should you even bother?

Is the online-banking-with-a-credit-card-thing a feature that you should look into? Does it really save you time? Is it a good deal? Inquiring minds want to know, so I'll tell you what I think. (I should point out that what I'm about to say next is just my humble opinion.)

I think that online banking is well worth the fee you probably have to pay for the service when you consider the time savings. Shoot, if you're a heavy hitter running $20,000 or $30,000 a month in charges through your account, your time savings will be substantial. And you'll probably pay only a few dollars a month. (What you pay depends on the bank issuing the credit card.)

Something bothers me about the whole deal, however: You really just receive an electronic version of your statement, which means — at least from my perspective — that you're more likely not to see erroneous transactions. And reconciling your bank statement against, well, your bank statement isn't going to make a whole heck of a lot of sense. (Golly gee, Batman, the charge to Edna's Pet School appears on both statements, too!)

You also have some extra, very minor, fiddling to do. Grabbing credit card charges off another computer is not particularly complicated. Nor do you need to know any special magic tricks to use a modem. (Your computer and the bank's credit card computer do exchange a secret handshake every time they want to talk, but you'll get the scoop on this after you join the club.) Nevertheless, setting it all up does take some time.

How to use Online Account Access with your credit card

Okay, so you've listened to my side of the story, but you still want to use the Quicken Online Account Access feature with your credit card — and your bank is one that provides this service. "What next?" you're wondering.

Actually, the whole process is pretty simple. You need to contact your bank and tell it that you want the service. You have to fill out some paperwork, and then, a few days later, you receive some information that you need as you set up the credit card. (If you've already set up the credit card account, you can add the information you need by displaying the Accounts window, selecting the credit card account, and clicking the Edit button.) I talk about the Online Account Access options earlier in the chapter, so I won't go into that again here.

After you have the account set up for online banking, you just choose Banking Banking. The first time you choose this command, Quicken has you sign up for something called an Intuit Online Services Membership. To sign up, you simply fill in the blanks on a window that asks for your name and address. (This sign-up just lets Intuit and the bank know who you are.)

After Quicken displays the Online Financial Center window, identify your bank by using the drop-down list box, select the credit card account from the list box (if you have more than one online account), and then click the Update button. Quicken grabs your data from the bank. After it finishes, Quicken displays something called a Transmission Summary window (which does just what its title suggests). If you click OK, you can peruse the credit card transactions that Quicken downloaded. (*Downloading* just means that your computer grabs information from another computer. Because *grabbing* doesn't sound as cool, however, computer geeks long ago decided to call this process *downloading*.)

Note: For more information about the Quicken Online Account Access feature, see Chapter 6.

Chapter 12

Other People's Money

A popular financial self-help writer thinks that one of the secrets to financial success is using other people's money: the bank's, the mortgage company's, the credit people's, your brother-in-law's. . . . You get the idea.

Me? I'm not so sure that using other people's money is the key to financial success. I do know that borrowing other people's money can turn into a nightmare.

Quicken can help you here. No, the folks at Intuit won't make your loan payments for you. But in a way, they do something even better. They provide you with a tool to monitor the money you owe other people and the costs of your debts.

Should You Bother to Track Your Debts?

I think that tracking your debts is a good idea — car loans, mortgages, student loans, and so on — when lenders fail to tell you the amount that you're paying in annual interest or the amount you owe after each and every payment.

If your lenders are doing a good job at keeping you informed, I don't think that using Quicken for this purpose makes much sense. Heck, it's their money. They can do the work, right?

Let me make one more observation. If lenders have half a clue, they send you a 1098 tax form at the end of every year. The number shown on that form equals your tax deduction if the interest stems from a mortgage, business, or investment loan. Note that personal interest expenses aren't deductible anymore, so you shouldn't track them unless you really want to be mean to yourself.

How Do I Get Started?

To track other people's money with Quicken, you must set up a *liability account*. Setting up one of these babies is easy. Just remember that you must set up a liability account for every loan or debt: your mortgage, your car loan, your student loan, and so on.

Setting up a liability account for an amortized loan

An *amortized loan* is one on which you make regular, equal-sized payments. Over time, the principal portion of each payment pays off, or amortizes, the loan principal. If you borrowed money to purchase a house, a car, a Winnebago, or anything else that's really expensive and that you pay off over several years, chances are that your loan is of the amortizing variety.

Let me say just one more thing. Setting up a loan account requires a couple of dozen steps. But none of the steps is difficult. And none takes that much time to complete. As long as you have your loan information handy — the loan amount, interest rate, balance, and so on — setting up this type of account is a snap.

Here's the recipe for setting up a liability account:

1. **Choose Finance⇨Account List or press Ctrl+A.**

   Quicken displays the Account List window.

2. **Click the New button in the Account List window.**

   Quicken, with little or no complaint, displays the Create New Account dialog box that asks which type of account you want to create.

3. **Select the Liability option button, the Next button, and then the Summary tab.**

   Quicken displays the Liability Account Setup dialog box, as shown in Figure 12-1.

4. Name the liability.

Type something clever (and, hopefully, useful) in the Account Name text box.

5. Enter an account description (optional).

If the account name isn't descriptive enough, you can enter the account number or the name of the lender, for example. And if that's not enough, you can click Info to store additional information or click Tax to associate a tax form and line with the liability account payment. Just fill out the dialog box that Quicken displays.

6. Enter the balance of your loan after your last payment.

(If you don't have this figure — and who does? — call your lender.) Move the cursor to the Balance text box and then type the amount that you owe.

7. Enter the date of your last payment in the as of text box.

This date is the date as of which you owe the balance that you entered in Step 6. Type the date in MM/DD/YY fashion. (For example, type **7/1/00** for July 1, 2000.)

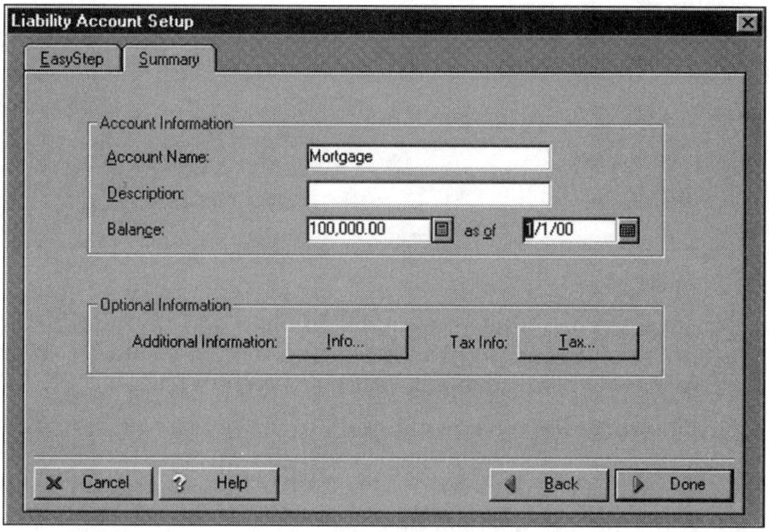

Figure 12-1:
The Liability
Account
Setup dialog
box.

8. Click Done.

Quicken displays a message box that asks if you'd like to set up an amortized loan for the new liability account.

9. If you want to set up an amortized loan, click Yes.

An amortized loan is just a loan with regular monthly payments that include both principal and interest. If you don't want to do this, click No. You're done. You can skip the rest of the steps. If you click Yes, Quicken displays the Loan Setup dialog box. Click the Summary tab to see the dialog box exactly as it's shown here (see Figure 12-2).

10. **Provide some basic background information.**

Use the Loan Type option buttons to specify whether you're borrowing money or lending money. And use the Have Any Payments Been Made? option buttons to indicate, well, whether you've started making payments yet. (You shouldn't need to do anything with the Account buttons and boxes.) Then click Next. Quicken displays another set of boxes and buttons, as shown in Figure 12-3.

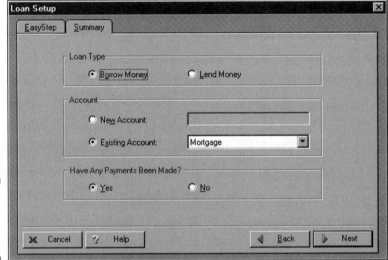

Figure 12-2:
The Loan Setup dialog box.

11. **Enter the date that you borrowed the money in the Opening Date text box or, if your loan has a grace period (like a student loan), enter the date when your loan enters the repayment period.**

Quicken needs to know this date so that it can calculate the interest the loan started to accrue when you borrowed the money. The program suggests the as of date you supplied when you set up the liability account.

12. **Enter the original loan balance.**

Quicken plugs the number you set as the liability account starting balance into the Original Balance text box. If this amount isn't correct, no problem. Move the cursor to the Original Balance text box and then type the amount that you originally borrowed.

13. **Enter the loan term in years in the Original Length text box.**

If you set up a 30-year mortgage, for example, type **30**. You have to perform one tiny trick when entering this figure: If you set up a loan that includes a balloon payment, enter the number of years over which the loan will be fully paid. For example, loan payments may be calculated based on a 30-year term, but the loan may require a balloon payment at the end of seven years. In this case, type **7** in the Original Length text box.

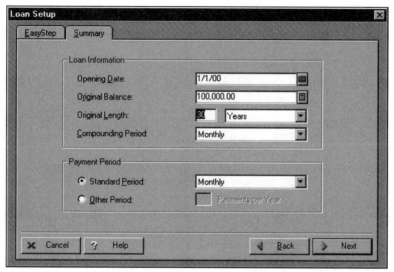

14. **Indicate how often the bank calculates loan interest.**

    The interest compounding period usually equals the payment period.

15. **Describe how often you make a loan payment by using the Payment Period options.**

    If you make regular monthly payments, for example, select the Standard Period option button and then open the Standard Period drop-down list box and select Monthly. If you can't find an entry in the Standard Period drop-down list box that describes how often you make payments, select the Other Period option button and then enter the number of payments you make each year in the Payments per Year text box.

16. **Click Next.**

    Quicken displays another set of boxes and buttons in the Summary tab (see Figure 12-4).

17. **Describe the balloon payment — if you have one.**

    The balloon payment option buttons and boxes let you alert Quicken to any balloon payment you must make in addition to the last regular loan payment. If the loan doesn't have a balloon payment, ignore this stuff. If the loan does have a balloon, select the Amortized Length option button; then use the Amortized Length text box and drop-down list box to specify the number of years or months (or whatever) the loan is amortized over.

If you know that you have a loan payment (and know the loan payment amount) but don't know what or when it occurs, select the Calculate option button.

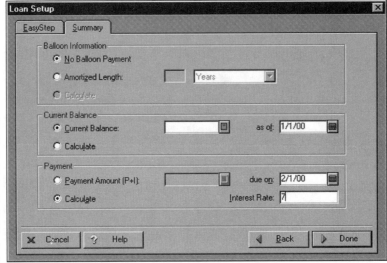

Figure 12-4:
Some more
buttons and
boxes you
can use to
describe the
amortized
loan.

18. **Enter the current balance if you've made any payments.**

If you indicated that you have already made payments on the loan, specify how much you still owe on the loan after making the last payment by using the Current Balance text box. If you haven't made any payments yet, skip to Step 20. You know the drill by now. Just move the cursor to the text box and pound a few number keys.

19. **Enter the date as of which the current balance is, well, current.**

Use the As Of date field to indicate the date for which you've entered the current balance. By the way, all the standard date entry and date editing tricks apply to this text box. You can press the + and - keys, for example, to move the date ahead and back by one day. And you can click that icon at the right end of the As Of date text box to display a pop-up calendar.

20. **Specify the interest rate.**

Enter the loan's interest rate into the Interest Rate text box. The loan interest rate, by the way, isn't the same thing as the APR, or annual percentage rate. You want to enter the actual interest rate used to calculate your payments. Enter the interest rate as a decimal amount. For example, don't type 7¾, type **7.625**. You should be able to get this amount from the lender or the prospective lender.

21. Describe the payment — if necessary.

If you've entered all the loan information that Quicken has requested in the preceding steps, you can just select the Calculate button and click Done. Quicken then calculates the loan payment by using the loan balance, term, balloon payment information, and interest rate you've already entered. If you haven't entered all this information — say you left out the balloon payment information because you don't know what it is — select the Payment Amount (P+I) button and then enter the loan principal and interest amount into the Payment Amount (P+I) text box. If necessary, edit the next payment date in the Due On drop-down list box.

22. Click Done.

If you asked Quicken to calculate anything for you, a dialog box will pop up telling you Quicken did so. Click OK to get back to the Loan Setup. Make sure that the Quicken calculations make sense and then click Done. Quicken displays the Set Up Loan Payment dialog box (see Figure 12-5).

23. Verify the principal and interest payment calculated by the program.

If it's wrong, you can keep going, but let me point out a minor yet annoying problem. You probably entered one of the loan calculation inputs incorrectly, such as the loan balance, the loan term, or the interest rate. Fortunately, these errors are only a minor bummer. Later in the chapter (in the "Fixing loan stuff" section), I describe how to restart.

24. Indicate any amounts you pay besides principal and interest (optional).

Click the Edit button. Quicken displays the Edit dialog box, which you can use to describe any additional amounts the lender requires you to pay. In the case of a mortgage, for example, you may be required to pay property taxes or private mortgage insurance. After you enter the information and click OK, Quicken calculates the full payment and redisplays the Set Up Loan Payment dialog box.

25. Indicate how you make payments in the Type drop-down list box.

Select one of the payment transaction types listed in the Type drop-down list box. Payment means that you hand-write checks; Print Check means that you print checks by using Quicken; and Online Pmt means that you use Quicken Online Banking to make electronic payments.

If you print checks by using Quicken and want to put the payee's address on the check, click the Address button in the Set Up Loan Payment dialog box. Quicken displays a dialog box that you can use to input the payee's address.

26. Type the lender's name in the Payee text box.

The payee is just the name of the person or business who loaned you the money.

27. Enter a memo description (optional).

Does the lender always get mixed up when you send the check? Stick the loan account number in the check's Memo text box. I would refrain from using this text box to comment on the fairness of the bank's interest rate, to mock the intelligence of the loan payment processors, or to perform other emotionally gratifying, but generally unproductive, acts.

28. Enter the date of your next loan payment in the Next Payment Date text box.

29. Enter the interest category.

Open the Category for Interest drop-down list box and select the appropriate category.

Quicken lets you schedule (have Quicken automatically enter) or memorize (just have Quicken remind you to enter) loan payments and electronic payments. I'm going to assume that you don't want to be doing this kind of stuff — at least not yet. If I'm assuming incorrectly, click the Payment Method button. Then fill out the dialog box that appears. It's not all that difficult.

If you're still confused, I talk about how you can use the Financial Calendar to schedule loan payments later in this chapter.

30. With the Set Up Loan Payment dialog box displayed, click OK.

Quicken removes the Set Up Loan Payment dialog box and asks if any asset is associated with the loan. If you want to associate an asset with your loan, Quicken walks you through the steps for setting up an asset account. But you know what? Don't worry about setting up an asset account. It actually isn't worth it. Just click No. Quicken re-displays the Account List window.

31. **Double-click the Liability account's name to display its register (see Figure 12-6).**

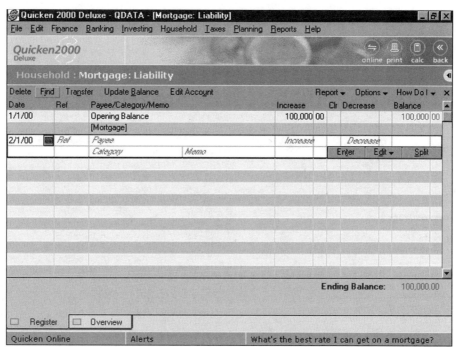

Figure 12-6:
The Liability register.

Fixing loan stuff

Nobody's perfect, right? You may have made a tiny little mistake in setting up either the loan or the loan payment. This mistake doesn't need to be a major financial or personal crisis, however. Just use the View Loans window to identify the incorrectly described loan and then make your corrections (see Figure 12-7). To display the View Loans window, just choose Household⇨Loans.

If you have multiple loans set up, click the Choose Loan [x] button and select the loan that you want to change. Quicken gives you all the dirt on the selected loan in the View Loans window's Loan Summary and Payment Graph tabs.

Hey, can I mention one other thing about the View Loans window? Do you see those two tabs labeled Payment Schedule and Payment Graph? You can probably guess what they do, but if you click the Payment Schedule tab, Quicken displays an amortization schedule showing the interest and principal portions of each loan payment. If you click the Payment Graph tab, Quicken displays a line chart that shows how you pay off the loan balance over time. You may want to take a minute and experiment with these two tabs. They're pretty neat.

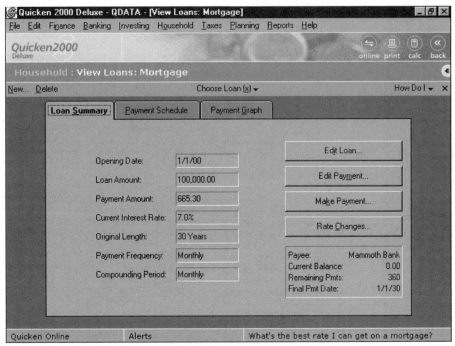

Figure 12-7:
The View
Loans
window.

Changing loan or loan payment information

If you want to change something about the loan, click the Edit Loan button. Quicken displays the Edit Loan dialog box, which works exactly like the Loan Setup dialog box shown in Figures 12-2 and 12-3. Make your changes and click OK.

To change something about the payment, click the Edit Payment button. Quicken displays the Edit Loan Payment dialog box. Make your changes and click OK.

Working with adjustable rate loans

Before I wrap up this discussion, let me mention a couple other things. If you're working with a variable rate loan, you can click the Rate Changes button to display the Loan Rate Changes dialog box (see Figure 12-8). This dialog box has a very simple purpose in life: It lists the interest rates you entered for a loan and the dates these interest rates were used in loan calculations.

If you want to record new interest rates — because you have a variable rate loan and the interest rate changes, for example — follow these steps:

1. **Indicate that you want to record a new interest rate.**

   Right-click in the dialog box and choose New from the shortcut menu. Quicken displays the Insert an Interest Rate Change dialog box, as shown in Figure 12-9.

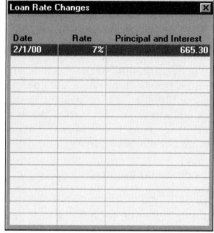

Figure 12-8:
The Loan
Rate
Changes
dialog box.

If you want to record new interest rates — because you have a variable rate loan and the interest rate changes, for example — follow these steps:

1. Indicate that you want to record a new interest rate.

Right-click in the dialog box and choose New from the shortcut menu. Quicken displays the Insert an Interest Rate Change dialog box, as shown in Figure 12-9.

Figure 12-9:
Use this
dialog box
to change
the interest
rate on
your loan.

Insert an Interest Rate Change			
Effective Date:	2/1/00	✓	OK
Interest Rate:	8%	✗	Cancel
Regular Payment:	733.76	?	Help

2. Provide the effective date of the interest rate change.

Use the Effective Date text box to indicate when the new interest rate becomes effective. You can either type in a date or open the drop-down list box and select a date from the calendar.

3. Give the new interest rate.

Enter the new interest rate in the Interest Rate text box. Quicken then recalculates the loan payment and sticks the new loan payment figure into the Regular Payment text box.

Adding and removing loans

You can add and delete loans by using the View Loans window.

Delete a loan that you no longer need or shouldn't have added in the first place by clicking the Choose Loan [x] button and selecting the loan account. Then click Delete. Quicken then warns you that you're about to delete your loan and asks you if you'd like to save the account for your records. Saving the account keeps the account available in your Accounts window, but eliminates it from your View Loans window. You can hide the saved account later if you'd like it to disappear from your Accounts window.

You can add loans from the View Loans window, too (refer to Figure 12-7). To do so, click the View Loans window's New menu. Quicken displays the Loan Setup dialog box and walks you through that sequence of steps that I describe earlier to set up the loan. For example, you fill out both the Loan Setup dialog box (refer to Figures 12-2 and 12-4) and the Set Up Loan Payment dialog box (refer to Figure 12-5).

Delivering a Pound of Flesh (Also Known as Making a Payment)

After you set up a liability account, you're ready to hand over a pound of your flesh — that is, make a payment. Before you say that this phrase is just some sort of populist bull-dweeble, I want to remind you that this metaphor comes from Shakespeare's *The Merchant of Venice,* in which a loan is guaranteed with a pound of human flesh.

Recording the payment

After you set up the loan and the loan payment, you're ready to record the payment in (drumroll, please) the register.

I'm trying to make the old Quicken register more exciting for you because you're probably becoming pretty darn familiar with it. And familiarity, as they say, breeds contempt.

Anyway, complete the following steps to record a payment:

1. **Display the View Loans window by choosing Household⇨Loans.**

2. **Display the loan you want to pay.**

3. **Click the Make Payment button.**

Quicken displays a message box that asks whether the payment you're making is a regular payment (one the lender expects) or an extra payment (perhaps to more quickly amortize the loan). After you select the payment type, Quicken displays the Make Regular Payment or Make Extra Payment dialog box. Figure 12-10 shows the Make Regular Payment dialog box; the Make Extra Payment dialog box looks almost exactly the same.

Figure 12-10:
The Make
Regular
Payment
dialog box.

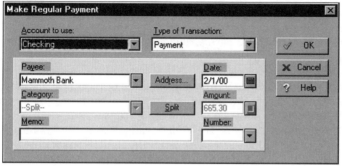

4. **Describe the loan payment.**

   I'm not going to give you the blow-by-blow account here. If you've gotten this far, you don't need my help. (Mostly, as you know, you just type stuff in boxes.)

5. **Click OK.**

   Quicken enters the loan payment in the Liability register and Bank Account register. You're done.

Handling mortgage escrow accounts

I should talk about one minor mortgage record-keeping annoyance — mortgage escrow accounts.

If you have a mortgage, you know the basic procedure. Although your mortgage payment may be $700 a month, your friendly mortgage company (while insisting that it trusts you completely) makes you pay an extra $150 a month for property taxes and other such things. In other words, even though you're paying only $700 a month in principal and interest, your monthly payment to the mortgage company is, according to this example, $850 ($700 + $150).

The mortgage company, as you probably know, saves this money for you in an escrow account or a set of escrow accounts. A couple of times a year, the mortgage company pays your property taxes, and a time or two a year, it pays your homeowner's insurance. If you have private mortgage insurance, it may pay this fee every month as well. And so it goes.

The question, then, is how to treat this stuff. As with most things, you can take the easy way, which is rough, dirty, and unshaven, or the hard way, which is precise, sophisticated, and cumbersome.

You can choose whichever method you want. It's your life.

The rough, dirty, and unshaven method

Suppose that you do pay an extra $150 a month. You can treat this extra $150 as another expense category, such as Other Housing or Property Expenses. (I'm just making up these categories. If you can think of better ones, use your own.)

Nice. Easy. No fuss. These words and phrases pop into my head when I think about the rough, dirty, and unshaven method of mortgage escrow record keeping. Figure 12-11 shows a sample Split Transaction window filled out this way. (The payment isn't exactly $850 because the earlier example loan payment isn't exactly $700 — it's $699.21.) If the Split Transaction window seems like too much of a fuss for you, you might want to mosey on over to Chapter 4 where I give you the rundown on using it.

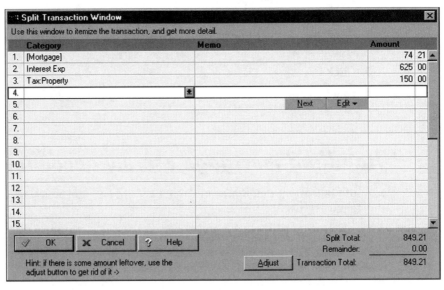

Figure 12-11: A mortgage payment with an escrow account treated as an expense.

I use the rough, dirty, and unshaven method. Let me make a confession, though. This approach doesn't tell you how much moola you have stashed away in your escrow accounts. It also doesn't tell you how much you really spend in the way of homeowner's insurance, what you're entitled to claim as a property tax deduction, or how much they're bleeding you for private mortgage insurance.

To get these figures, you have to peruse the monthly and annual mortgage account statements — that is, if you get them. Or you have to call the mortgage lender and rattle a cage or two.

Still, with all its shortcomings, I like the easy-to-use, rough, dirty, unshaven method.

The precise, sophisticated, and cumbersome approach

You say you can't live with the uncertainty, the stress, the not knowing? Then I have another approach just for you.

You can set up an *asset account* for each of the escrow accounts for which the mortgage company collects money.

You set up asset accounts as you set up a checking account. And, in fact, you should think of escrow accounts as, essentially, special checking accounts into which your lender deposits money collected from you so it can pay your property taxes and insurance.

Because I explain this "setting up a checking account" process in Chapter 1, I'll just refresh your memory quickly. You need to set up an asset account with its starting balance equal to the current escrow account balance. To do so, display the Account List window and click the New button to indicate that you want to create a new account. Identify the account as an asset account and give it a name. Then tell Quicken how much money is in the account as of a specific date.

If you've set up an account or two in your time, this process should take you about 40 seconds.

After you set up your asset account and record its current balance, you're ready to cruise. Record payments in the escrow as account transfers whenever you record the actual loan payment.

You need to do one other thing. When you set up an escrow account, you must record the payments that the bank makes from your escrow account to the county assessor (for property taxes) and to the insurance company (for things such as homeowner's and private mortgage insurance). You don't know when these payments are really made, so watch your monthly mortgage account statements.

When the mortgage company disburses money from the escrow account to pay your first property tax assessment, for example, you need to record a decrease equal to the payment for property taxes and then categorize the transaction as a property tax expense. This process isn't tricky in terms of mechanics. The account increases after every loan payment and decreases after a disbursement.

Basically, the Asset Account register mirrors the Checking Account register. The only difference is that the Payment and Deposit fields in the latter are labeled Decrease and Increase in the former.

This second approach doesn't seem like all that much work, does it? And if you use this approach, you can track escrow balances and escrow spending precisely. You can, for example, pull your property tax deduction right from Quicken. Jeepers, maybe I should try the sophisticated approach next year.

Your Principal-Interest Breakdown Won't Be Right

I don't want to bum you out, but your principal-interest breakdown will often be wrong. You may calculate interest expense as $712.48, for example, when your bank calculates it as $712.47. A few pennies here, a few pennies there, and pretty soon your account balance and interest expense tallies are, well, a few pennies off.

So you can't change the world

You can try calling the bank, telling whomever you talk to what a bozo he (or she) is, and then demanding that someone there correct your balance. (If this approach works for you, let me know.)

Or (and this method is really more practical) you can adjust your records to agree with the bank's. Here's how:

1. **Display the register for the liability.**

2. **Click the Update Balance button.**

   (Go ahead. Tap your keys very hard if you're angry that the bank won't adjust its records.) Quicken displays the Update Account Balance dialog box, as shown in Figure 12-12.

3. **Enter the correct account balance (that is, the one that the bank says is correct).**

   Type the correct figure in the Update Balance To text box. (The amount probably comes from the year-end or month-end loan statement.)

4. **Enter the last day of the month or year for which you're making the adjustment.**

   Enter a transaction date in the Adjustment Date text box. (The trick here is to use a transaction date that sticks the adjustment transaction — which fixes the principal-interest split — into the right month or year.)

Figure 12-12:
The Update
Account
Balance
dialog box.

5. **Enter your interest expense category.**

   Type the correct category name in the Category for Adjustment text box. (To see a list of categories, open the drop-down list box.)

6. **Record the adjustment.**

   When the Update Account Balance dialog box correctly describes the needed adjustment, click OK.

Do you think this adjustment business is kooky?

Does the whole adjustment transaction business make sense to you? At times, it can seem kind of backwards, so let me throw out a quick observation.

As you record loan payments, you split the loan payment between the interest expense category and a principal account transfer that reduces the liability. Here's the tricky part: When the liability gets reduced either too much or not enough, you need to fix both the liability balance *and* the principal-interest split.

Let me give you an example. Suppose that over the course of a year, you record $.17 too little interest expense and, therefore, record $.17 too much principal reduction, despite your best efforts to be accurate. You need to increase the liability account balance by $.17 in this case, but you also need to increase the interest expense figure by $.17. By entering the interest expense category in the Category for Adjustment field, Quicken does these adjustments for you. Pretty cool, huh?

Automatic Loan Payments

Quicken has a couple of nifty features called Scheduled Transactions and the Financial Calendar that can help you with automatic loan payments.

The Financial Calendar and Scheduled Transactions features may be useful in other instances as well. For example, a business may use the Scheduled Transactions and the Financial Calendar features to schedule and plan employee payroll checks, tax returns, and deposits.

But I think that they're both most useful in the case of a loan. So I talk about both of them here.

Scheduling a loan payment

If a loan payment occurs regularly, you can set it up as a scheduled payment. When you do so, Quicken automatically records the payment for you based on a schedule.

Consider this example. Suppose that on the fifth day of every month your mortgage company taps your checking account for the full amount of your mortgage payment. (You, of course, have already authorized it to do so. The mortgage company can't take your money willy-nilly.) In this case, you can tell Quicken to record the mortgage payment on the fifth of each month. Kind of handy, right?

Follow these steps to set up such a scheduled transaction:

1. **Choose Fi_nance_⇨ _F_inancial Calendar or press Ctrl+K.**

   Quicken displays the Financial Calendar window, as shown in Figure 12-13. The figure shows a calendar for the current month and a list of transactions.

2. **Display the first month for which you want to schedule the transaction.**

   Using the Prev Month and Next Month buttons, select the starting month for the scheduled transaction. You can also click the Go to Date button. If you do so, Quicken displays a dialog box that you can use to specify the precise date you want to schedule a payment for.

3. **Identify the scheduled transaction and date.**

   Select the transaction for which you want to create a schedule. In Figure 12-13, for example, you may want to schedule the loan payment transaction to Mammoth Mortgage to fall on the 5th. To do so, select the transaction by clicking it. Then drag the transaction to the 5th. When you release the mouse button, Quicken displays a dialog box that asks you to confirm the principal and interest breakdown. You won't know whether the breakdown is correct until you see the bank statement, so click OK. Quicken displays the New Transaction dialog box (see Figure 12-14).

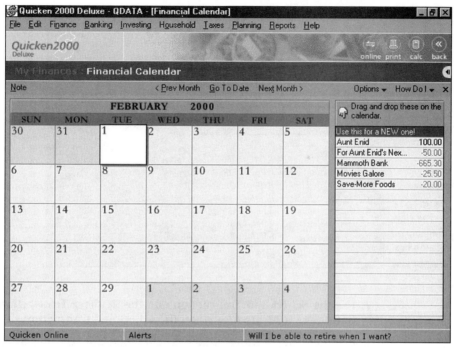

4. **Identify the account from which the payment should be made.**

   Open the Account to Use drop-down list box and then select the appropriate account.

5. **Verify that the transaction type is Payment.**

   Open the Type of Transaction drop-down list box and select Payment. (Of course, if you were setting up some other type of payment, you might choose something else.)

6. **Verify that the Payee, Date, and Memo fields are correct.**

   They probably are. But I have kind of a compulsive personality. Because I've been telling you to check all this other stuff, I thought I'd also suggest that you check these three fields.

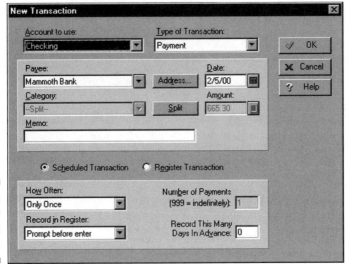

7. **Use the Scheduled Transaction and the Register Transaction option buttons to indicate how often the scheduled transaction should occur.**

   If you indicate a transaction is a scheduled transaction, use the How Often drop-down list box and the Number of Payments text box to indicate the payment frequency and the number of payments.

8. **Tell Quicken whether you want to double-check the scheduled transaction before it actually gets entered in the register.**

   Doing so is easy. Just open the Record in Register drop-down list box to select the Prompt before Enter choice.

9. **Indicate the number of days in advance you want to be reminded of the scheduled payment.**

   Move the cursor to the Record This Many Days in Advance text box and enter a number. This input actually determines how many days in advance Quicken displays a Reminder window to jog your memory about a scheduled transaction. (The Reminders window appears when you first start Quicken, as I mention in Chapter 1. It also appears whenever you choose Finance➪Reminders.)

10. **Click OK.**

    Quicken adds the transaction to its scheduled transaction list.

Quicken takes the Paul Masson approach to finance — it will enter no transaction before its time. So when the time is right — meaning next month on the 5th, for this example — Quicken enters the transaction automatically. Furthermore, Quicken enters the transaction automatically each month until you tell it to stop.

Updating your scheduled transactions

You already know the most important thing about scheduled transactions: how to set one up. Here are some other nuggets of knowledge that you may find useful.

You can edit or delete a transaction scheduled for a particular day by double-clicking the day on the calendar, selecting the transaction from the list in the dialog box Quicken displays, and then clicking the Edit or Delete button, depending on what you want to do.

Another thing: You don't have to use the Financial Calendar to set up scheduled transactions. You can choose Banking⇨Scheduled Transaction List instead. This command displays a window that lists all scheduled transactions and provides buttons that you can use to add, edit, or delete scheduled transactions. The functions of this window are pretty straightforward. To delete a scheduled transaction, for example, just select it from the list and click the Delete button.

Checking out the Financial Calendar

The bar along the top of the Financial Calendar provides some other tools that you may want to use. I'm not going to spend much time on them; you'll have more fun trying them out yourself than you would reading about them. Nevertheless, let me give you a bird's-eye view:

- ✔ The Options button displays a menu of commands that let you specify which transactions should appear in the calendar, add an account balances graph to the calendar window, and fiddle with the memorized transactions list. The transactions shown in that list box along the right edge of the Financial Calendar window, by the way, are memorized transactions (Chapter 4 briefly discusses memorized transactions).

- ✔ The Note button lets you post a note on a calendar day. You use this feature to create reminder notes. For example, you may want to post a note saying "Remember Wedding Anniversary" on the big day. After you click this button, Quicken displays a dialog box in which you type the message. Then you click Save. The Quicken Billminder utility displays your calendar notes. The program also marks the calendar day with a little yellow square — a miniature stick-on note. Click the square to read the message.

- ✔ The Close button removes the Financial Calendar from the Quicken desktop. But, shoot, you probably figured that out already, didn't you?

Chapter 13

Mutual Funds

● ●

In This Chapter

▶ Knowing when to use Quicken investment record keeping

▶ Setting up a mutual fund investment account

▶ Recording your initial mutual fund investment

▶ Buying mutual fund shares

▶ Recording mutual fund profits

▶ Selling mutual fund shares

▶ Adjusting your mutual fund shares

▶ Adjusting mutual fund price information

● ●

I don't mean to scare you, but I think that investment record keeping is the most complicated Quicken feature. So it's time to get down to business. Time to stop pussyfooting around. Time to earn my pay.

Deciding to Use Investment Features

The Quicken investment record keeping feature lets you do three important things:

▶ Track your interest and dividend income

▶ Track real and potential capital gains and losses

▶ Measure an investment's performance by calculating the annual return from an investment

If you're a serious investor, these things probably sound worthwhile. But before you invest any time learning how Quicken investment record keeping works, be sure that you need all this power.

Are your investments tax-deferred?

If your investments are tax-deferred — if, for example, you're using individual retirement accounts (IRAs), 401(k)s, or Keoghs — you don't really need to track investment income and capital gains and losses. Tax-deferred investments have no effect on your personal income taxes. You get a tax deduction for the money you stick into IRAs, for example, and anything you take out is taxable.

With tax-deferred investments, you record all that you should need to know via your checking account. Checks earmarked for investment are categorized as "IRA Deductions," for example, while investment account withdrawals deposited into your checking account are categorized as "IRA Distributions." In other words, you don't need to set up special accounts for tracking your investments. Your bank accounts track everything you need to keep track of.

Are you a mutual fund fanatic?

If you're a fan of mutual funds, you don't need Quicken to measure the funds' annual returns. Fund managers provide these figures for you in quarterly and annual reports.

Some investors don't need Quicken

Let me give you an example of someone who doesn't need to use Quicken's investments feature — me. Once upon a time, I bought and sold common stocks, fooled around with half a dozen mutual funds, and learned firsthand why junk bonds are called junk bonds. Over the last few years, though, I've simplified my financial affairs considerably.

I typically don't invest directly in stocks, bonds, or mutual funds these days; instead, I stick money into an IRA. My investments don't produce taxable dividends or interest income, nor do they produce taxable or tax-saving capital gains or losses. Money I put into the IRA is tax-deductible. And money I ultimately take out of the IRA will be taxable.

I'm also sticking with a handful of mutual funds, but I don't need to calculate the annual return — that's what mutual fund managers do. So I don't need to separately figure, for example, what my shares of Vanguard Index Trust delivered as an annual return when I include both the 3 percent dividend and the 10 percent price drop.

Because I don't need to track investment income, or track capital gains and losses, or calculate the progress of my investment portfolio, I don't need Quicken investment record keeping for my personal use.

Many investors do need Quicken

Of course, many people do benefit from Quicken investment record keeping. If you routinely buy stocks and bonds, you probably want to calculate your annual returns. What's more, if you try to monitor your capital gains and losses intelligently — and you should — you want to know both what you originally paid for your securities and what they're worth currently.

The size of your investment portfolio isn't an issue. For example, I have two daughters who are saving money for college. (Actually, in a cruel twist of fate, *I* am saving; they're simply accumulating.) Although Beth and Britt haven't saved much money, and although they use mutual funds to keep things simple, they do three things that cause nightmarishly complex record keeping for their poor, overworked, and grossly underpaid accountant — Dad: They reinvest their quarterly dividend income, pay annual maintenance fees, and coerce their parents into adding more and more money to their investment portfolios.

What's the big deal? All three things adjust the *basis* in the fund. And when Beth and Britt sell their mutual fund shares, their gain (or loss) will be determined by subtracting the *basis* (the purchase price and all out-of-pocket costs) from the sales proceeds.

The bottom line: Even though Beth and Britt don't have much money, I need to use Quicken to track their investments.

Tracking a Mutual Fund

If you need to track a mutual fund investment, you need to know how to set up a mutual fund account and then record your investment activities.

Even if you don't invest in mutual funds, you shouldn't skip this section. Understanding how mutual fund record keeping works makes tracking other, more complicated investments much, much easier for you. Like stocks. Bonds. Krugerrands. Commodity options.

Setting up a mutual fund investment account

Setting up an investment account works the same way as setting up any other account:

1. **Choose Fi<u>n</u>ance⇨<u>A</u>ccount List or if you see the Accounts Feature Tab listed with the QuickTabs along the right edge of the Quicken program window, click it.**

   Quicken, ever the faithful companion, displays the Account List window.

2. **Click the <u>N</u>ew button on the Account List window.**

   Quicken dutifully displays the Create New dialog box that you use to indicate you want to create a specific type of account. If you've seen one of these Account dialog boxes, you've seen them all — so I won't show them all as figures.

3. **Click the <u>O</u>ther Investment button and click Next.**

   After Quicken displays the Investment Account Setup dialog box, click the Summary tab (see Figure 13-1).

   Note: Quicken lets you set up a 401(k) type account. Although I recommend you not go to the work of tracking tax-deferred investments — especially when someone else already does the record keeping for you — you can set up an account for a 401(k) account. And then you can use that account to monitor the account's performance. The steps I describe here for working with a mutual fund investment are the same basic steps you use for working with a 401(k) account.

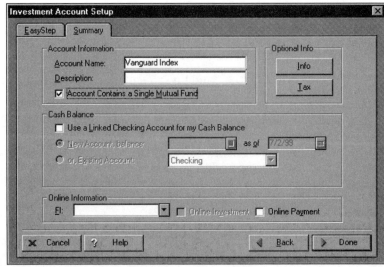

Figure 13-1:
The Investment Account Setup dialog box.

4. **Name the investment.**

   Move the cursor to the Account Name text box and enter a name for the mutual fund. If you're investing in the Vanguard Index 500 Trust mutual fund, for example, you might type **Vanguard Index**.

5. **Enter a description for the account (optional).**

   Move the cursor to the Description text box and type a description.

6. **Select the Account Contains a Single Mutual Fund check box.**

   Doing so tells Quicken, "Yeah, this is a mutual fund investment account."

7. **Indicate whether you have a cash account attached to this mutual fund by clicking the Use a Linked Checking Account for My Cash Balance check box.**

   You probably don't, by the way. This "linked checking account" business typically applies to brokerage accounts. With a brokerage account, you need someplace to store the cash that you receive from selling securities and from receiving investment income. And you need someplace from which to get the cash you'll need when you purchase additional shares of some hot, new mutual fund. If you do indicate that you have a linked checking account, you need to describe or identify the account. If this mutual fund investment is new and, therefore, a new linked checking account, click the New Account button and then use the Balance and As Of boxes to give the opening balance and transaction date. If the linked checking account is an existing checking account, click the Existing Account button and then select the account from the Existing Account drop-down list box.

8. **Provide any additional account information (optional).**

   You can click the Info button to display the cleverly named Additional Account Information dialog box. You can then use its text boxes to collect and store a bunch of additional information about the mutual fund account: the mutual fund management company, the account number, telephone number, and so forth.

9. **Click the Tax button.**

   Quicken displays the Tax Schedule Information dialog box (see Figure 13-2).

10. **Select the Tax-Deferred Account – IRA, 401(k), etc. check box if the investment is tax-deferred.**

    Doing so tells Quicken that this information doesn't affect your taxes. As I mention earlier, I can't think of a good reason for tracking a tax-deferred mutual fund. But, hey, I just work here.

Figure 13-2:
The Tax
Schedule
Information
dialog box.

Tax Schedule Information

☐ Tax-Deferred or Tax-Exempt Account - 401(k), IRA, etc.

(Optional) Choose the tax schedules to be associated with transfers in and out of this account:

Transfers In:

Transfers Out:

✓ OK   ✗ Cancel   ？ Help

11. **Indicate how transfers into this account and transfers from this account are reported on your tax return.**

   If this mutual fund is really an IRA, for example, and you've decided to track it with Quicken, activate the Transfers In drop-down list box and select the entry that describes the tax form and tax form line you'll use to report transfers into this account. (For example, in the case of an IRA, you may choose Form 1040: IRA Contribution Self.) Then activate the Transfers Out drop-down list box and select the entry that describes the tax form and tax form line you'll use to report transfers out of this account. You're doing this, by the way, so that Quicken reports will show all your tax deductions and so that you can export data from Quicken to TurboTax. When you finish, click OK to close the Tax Schedule Information dialog box.

12. **Click Done.**

   Quicken displays the Set Up Mutual Fund Security dialog box, shown in Figure 13-3. The Name text box shows the name you entered back in Step 4.

13. **Enter the mutual fund symbol (optional).**

   If you're going to download share price information via a modem — such as information from Quicken Online Quotes and News Service — move the cursor to the Symbol text box and enter the mutual fund's stock symbol.

14. **Indicate the type of investment you're setting up.**

   Choose an investment type (Bond, CD, Employee Stock Options, Market Index, Mutual Fund, Other, or Stock) from the Type drop-down list box.

15. **Indicate why you're investing (optional).**

   Choose your goal (College Fund, Growth, High Risk, Income, or Low Risk) from the Goal drop-down list box. This investment stereotyping seems sort of goofy, though. Does anybody really want high-risk investments? Reminds me of an old joke: How do you accumulate a million dollars in the stock market? Start with two million in the stock market.

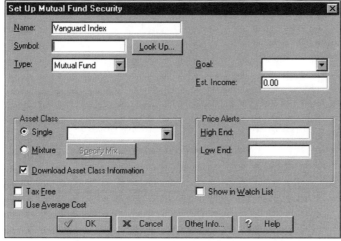

16. Describe the mutual fund's principal investment (optional).

If you are going to track more than one investment with Quicken and want to monitor the amount you've invested in different asset classes, or investment categories — domestic bonds, domestic large cap, domestic small cap, global bonds, and so forth — activate the Asset Class Single drop-down list box. Then select the asset class that most closely matches the mutual fund's principal investment. (***Note:*** If a mutual fund actually consists of several asset classes, you can click the Mixture button and then click the Specify Mixture command button. When you do so, Quicken displays a dialog box you can use to say, basically, "Oh this mutual fund is 40 percent bonds and 60 percent stocks.") And one final comment: If this "asset class" business just seems confusing, don't worry about it.

You can get lots of good investment information online at different mutual funds' web sites. One of the best, in my opinion, is Vanguard at www.vanguard.com.

17. Describe the high-end price and low-end price you'll use to trigger alert messages from Quicken concerning the price of the mutual fund (optional).

Does this step make sense? In other words, if you want to take your profits should the mutual share price rise to a specific level or you want to cut your losses should the share price fall to a specific price level, enter these share prices into the High End Price and Low End Price text boxes. Quicken will then alert you if the mutual fund share price moves above or below these amounts, assuming you've got an Internet connection. (Quicken will automatically get mutual fund share prices if you have an Internet connection and supply the mutual fund security symbol.)

18. Click OK.

Quicken redisplays the Account window — except now it lists the new investment account.

Recording your initial investment

After you set up a mutual fund investment account, you can record an initial purchase of fund shares.

Of course, you need to know the original price of those first shares. So dig through that kitchen drawer where you stuff bank statements, financial records, and those kooky birthday cards from Aunt Enid.

When you find the proper paperwork that shows the number of shares you purchased and the price per share, here's what you do:

1. Open the investment account.

Display the Account window; then select the investment account (with the arrow keys or by clicking the mouse). Click the Open button. Quicken displays the Create Opening Share Balance window. You don't — I repeat, *don't* — want to record your initial purchase with this dialog box. Just click Cancel to keep on moving to the investment account register (see Figure 13-4). You're in the big leagues now.

2. Enter the date you first purchased fund shares into the first row's Date field.

Move the cursor to the Date field and enter the date by using the MM/DD/YY format. Enter May 23, 1999, for example, as **5/23/99**. You may also select the date from the pop-up calendar.

3. Indicate that you're recording the prior purchase of shares.

When you move the cursor to the Action field, Quicken displays a down-arrow box, indicating a drop-down list box. From the drop-down list box, select ShrsIn. Doing so tells Quicken, "Yeah, I've purchased some shares of this mutual fund, but I don't want you to adjust my checking account because I bought them a long, long time ago and I recorded the transaction then." In some Quicken windows, drop-down list boxes don't appear until you move the cursor onto the field.

4. Accept the suggested security name.

The *security name* is the mutual fund account's name. Move the cursor past the Security field to the Avg. Cost field. (Quicken changes the name of this field from Price to Avg. Cost when you select ShrsIn.)

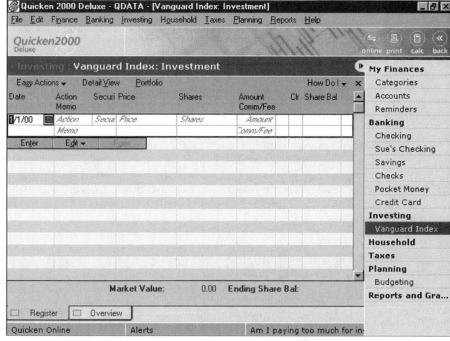

Figure 13-4:
The
investment
account
register
window.

5. **Indicate what you paid per share.**

   With the cursor on the Avg Cost field, enter the share price. You can type a fractional price — such as **10 1/4** — but your mutual fund shares probably cost something in dollars and cents, such as 10.25.

6. **Indicate the size of your purchase.**

   Tell Quicken the size of your initial investment — either total number of shares or total price.

   - To enter the total number of shares, move the cursor to the Shares field (fractional shares are okay).

   - To enter the total price, move the cursor to the Amount, or after you select the ShrsIn action, the Basis field.

   Quicken calculates the piece of data you didn't enter. Suppose, for example, that you spent $500 to purchase 5 shares of a mutual fund that cost $100.00 per share. If you enter the share price as **100.00** and the number of shares as 5, Quicken calculates the total price. If you enter the share price as **100.00** and the total purchase as **500**, Quicken calculates the number of shares purchased.

   Life doesn't get much better than this, huh?

7. Enter a memo description (optional).

If you want to tie the purchase to a confirmation order number, for example, enter the data into the Memo field. I suppose that you could use this field to record anything: Kilroy was here. Save the Whales. Don't tread on me.

8. Record the initial purchase of mutual fund shares.

Click the Enter button.

Quicken makes the familiar "ch-ching" cash register sound and records the transaction into the register. Figure 13-5, for example, shows a register that records a $500 purchase of shares in the Vanguard Index mutual fund. Note that I've removed the QuickTabs pane from the program window. You can add and remove the QuickTabs by clicking the arrowhead at the top of the QuickTabs row.

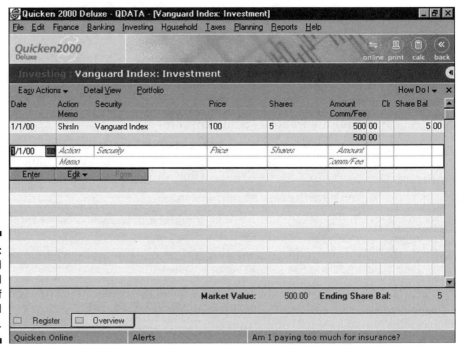

Figure 13-5:
The record of an initial purchase of mutual fund shares.

Buying investments

As you purchase shares — by sending a check to the mutual fund management company or by reinvesting dividends and capital gain distributions — record the transactions in the investment account register.

By writing a check

If you buy shares by writing a check, you have two ways to enter a description of the shares you purchase.

I think the easier way is to enter the transaction directly into the investment account register, much as you enter checks and deposits into a bank account register. (To display the investment account register, click its QuickTab.) To record the purchase this way, follow these steps:

1. **Enter the purchase date into the first empty row's Date field.**

2. **Indicate that you're purchasing new shares by check.**

   Move the cursor to the Action field. From the Action drop-down list box, select the BuyX action. (You also can type the Action abbreviations directly into the field.)

3. **Accept the suggested security name.**

4. **Indicate what you paid per share.**

5. **Indicate the size of your purchase by using either the shares or the Price field.**

   Tell Quicken the size of your investment — either the total number of shares or the total price.

6. **Enter a memo description (optional).**

7. **Enter the bank account on which you'll write the check that pays for the shares.**

   Select the account name from the Xfer Acct drop-down list box.

8. **Enter the account transfer amount.**

   Move the cursor to the Xfer Amt field and enter the transfer amount.

9. **Enter the commission or fee that you paid.**

   Move the cursor to the Comm/Fee field and enter the commission or fee you paid to purchase the shares. (The amount shown in the Amount field includes this figure.)

10. Record the purchase.

Click the Enter button. Quicken beeps with enthusiasm and then records your purchase of new shares. You are now, by definition, a capitalist. Congratulations.

Figure 13-6 shows a new shares purchase transaction recorded in the investment account register.

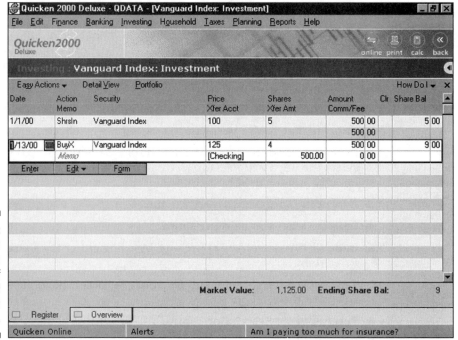

Figure 13-6: The record of a purchase of additional mutual fund shares.

Quicken offers another way to record a shares purchase: The Buy/Add Shares dialog box (see Figure 13-7) prompts you to enter the same information that you record when entering a mutual fund shares purchase transaction directly into the investment account register. Quicken then records the transaction into the register.

To display the Buy/Add Shares dialog box, click the Easy Actions button, which appears at the top of the investment account register window. When Quicken displays a list of investment actions, choose the Buy/Add Shares action and click the Summary tab. To record an investment purchase with the Buy/Add Shares dialog box, you just describe the purchase by using the dialog box's buttons and boxes.

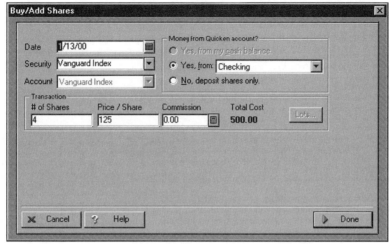

Figure 13-7:
The
Buy/Add
Shares
dialog box.

By reinvesting dividends, interest, or capital gains

When you reinvest your dividends, interest, or capital gains, you also have two methods available for recording the transaction: using the register or using the Reinvest Income dialog box. Here again, I like the register approach, so I'll describe it first. (Remember that you get to the investment account register by clicking its QuickTab.)

You can record your reinvestment transactions, in which you're buying new shares, by first displaying the investment account register and then by following these steps:

1. **Enter the purchase date (in this case, the reinvestment date) into the next empty row's Date field.**

2. **Tell Quicken that you're purchasing new shares by reinvesting.**

   Open the Action drop-down list box and select one of the following Reinvest actions:

   - **ReinvDiv:** Reinvest dividends

   - **ReinvInt:** Reinvest interest

   - **ReinvLg:** Reinvest long-term capital gains

   - **ReinvSh:** Reinvest short-term capital gains

   Use the arrow keys or the mouse to select the appropriate reinvestment action and press Enter. Quicken enters the reinvestment abbreviation in the Action field. You also can type these abbreviations directly in the field once you memorize them.

You don't need to determine whether the amounts you reinvest are dividends, interest, long-term capital gains, or short-term capital gains because the mutual fund statement gives you this information. If you reinvest more than one type of gain, however, you need to record more than one transaction. For example, if the $50 you reinvest is part long-term capital gain and part dividend income, you need to record two transactions: one for the long-term capital gain reinvestment and one for the dividend income reinvestment.

3. **Accept the suggested security name, which Quicken places in the Security field.**

4. **Using the Price field, indicate the price per share that you paid.**

5. **Indicate the size of your purchase.**

   You can give Quicken either the number of shares you're purchasing (using the Shares field) or the total dollar amount of the transaction (using the Amount field).

6. **Type a brief explanation of the transaction into the Memo field (optional).**

7. **Enter the commission or fee that you paid in the Comm/Fee field.**

   The figure shown in the Amount field includes the commission fee.

8. **Record the reinvestment transaction.**

   Click the Enter button.

Figure 13-8 shows $50 of dividends being reinvested in the mutual fund by buying shares that cost $120 apiece. (Because the shares cost more money than the $50, of course, only a fractional share is purchased.) Other reinvestments work basically the same way — except you use a different reinvestment action.

As I mention earlier, you also can record amounts that you reinvest by clicking the Easy Actions button and then selecting the Reinvest Income option. After you choose this command, Quicken displays the Reinvest Income dialog box (see Figure 13-9).

To describe an amount that you're reinvesting, just fill in the text boxes, which are similar to the fields you fill in when you record the reinvestment directly into the register. After you click OK, Quicken takes the information you entered into the text boxes and records the reinvestment into the investment account register.

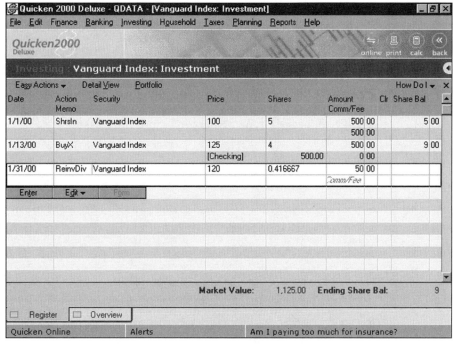

Figure 13-8:
How you record dividend reinvestment.

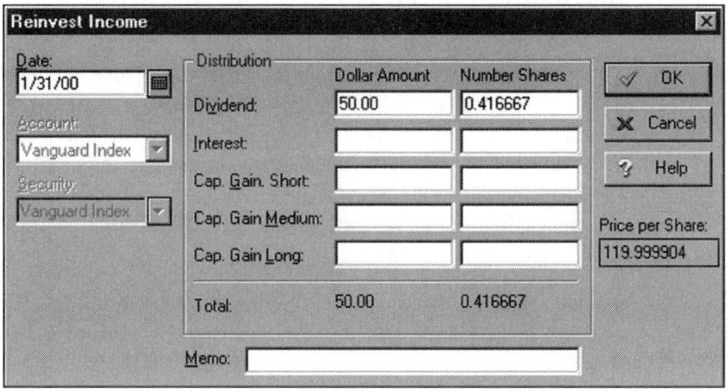

Figure 13-9:
You can also use the Reinvest Income dialog box to record a reinvestment.

Although you can record reinvestment transactions directly into the register, using the Reinvest Income dialog box does possess a noteworthy advantage. When you use the register approach, you need to record one transaction for each type of income that you reinvest. When you use the Reinvest Income dialog box, however, you can record the reinvestment of each type of income at the same time: dividends, interest, short-term capital gains, and long-term capital gains. All you need to do is fill out more than one set of Dollar Amount and Number Shares text boxes. Quicken then enters the separate transactions — one for each type of income — into the register.

Recording your profits

Every so often, you may receive distributions directly from the mutual fund company. Retirees, for example, often direct mutual fund managers to send dividend checks and capital gains directly to them rather than reinvesting the amounts.

To record these kinds of distributions, you go through a process very similar to those I describe earlier in this chapter. For example, if you want to record an income transaction directly into the investment account register, you follow these steps:

1. **Enter the distribution date into the next empty row's Date field.**

2. **Tell Quicken that you're receiving a distribution from the mutual fund.**

   Open the Action drop-down list box and select the appropriate action to describe the distribution: DivX, to indicate that you're depositing dividends; CGLongX, to indicate that you're depositing long-term capital gains; CGMedX to indicate you're depositing medium-term capital gains, or CGShortX, to indicate that you're depositing short-term capital gains. Again, when you memorize these abbreviations — DivX, CGLongX, CGMedX, and CGShortX — you also can type them directly into the Action field.

   You don't need to determine for yourself whether a distribution is a dividend, a long-term capital gain, or a short-term capital gain because the mutual fund statement makes the distribution clear.

3. **Indicate the dividend or capital gains distribution amount.**

   Enter the amount in the Amount text box.

4. **Type a brief description of the distribution in the Memo field (optional).**

   Be creative — type your wedding anniversary, the name of your dog, or even a piece of data related to the dividend or distribution.

5. **Indicate into which bank account you'll deposit the dividend or distribution.**

   Open the Xfer Acct, or Transfer Account, drop-down list box and select the account into which you'll deposit the money.

6. **Record the dividend or distribution transaction.**

   You can record the dividend in a bunch of ways, but why not just click the Enter button? Quicken records the reinvestment — bip, bap, boom. It's just that quick.

Figure 13-10 shows you depositing $50 of dividends into your checking account.

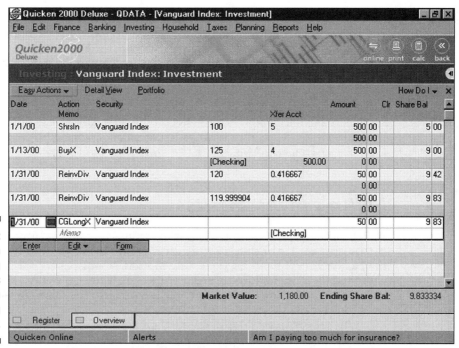

Figure 13-10: A transaction for depositing dividends into a checking account.

If you don't want to enter the transaction directly into the investment account register, click the Easy Actions button and choose the Record an Income Event action. Quicken displays the Record Income dialog box (see Figure 13-11).

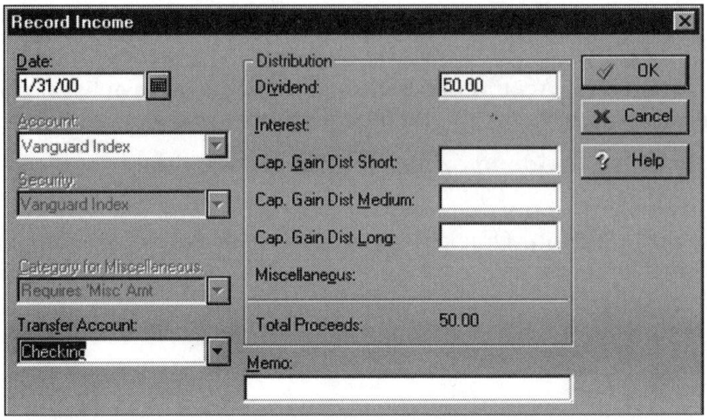

Figure 13-11:
The Record
Income
dialog box.

You record an income transaction in the Record Income dialog box in the same way that you record it directly in the register. You describe the income amount, the category, and the account into which you are depositing the dividend, interest, or capital gains check.

As with the Reinvest Income dialog box, you can record several types of income in one fell swoop with the Record Income dialog box. Quicken uses the information that you type in the Record Income dialog box to enter up to four income transactions into the investment account register.

Selling investments

Selling mutual fund shares works basically the same way as buying them. You can record the sale of shares either directly into the register or by clicking the Easy Actions button and selecting the Sell/Remove Shares action. (You get to the investment account register by clicking its QuickTab.) To record the sale of shares directly into the register, perform the following actions:

1. **Enter the sale's date into the next empty row's Date field.**

2. **Tell Quicken that you're selling shares.**

   Open the Action drop-down list box and select the SellX action. (***Note:*** You also can type **SellX** directly into the field.)

3. **Accept the suggested security name, which Quicken places into the Security field.**

4. **Indicate the price per share that you received by using the Price field.**

   With a little luck, your selling price is more than you paid.

5. **Indicate the size of your sale by giving Quicken either the number of shares you sold or the total dollar amount of the sale.**

   Quicken calculates whatever you don't enter. For example, if you tell Quicken how many dollars you sell (using the Amount field), it calculates the number of shares you sell by dividing the total sales amount by the price per share. If you tell Quicken how many shares you sell (using the Shares field), it calculates the total sales amount by multiplying the number of shares by the price per share. I guess this feature is handy.

6. **Type a brief description of the sale in the Memo field (optional).**

7. **Enter the bank account into which you are going to deposit the sale's proceeds.**

   Open the Xfer Acct drop-down list box and select the appropriate account.

8. **Enter the account transfer amount.**

   Move the cursor to the Xfer Amt field and type the transfer amount. This amount is what you are actually going to deposit into the transfer account. The transfer amount equals the total sales price less the commission you paid.

9. **Enter the commission or fee you paid to sell the shares in the Comm/Fee field.**

   No wonder Bernie, your broker, does so well, huh? He makes money even if you don't.

10. **Click the Enter button.**

    Quicken displays the Sell Shares dialog box (see Figure 13-12), which lets you create some degree of control over how Quicken calculates the basis of the shares you sell.

Figure 13-12:
The Sell
Shares
dialog box.

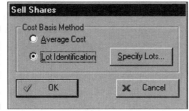

11. Indicate whether you want to use specific identification (optional).

When Quicken displays the Sell Shares dialog box, which basically asks how you want to calculate the cost of the shares you're selling:

- Click Average Cost if you're selling all the shares because specific identification makes no difference in your case.

- Click Lot Identification and then the Specify Lots if you aren't selling all your shares. Now you can pick and choose which shares to sell so that you can minimize the capital gains taxes you'll owe (good idea, huh?). Quicken displays the Specify Lots for Investment dialog box, shown in Figure 13-13.

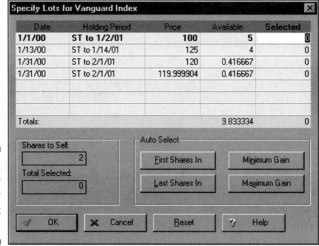

Date	Holding Period	Price	Available	Selected
1/1/00	**ST to 1/2/01**	**100**	**5**	**0**
1/13/00	ST to 1/14/01	125	4	0
1/31/00	ST to 2/1/01	120	0.416667	0
1/31/00	ST to 2/1/01	119.999904	0.416667	0
Totals:			9.833334	0

Shares to Sell: 2
Total Selected: 0

Auto Select
First Shares In — Minimum Gain
Last Shares In — Maximum Gain

OK — Cancel — Reset — Help

Figure 13-13: The Specify Lots for Investment dialog box.

12. Identify which lots you're selling (optional).

You can pick and choose which lots to sell to minimize the capital gains taxes you owe. A *lot* is simply a batch, or set, of shares that you purchase at one time. If you sell the most expensive lots, you reduce your capital gains and the taxes on those gains.

- To pick an entire lot, double-click it. (You need to double-click the date field, by the way.)

- To pick a portion of a lot, select it and then type the number of shares from the lot you want to sell in the Selected box.

- To clear your selections and start over, click the Reset button.

The Specify Lots for Investment dialog box also provides four nifty command buttons for automating the process of selecting lots. If you click the Maximum Gain or Minimum Gain button, Quicken picks lots for you in a way that produces the largest possible or smallest possible capital gain. Alternatively, you can click the First Shares In or Last Shares In button to sell either the oldest shares or newest shares first. This business about picking the lots you sell is rather arbitrary, of course. By letting Quicken pick lots, you can manipulate the capital gain you'll have and the capital gains taxes you'll pay. But it's all legal. And honorable. And it can save you money because you can time your capital gains so that they occur when they'll cost you least.

After the Specify Lots for Investment dialog box correctly shows all the shares you want to sell, click OK. Quicken records the sell transaction in the register.

Figure 13-14 shows shares being sold to pay for Beth's first-quarter community college tuition. Just a few pages ago, she was a little girl, and now she's leaving home. They grow up fast, don't they?

If you don't want to record a sell transaction directly into the register, you can click the Easy Actions button and then click the Sell/Remove Shares command. After you choose the command, Quicken displays the Sell/Remove Shares dialog box. Click the Summary tab and you can enter the same information in the text boxes that you enter in the register's fields (see Figure 13-15). To identify shares specifically, click the Specify Lots button.

Correcting a mistake

If you make a mistake, don't worry — it's not a problem. You can edit an investment transaction in the investment account register the same way that you edit check and deposit transactions in a bank account register. For example, you can click the fields with the incorrect entries, fix them, and then record the new, corrected transaction.

You also can select the transaction and click the Form button. Quicken then displays the investment dialog box that lets you change each of the pieces of the transaction. The dialog box that Quicken displays mirrors the investment dialog box you could have used originally to record the transaction. For example, the dialog box to edit a sell shares transaction looks much like the Summary tab of the Sell/Remove Shares dialog box, shown in Figure 13-14.

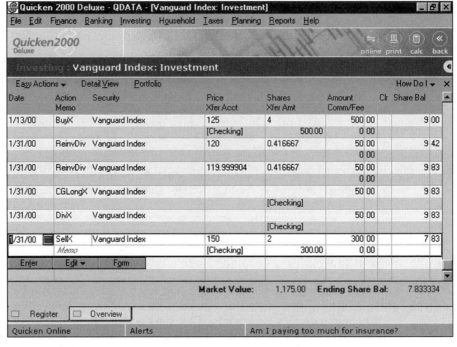

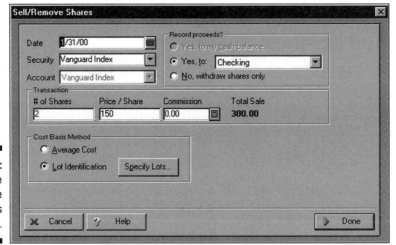

Working with slightly tricky mutual fund transactions

I haven't described every possible mutual fund transaction — although I have described every one I've encountered in the last 10 or 12 years. You should know, however, that Quicken does let you record three additional transactions by specifying several almost-magical actions: shares out, stock split, and reminder transactions.

How do I remove shares from an account?

You can tell Quicken to remove shares from an account — without moving the money represented by the shares — to some other account. Why would you want to remove a *shares-out* transaction? I can think of two situations:

- You erroneously added shares to the account with the shares in (ShrsIn) action and now you need to remove them.

- You are using an investment account to record old investment activity, such as activity from last year.

The first instance is self-explanatory because you are simply correcting an error that you made. In the second case, however, you don't want to transfer the proceeds of a mutual fund sale to a checking account because the money from the sale is already recorded as a deposit at some point in the past.

You can record a shares-out transaction directly into the register by moving the cursor to the next empty row of the register and specifying the action as ShrsOut. Then fill in the rest of the fields in the investment account register the same way that you would for a regular ol' sell transaction. The only difference is that you won't give an Xfer Account.

You also can record a shares-out transaction with a dialog box. Click the Easy Actions button, choose the Sell/Remove Shares action, and fill in the Date and Transaction text boxes in the dialog box, leaving the Record Proceeds? button set to No.

What? The stock split and then doubled?

Stock splits don't occur very often with mutual funds; however, when they do occur, the mutual fund manager, in effect, gives you a certain number of new shares (such as two) for each old share you own.

To record a stock split, you use the StkSplit action. Then you indicate the ratio of new shares to old shares. For a two-for-one split, for example, you indicate that you get two new split shares for each old unsplit share. The whole process is really pretty easy.

You can record a stock split by moving the cursor to the next empty row of the register and using the StkSplit action. You can also click the Easy Actions button, select the Stock Split action from the menu, and fill out the dialog box that asks about the split date, the new shares, the old shares, and, optionally, the share price after the split.

Quicken, will you remind me of something?

A *reminder* transaction is the electronic equivalent of a yellow stick-on note. If you put a reminder transaction in the investment account register, the Quicken Billminder utility gives you a reminder message on the reminder date. You can't goof up anything by trying out reminders, so if you're curious, enter a reminder transaction for tomorrow and see what happens.

You can post a reminder note by moving the cursor to the next empty row of the register and using the Reminder action. Or you can click the Easy Actions button and choose Advanced⇨Reminder Transaction from the menu. Then fill out the dialog box that asks you for information about the reminder.

Reconciling an account

You reconcile a mutual fund investment account the same basic way that you reconcile a bank account. The only real difference — and it doesn't affect reconciliation mechanics — is that you focus on mutual fund shares and not on account balance dollars. To begin reconciling a mutual fund investment account, choose Investing⇨Investing Activities⇨Reconcile an Investment Account. If you have questions about what to do next, refer to Chapter 8. It describes how you reconcile a bank account, but the same procedures apply to a mutual fund account.

Trying reports

I just want to say one thing about Quicken reports as they relate to your investments: *Remember that the reports are available.* (For more information, see Chapter 7.)

Using menu commands and other stuff

For the most part, the commands and menus available for an investment account are the same as those available for all the other accounts Quicken supplies. I write about the commands that I think are most helpful to new users in the preceding chapters of this book. If you have a question about how the Void Transaction command works, for example, refer to the Index, which directs you to a specific discussion of that command.

Updating Securities Prices

You can collect current market prices and store this information with your accounts. Just display the investment account that has the mutual fund shares. Then click the Portfolio button or choose Investing➪Portfolio View. Either way, Quicken displays the Portfolio View window (see Figure 13-16).

To record the current market price for a security, use the arrow keys or click the mouse to select the security. Then move the cursor to the Price field and enter the current price.

Quicken updates the Mkt Value field in the Portfolio View window as well as the Market Value figure at the bottom of the register window. After you update the market price, you can return to the register by clicking the Register button.

If you invest exclusively in mutual funds, the information in this chapter should be all you need. If you also invest directly in such things as stocks and bonds, you may want to turn to the next chapter. It describes how you use a Quicken investment account to track a brokerage account.

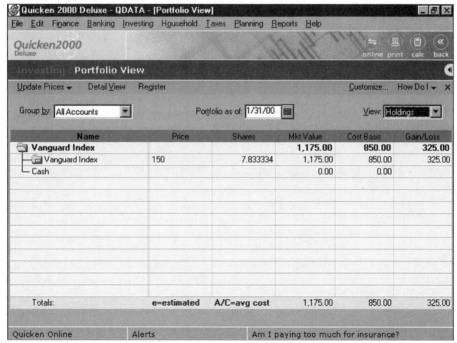

Figure 13-16:
The Portfolio View window.

The Portfolio View window

You can do more with the Portfolio View window than just update share prices.

The Portfolio As Of field lets you specify the date on which you want to see and set market prices and values. The Group By drop-down list box lets you customize the way Quicken displays your list of securities in the Portfolio View. And the Detail View button displays the Security Detail View, where you can review the details of each security.

The Customize button displays a dialog box that lets you create a customized view of the Portfolio View window. You can select what

information you want Quicken to display in the Portfolio View window and which order you want the information in. The Update Prices button displays a menu of commands that let you download securities prices from the Internet and that let you see and modify a historical list of share prices.

I'm not going to go into more detail here about what all these extra bells and whistles do. If you're a serious investor, however, take the time to explore these commands. You may gain some interesting insights into your financial investments.

Chapter 14

Stocks and Bonds

- -

In This Chapter

▶ Setting up a brokerage account

▶ Describing the securities in a brokerage account

▶ Transferring cash to and from a brokerage account

▶ Buying stocks and bonds from a brokerage account

▶ Recording income from securities held in a brokerage account

▶ Recording margin interest, miscellaneous income and expenses, and return of capital

▶ Updating securities prices

▶ Adjusting your brokerage cash balance

▶ Adjusting your brokerage account shares

▶ Investing online with Quicken

- -

*A*fter you understand how Quicken handles mutual fund investments, working with a brokerage account (or *cash investment account,* as Quicken calls it) is a snap.

Setting Up a Brokerage Account

Setting up a brokerage account is similar to setting up a regular mutual fund account except for a couple of minor — but predictable — differences. Because you're still fairly new to this process, I'll go through it step-by-step:

1. **Choose Finance⇨Account List, press Ctrl+A, or click the Accounts Feature tab if it appears with the other QuickTabs along the right edge of the Quicken program window.**

    Quicken, the ever faithful companion, displays the Account List window.

2. **Click the New button in the Account List window.**

    Quicken displays the familiar Create New Account dialog box that you use to specify what type of new account you want to create.

3. **Click the Brokerage button and click Next.**

   When Quicken displays the Investment Account Setup dialog box, click the Summary tab. You don't need to step through the other tabs unless you're someone who loves excessive hand-holding.

   Quicken displays the Investment Account Setup dialog box (see Figure 14-1).

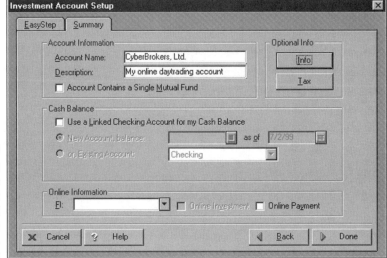

Figure 14-1: The Investment Account Setup dialog box.

4. **Name the investment.**

   Move the cursor to the Account Name text box and type the broker's name. Or, if you have trouble remembering your broker's name, you can identify this account as the one you use to track your brokerage account with a name such as Brokerage.

5. **Enter a description of the account (optional).**

   You can use the Description text box to store extra information about the account.

6. **Leave the Account Contains a Single Mutual Fund check box unselected.**

   Leaving this check box unselected tells Quicken that you are using the investment account to track a brokerage account.

7. **Indicate whether you have a cash management account (or some similarly titled cash account) attached to your brokerage account.**

   To do so, select the Use a Linked Checking Account for my Cash Balance check box. Most brokerage accounts — maybe all brokerage accounts — have a linked cash account. You need someplace to store the cash that you receive from selling securities and the cash you receive because you've earned dividend or interest income. Your brokerage outfit, of course, also wants someplace where it can quickly grab the cash whenever you buy anything.

8. **Describe the linked checking account (optional).**

   If you indicate that you have a linked checking account, you need to describe or identify the account. If this account is a new brokerage investment and, therefore, a new linked checking account, click the New Account button and then use the Balance and As Of boxes to give the opening balance and transaction date. If the linked checking account is an existing checking account, click the Existing Account button and then select the account from the Existing Account drop-down list box.

9. **Click the Tax button.**

   Quicken displays the Tax Schedule Information dialog box (see Figure 14-2).

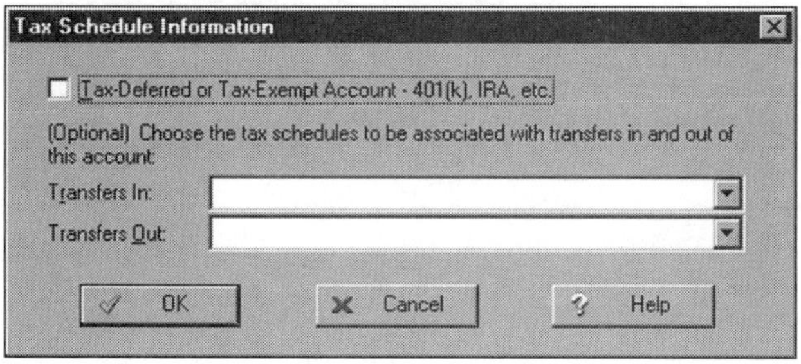

Figure 14-2:
The Tax
Schedule
Information
dialog box.

10. **Select or deselect the Tax-Deferred or Tax-Exempt Account — 401(k), IRA, etc. check box as appropriate.**

    Basically, this check box tells Quicken whether the dividends, interest, and capital gains for this account affect your taxable income.

11. **Indicate where you report a tax-deferred account's transfers for tax purposes and click OK.**

    Okay. This is kind of confusing. But here's the deal. If you have your IRA money (or something like that) invested in a tax-deferred brokerage account, any time you add money to the account, that transfer may result in a tax deduction. And any time you take money out of the account, that transfer may result in taxable income.

    So, as you move money into and out of the brokerage account, you produce transactions that you need to report on your tax return at the end of the year. Quicken tracks these transactions for you, but you need to tell it where to stick the numbers it tallies. To do so, you first open the Transfers In drop-down list box and select the entry that describes the tax form and tax form line you use to report transfers into this account. (For example, in the case of an IRA, you may choose "Form 1040: IRA Contribution Self.") Then you open the Transfers Out drop-down list box and select the entry that describes the tax form and tax form line you use to report transfers out of this account. Whew.

12. **Click Done.**

Quicken displays the Security Setup dialog box, which you can use to describe the individual investments you hold in your brokerage account. But I know an easier way. Click the Cancel button. Quicken redisplays the Account List window. If you want to begin entering investment transactions, select the account and then click the Open button. Quicken displays an investment account register window, as shown in Figure 14-3.

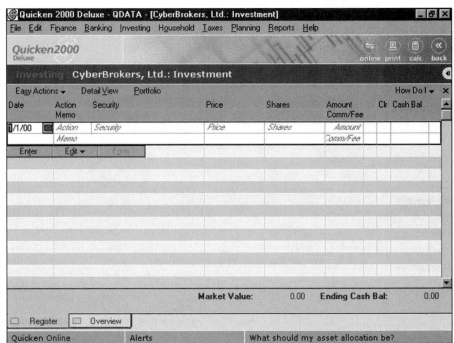

Figure 14-3:
The investment register.

Trying the Portfolio View

In Chapter 12, I briefly mention the Portfolio View window. My superficial coverage of the Portfolio View window stems largely from the fact that, for mutual funds, working from the register is easier. You already know how the register works, for example, if you've been tracking a bank account with Quicken. And for a single mutual fund, using the Portfolio View window is overkill (sort of like using industrial solvent to clean your kitchen floor).

When it comes to a brokerage account, however, the Portfolio View window makes more sense to use. Sure, you need a few minutes to get used to the Portfolio View window, but once you do, you'll find it much easier to work with.

To switch to the Portfolio View window, by the way, display the investment account you want to work with. Then click the Portfolio button. If you don't have any securities set up yet, Quicken will probably pop up the Security Setup window. Just click Cancel to move on by. Quicken then displays the Portfolio View window, as shown in Figure 14-4.

The really neat thing about a Portfolio View window — at least as it applies to investment portfolios — is that it lets you look at your investment portfolio as a set of securities. In contrast, a register simply lists the investment trans-actions for an account.

Setting up security lists

Your account contains more than one type of *security*. You may have shares of Boeing, General Motors, or Chase Manhattan. You name it, and someone owns it.

You need to create a list of the securities — stocks, bonds, and so on — that your account holds.

To do so, set up the brokerage account, and then complete the following steps:

1. **Choose Investing⇨Security List.**

   Quicken displays the Security List window (see Figure 14-5). Note that any mutual funds you've already set up appear in the list as securities.

2. **Click the New button in the Security List window.**

   Quicken displays the Set Up a New Security dialog box, as shown in Figure 14-6.

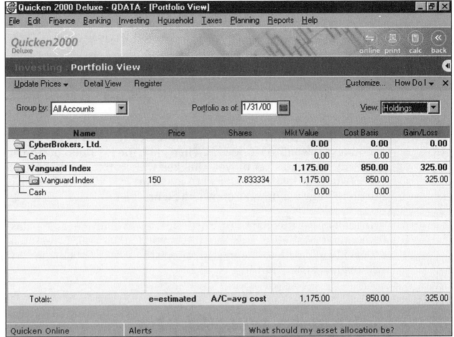

Figure 14-4:
The
Portfolio
View
window.

Figure 14-5:
The Security
List window.

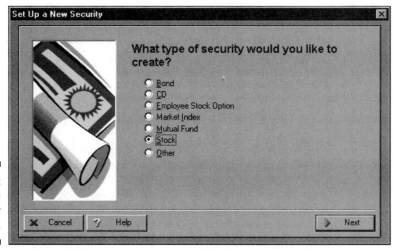

Figure 14-6:
The Set Up
Security
dialog box.

3. **Select the option button that corresponds to the type of security.**

   This makes sense, right? If you're setting up a bond, you click the Bond button. If you're setting up a CD, or certificate of deposit, you click the CD button. If you're not sure what you should pick, click the one that seems closest. If you have no idea which of Quicken's types are closest, click the Other button. Then click Next. Quicken displays a new set of boxes in the Set Up a New Security dialog box.

4. **Enter a name for the security in the Name text box.**

5. **Enter the stock symbol for the security in the Symbol text box (optional, and truthfully, probably crazy).**

   If you enter the symbol, you can download share price information from a modem. If you don't know the symbol, make sure that you have the name of the security correct and then click the Look Up button to search for the symbol on the Internet.

6. **Click Next to continue.**

   Quicken displays still another set up of boxes and buttons in the Set Up a New Security dialog box — this time, asking for asset class and investment goal investment. Yeah, like you're going to know this stuff off the top of your head.

7. **Use the Asset Class buttons and boxes to describe this security (optional).**

   If the security you're setting up is a large capitalization stock, for example, click the Single button and then select the Large Cap Stocks entry from the Single drop-down list box. Note that if the security that you're setting up is really a collection of asset classes — say you're setting up a mutual fund that will own securities in more than one class — you can click the Mixture button and then the Specify Mixture button to say, basically, "Oh, this security is 60 percent stocks and 40 percent bonds."

 8. **Indicate the purpose for which you're investing (optional).**

Open the Goal drop-down list box and then select one of the goals listed: College Fund, High Risk, Income, or Low Risk.

Excuse me, may I digress just for a moment? If you really are into high-risk investments, by the way, please write me in care of the publisher. I have an idea that I'm too conservative to test with my own money. Here it is: You take your money and go to Las Vegas. You place the minimum wager at a roulette wheel, betting on the color red. If you lose, you triple your wager and bet on red again. If you lose again, you triple your wager again and bet on red again. Assuming the table limit doesn't foul us up, you keep tripling your bets until we win. Then you start over again. I should tell you that I've created a computer model that simulates the aforementioned strategy. And it doesn't work. But it would sure be interesting to test the idea with real money. Yours.

Note: You can choose either Investing⇨Security Type or Investing⇨Investment Goal at any time after the initial Security setup to display lists of the security types and investment goals. You can also use these commands to create new security types and investment goals — Sure-fire, Easy money, or Unconscionable profits, for example.

I don't think this option is all that important. If you want to use it, choose Investing⇨Security Type or Investing⇨Investment Goal and then click the New button in the dialog box that appears. Quicken displays another dialog box, in which you enter your new type or goal.

 9. **Click Next to continue.**

Quicken displays yet another set of options, which you use to tell it how you want to track the costs of your securities.

10. **Tell Quicken that you want to use Lot Identification because you're the sort of person who doesn't like to pay too much in taxes.**

You should click the Lot Identification button if you're setting up a security that you'll hold in a taxable account. Specific identification of individual lots — a lot is just a batch you buy at the same time and price gives you the opportunity to time your capital gains. And timing your capital gains often lets you minimize your taxes.

If you're setting up a security for a tax-deferred account — like a self-directed IRA — you can use average costing. In this case, go ahead and mark the Average Cost button.

11. **Dude. Click Next to continue.**

After you select your costing method, click Next. Quicken next asks how you want to track the security (see Figure 14-7).

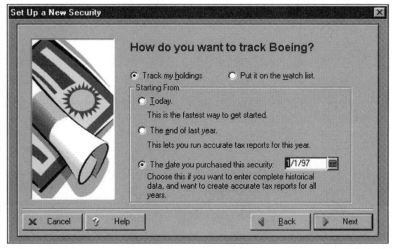

Figure 14-7:
The fifth
version of
the Set Up a
New
Security
dialog box,
but, hey,
who's
counting.

12. **Tell Quicken how you want to track the historical cost information of this security.**

    Okay, the first thing you need to do is indicate whether this security is, in fact, one you really own or just one you're watching. If you own the security, select the Track my holdings radio button. If you don't own the security but you want to monitor its price or news about the security, mark the Put it on the watch list radio button.

    Note: The Investing Activity Center provides a hyperlink to your watch list. You can also view your watch list from the Portfolio View window.

    If you're tracking a security you own, you'll need to indicate how closely you want to record the historical cost information about the security. If you're setting up a security that's inside a tax-deferred account, you can select the Today option. This is sloppiest, but, as Quicken indicates, it's also fastest. The Today option is also acceptable when you don't need to monitor the historical cost basis of the security.

    If you're setting up a security that's inside a regular, taxable account, you should select the The date you purchased this security radio button and then give the date.

13. **Click Next to plod even further into this wizard.**

    When you do, Quicken displays the sixth Set Up a New Security dialog box. This one lets you indicate which investment account you want to use to record your current holdings of the security.

14. **Tell Quicken which investment account you'll use to hold the security.**

    To do this, activate the Account Name drop-down list box and select the account. Then click Next.

15. Give Quicken the number of shares, price per share, and commission.

When Quicken displays the seventh Set Up a New Security dialog box (see Figure 14-8), provide the number of shares, cost per share, and commission information. Then click Next. If you've indicated that you want to use specific lot identification, Quicken should ask you to repeat this step for each lot. Unfortunately, as of this writing, it doesn't. Go figure. What you'll need to do is add the second and subsequent lots by following the same sequence of steps as described in Chapter 13 in the section, "Recording the Initial Investment."

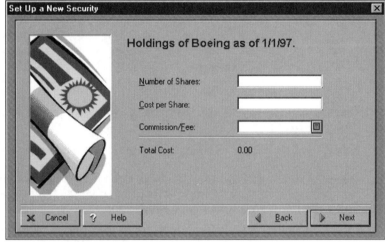

Figure 14-8:
The seventh version of the Set Up a New Security dialog box, and now I really am counting.

16. Confirm your description of the security.

When Quicken asks you to confirm your security description, do so by reading the summary information provided in the Set Up a New Security dialog box. If you need to make changes, click Back to return to the earlier dialog boxes you used to describe the security. If the security description is correct, click Done.

17. Indicate whether you want to set up additional securities.

After you describe a security, Quicken asks if you want to describe another one. If you do, click Yes and then repeat the preceding steps. If you don't, click No.

18. Download security information.

After you describe each of your securities, Quicken asks if you want to download security prices. If you have an Internet connection and you want to download these prices, click Yes.

Mutual (fund) acquaintance

Treat mutual fund shares that you hold in a brokerage account the same way that you treat other stocks and bonds that you hold in the account. If you're confused, think of it this way: Although brokers sell many mutual funds to their clients, the mutual fund manager sells some mutual funds directly to the public.

I don't want to get into the subject of load mutual funds versus no-load mutual funds — you pay a commission to buy load funds and you don't pay a commission to buy no-load funds — but if you're interested in how these two types of funds work, flip open *The Wall Street Journal* and look for advertisements from no-load fund

managers such as Vanguard, Scudder, and T. Rowe Price. Give them a call, and they'll tell you why they think that you should bypass the middleman — your broker. Next, talk to a broker, who will tell you why you *shouldn't* bypass the middleman. Then you make the decision.

What? You want *my* opinion? With much trepidation, I'll tell you: I always use no-load mutual funds because I'm a big fan of the do-it-yourself approach. However, I also think that a good broker — *good* is the operative word here — is well worth the commission fee if he or she helps you avoid expensive mistakes.

Working with cash

One of the differences between a brokerage account and a mutual fund account is that a cash management, or *money market,* account is attached to the brokerage account.

When you initially set up a brokerage account, your money goes into this account. (The broker buys you a doughnut and coffee in this meeting, remember?)

You purchase your first shares with the cash from this account. And when you sell shares, all cash proceeds go into this account.

Transferring cash to and from an account

Because you work with cash in a brokerage account, you need to know how to record the cash that flows into and out of the account.

To transfer cash to an account, follow these steps:

1. **Display the Portfolio View.**

   When you see the Portfolio View window, click its Detail View button to display the Security Detail View window (see Figure 14-9).

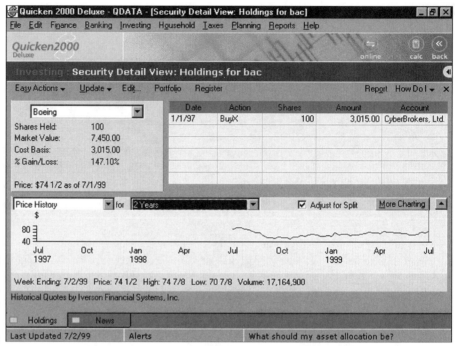

Figure 14-9:
The Security
Detail View
window.

2. Indicate that you're transferring money.

Click the Easy Actions button in the Security Detail View window, and choose Transfer Cash into Account. Quicken displays the Transfer Cash In dialog box (see Figure 14-10).

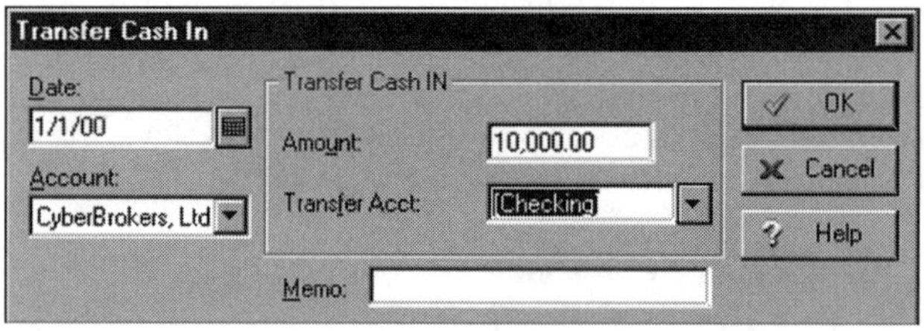

Figure 14-10:
The Transfer
Cash In
dialog box.

3. Record the transaction date, amount, and account.

To record the amount of a cash transfer, confirm the transaction date, enter the dollar amount in the Amount field, and then specify the investment account receiving the cash in the Transfer Acct drop-down list box. Then click OK.

To transfer cash from an account, follow these steps:

1. **Display the Portfolio View.**

   When you see the Portfolio View window, click its Detail View button to display the Security Detail View window (refer to Figure 14-9).

2. **Indicate that you're transferring money from an account.**

   Click the Easy Actions button (which appears at the top of the Security Detail View window) and choose the Transfer Cash from Account command. Quicken displays the Transfer Cash Out dialog box (see Figure 14-11).

3. **Record the transaction date, amount, and account.**

   To record the amount of a cash transfer, again confirm the transaction date, enter the dollar amount in the Amount field, and specify the investment account dispersing the cash in the Transfer Acct drop-down list box. Then click OK.

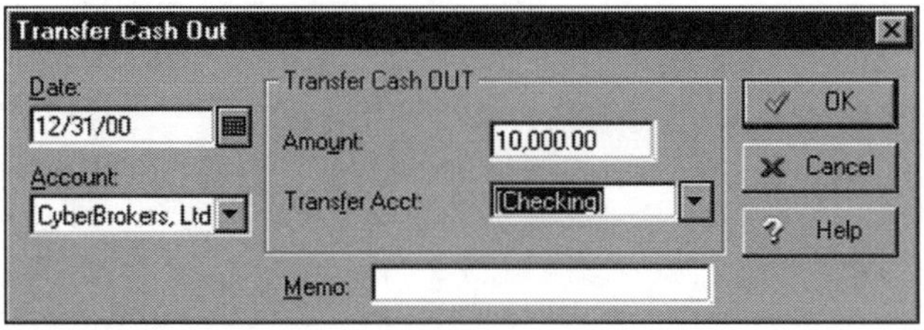

Figure 14-11:
The Transfer
Cash Out
dialog box.

I know it's not all that complicated, but you'll impress your friends.

Buying near and selling dear

Buying and selling securities in a brokerage account is very similar to buying and selling shares of a mutual fund. You fill out almost the exact same fields.

1. **Display the Security Detail View window and select the security by using the unnamed drop-down list box.**

2. **Click Easy Actions, select the Buy/Add Shares action, and click the Summary tab.**

   Quicken, ever responsive to your needs, displays the Buy/Add Shares dialog box (see Figure 14-12). When Quicken displays this dialog box, confirm that the Security drop-down list box identifies the stock, bond, or mutual fund you're purchasing. You use the # of Shares, Price/Share, and Commission boxes to describe your purchase. (You can get this information from your order confirmation slip.)

3. **Indicate whether Quicken should adjust a cash account.**

   Use the Money from Quicken account? buttons to specify, "No, Quicken shouldn't adjust some bank account's cash balance for this transaction." Or to specify, "Yes, Quicken should adjust some bank account's cash balance."

4. **Click Done when you're done.**

   Pretty simple, right?

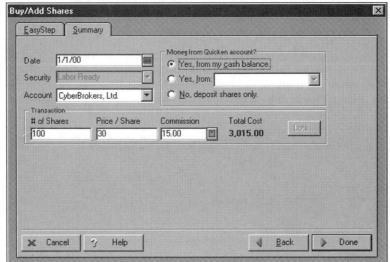

Figure 14-12:
The Buy/Add
Shares
dialog box.

Selling a security works in the same basic way as buying a security:

1. **Display the Security Detail View window and select the security.**

2. **Click the Easy Actions button and select the Sell/Remove Shares command.**

   When Quicken displays the Sell/Remove Shares dialog box (see Figure 14-13), click the Summary tab. The Security drop-down list box identifies the stock, bond, or mutual fund you're selling. You use the # of Shares, Price/Share, and Commission boxes to describe your sale and the Record Proceeds buttons and boxes to specify whether Quicken should adjust some bank account balance for this transaction.

3. **Click Done.**

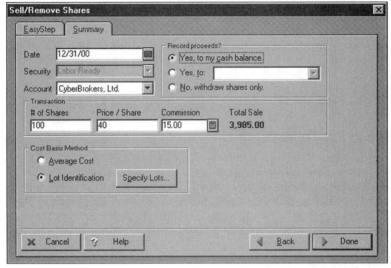

Figure 14-13:
The
Sell/Remove
Shares
dialog box.

If you want to control which lots are sold — a *lot* is just a chunk of securities you purchase together — you can click the Sell/Remove Shares dialog box's Specify Lots button. Clicking this button tells Quicken to display a dialog box that lets you specify which lots you're selling. (I describe how to use this dialog box in Chapter 13 if you need more information.)

Recording dividends, capital gains, and other goodies

Taking care of this stuff is easy. Any time you receive investment income, click the Easy Actions button and choose the Record an Income Event command. When Quicken displays the Record Income dialog box, use the Security drop-down list box to identify the stock, bond, or mutual fund producing income and use the Distribution boxes to record the amount and type of income (see Figure 14-14).

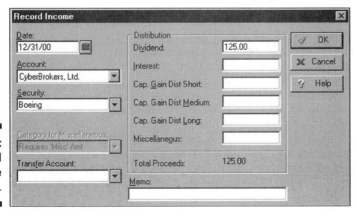

Figure 14-14:
The Record
Income
dialog box.

Recording other not-so-tricky transactions

Quicken lets you record all sorts of transactions in a brokerage account. Not only can you do reminder and stock split actions (which I describe for mutual fund accounts in Chapter 12), but you can also do a bunch of other things.

I'll briefly describe these other transactions and explain how to record them.

Bonds . . . James Bonds . . .

If you invest in bonds, you know that a bond's price is actually quoted as a percentage of its face value. A bond that sells for $950 with a face value of $1,000, for example, is quoted as 95 because the $950 price is 95 percent of the $1,000 face value. Quicken, however, doesn't let you describe a bond's price as a percent. You must enter the bond price as its price in dollars and cents.

Going for the gold

You can use Quicken to record precious metal investments. Suppose, for example, that you're hoarding *Krugerrands* (one-ounce gold coins minted in South Africa). For this investment, the price is the price per Krugerrand, and the shares figure is actually the number of ounces (equal to the number of Krugerrands). Because Quicken doesn't supply price-per-ounce and number-of-ounces fields, you insert the information into the Price and Shares fields on the investment register.

Recording margin interest expenses

The Margin Interest Expense action records margin interest expense. To record it, click the Easy Actions button and then choose Advanced⇨Margin Interest Expense. When you do, Quicken displays the Margin Interest Expense dialog box, which you use to describe the cost of your financial adventure. Only the most sophisticated investors should be using margin anyway. If you're one of these financial cowboys or cowgirls, then I assume that you're smart enough to figure this stuff out on your own.

Paying miscellaneous expense

Sometimes you need to pay an expense. I've never seen one occur for a stock or bond — but my investing has been pretty conventional. Expenses sometimes do arise with brokerage accounts, real estate partnership interests (which can be treated like common stock shares), or precious metal investments (which can also be treated like common stock shares).

If you need to pay a fee for account handling or for storing your stash of South African Krugerrands, for example, you can record such an expense by clicking the Easy Actions button, choosing the Miscellaneous Expense action command, and then filling out the boxes on the Miscellaneous Expense dialog box that Quicken displays.

Recording a return of capital

The old *return of capital* trick. Sometimes, the money you receive because you own a security isn't really income. Rather, it's a refund of part of the purchase price.

Consider this example: You buy a mortgage-backed security — such as a Ginnie Mae bond — for which the *mortgagee* (the person who borrowed the mortgage money) pays not only periodic interest but also a portion of the mortgage principal.

Obviously, you shouldn't record the principal portion of the payment you receive as income. You must record this payment as a mortgage principal reduction or — in the parlance of investment record keeping — as a return of capital.

As another example, suppose that you invest in a limited partnership or real estate investment trust that begins liquidating. Some of the money that the investors receive in this case is really a return of their original investment, or a return of capital.

To record a return of capital action, click the Easy Actions button and choose the Return of Capital action. When Quicken displays the Return of Capital dialog box, describe the security that's returning capital.

More Quick Stuff about Brokerage Accounts

Let me tell you a couple other quick things. You'll almost certainly find these tidbits helpful.

Monitoring and updating securities' values

Regardless of whether you're working with a mutual fund account or with securities in a brokerage account, you can collect current market prices and store them with the Quicken account information.

To do so, display the investment account with the mutual fund shares or the securities you want to update by using the Portfolio View window.

To record the current market price for a security, use the up-arrow and down-arrow keys to select the security (or click the security with the mouse). Then move the cursor to the Mkt Price field and enter the current price.

Quicken includes a couple of features that you can use to download updated security prices quickly. Just choose Investing⇨Investing Activities⇨Set Up My Quotes and News Download and use the Customize Quicken 2000 Download dialog box that Quicken displays to specify the securities for which you want to obtain updated information. (If you're missing the symbol for one of your securities, select the security and then click the Edit Security button. Enter the symbol in the Symbol box, or click the Look Up button to get the information from the Internet. When you finish, click OK.) Click OK to return to the main Quicken window. Click the Update Prices button and choose the Get Online Quotes and News command from the menu Quicken displays to download prices directly into the Portfolio View window. If you have Quicken Deluxe, you can also choose this comment to download the latest information about your holdings. Although the Quicken online quote services provide a handy way of updating your stock prices, try not to get too carried away. Tracking the day-to-day, week-to-week, or even month-to-month price fluctuations of your investments just doesn't make sense. Only the long-term growth really matters. You really only need to update your security prices once or twice a year — either by using Quicken Online Quotes and News feature or by looking up the prices in the newspaper and entering them manually into Quicken.

Adjusting errors

You can adjust the cash balance in a brokerage account and the shares balance in brokerage accounts if for some reason the figures are incorrect.

Oops, my brokerage cash balance is wrong

To adjust the cash balance in a brokerage account, open the brokerage account's register and choose Investing⇨Investing Activities⇨Update My Cash Balance.

Quicken next displays an Update Cash Balance dialog box, which lets you specify the correct cash balance and the date as of which the figure you enter is correct. Fill in the text boxes and click OK. Quicken adjusts the cash balance.

Oops, my brokerage account shares balance is wrong

To adjust the shares balance for a security in a brokerage account, open the brokerage account's register and choose Features⇨Investing⇨Update Share Balance.

Quicken next displays the Update Share Balance dialog box, which lets you specify the security, the correct shares balance, and the date for which you're entering the balance. Fill in the text boxes and click OK. Quicken adjusts the shares balance for the security you specified.

A few more words on the Portfolio View

If you've read through this whole chapter, you know that I've mostly described how you get information into the Portfolio View window. But before I stop talking about the Portfolio View window, I want to give you a little more information on how you can use the Portfolio View window to monitor your investments.

Okay, the first thing to notice is that two drop-down list boxes reside near the top of the Portfolio View window — just beneath the labeled command buttons. You see a Group By drop-down list box (which you open by clicking the down arrow), and the Portfolio As Of text box (which you open by clicking the Calendar button, or enter a date manually in the MM/DD/YY format that you should be pretty comfy with in this day and age). The Group By drop-down list box provides options for changing the view of Portfolio View window. The Portfolio As Of drop-down list box lets you specify the date as of which you want Quicken to display your investment information. Neither of these drop-down list boxes are difficult to use. The tricky part is realizing that they're there. But now that you're aware of that fact, just experiment a bit. You'll see exactly how they work. And don't worry. You can't mess up any of your investment records by playing with these boxes.

Putting the register to rest

Let me say one final thing about this investment record keeping business. When you enter stuff into the Security Detail View window, Quicken takes your information and records transactions in the investment accounts register. You don't ever actually have to look at this investment account register. But I thought I'd at least alert you to its presence because you may stumble on it some day quite by accident. If that happens, don't muck about with it. Just close the window and pretend you didn't see anything.

Maybe I should tell you one other thing, too. You can use the investment register, if you really want to, by entering transactions directly into it. However, using the Security Detail View window is really much easier.

Online Investing with Quicken

Before you and I wrap up this chapter, let me mention one other quick thing. If you have Quicken and you have an online investment account with someone who supports Quicken's Online Investing feature — and this should include just about everybody — you can download your investment transactions from your online broker's web site right into the appropriate Quicken investment account.

If you want to do this — first check with the online broker to see if they support this feature — choose the Investing⇨Online Investing Setup command. Then follow the on-screen instructions. Once you do this, you can easily download investment transactions from your online investment broker. Online investing works the same way that online banking does. (You can refer to Chapter 6 if you have questions.)

Let me just make one, tiny, up front warning. You know how your monthly brokerage statement has all those crazy transactions on it for moving money around. I mean, you buy a stock and you'd think they just deduct the funds from your cash account. But they don't, do they? Nosirree. You buy the securities on, say, Monday, creating a debit balance in your account or perhaps even a margin transaction. Then, later in the week you settle — and that's when the money comes out of your cash account and the debit balance or margin balance goes away. This time-delayed, slow motion, anal-retentive settlement process produces an avalanche of transactions. Which is no big deal — you're used to it, I'm sure — except I want to tell you that all of these transactions will appear in the set you download from your broker.

Is this avalanche of transactions worth it? Totally. Investment record keeping, even as good as Quicken is, sorely tests the man (or woman) and tries the soul. That Quicken and your online broker are coordinating to save you time and trouble; well, that's just great. You just need to be ready for the transaction volume.

Chapter 15

Petty Cash and Mad Money

● ●

In This Chapter

▶ Setting up a cash account

▶ Entering cash transactions

▶ Handling checks you cash

▶ Updating your petty cash or mad money balance

● ●

*Y*ou can track petty cash in your business as well as the petty cash in your wallet by using a special Quicken cash account. To track the cash, you must set up a cash account and then enter the increases and decreases into the cash account's register. Sure, this stuff isn't exactly rocket science, but shoot, I thought I'd just quickly go over it to show you how easy it really is. Okay?

Adding a Cash Account

To set up a cash account, you follow roughly the same steps as you do for setting up a bank account. Because you've probably already set up a bank account, you can move quickly through the following steps to set up a cash account:

1. **Choose Finance⇨Account List or, if you see it, click the Accounts Feature tab if it appears with the QuickTabs.**

   Quicken displays the Account List window. You remember this puppy, the one you've probably seen a thousand times already.

2. **Click the New button on the Account List window to set up a new account.**

   Quicken, of course, is no fool, so it displays the Create New Account dialog box shown in Figure 15-1.

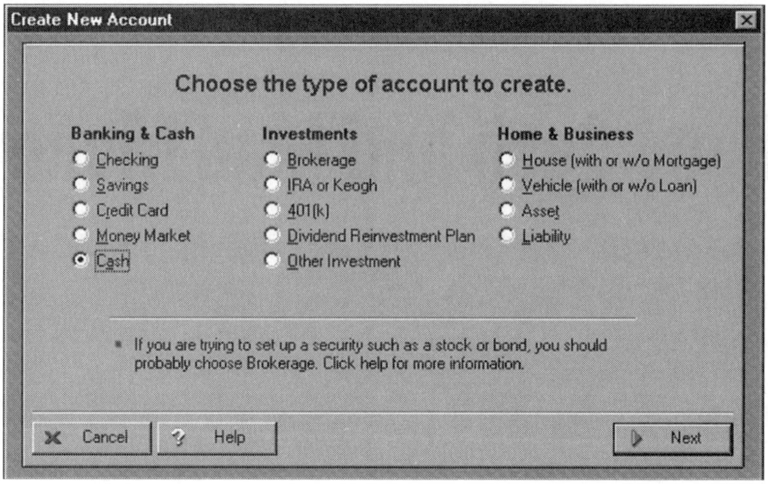

Figure 15-1:
The Create New Account dialog box.

3. **Select Cash.**

You know how to do this, don't you? You just click the Cash button and then click the Next button. Quicken, ever mindful of your purpose, displays the Cash Account Setup dialog box.

4. **Click the Summary tab.**

Quicken moves you to the Summary dialog box tab in which you'll describe the cash account as shown in Figure 15-2.

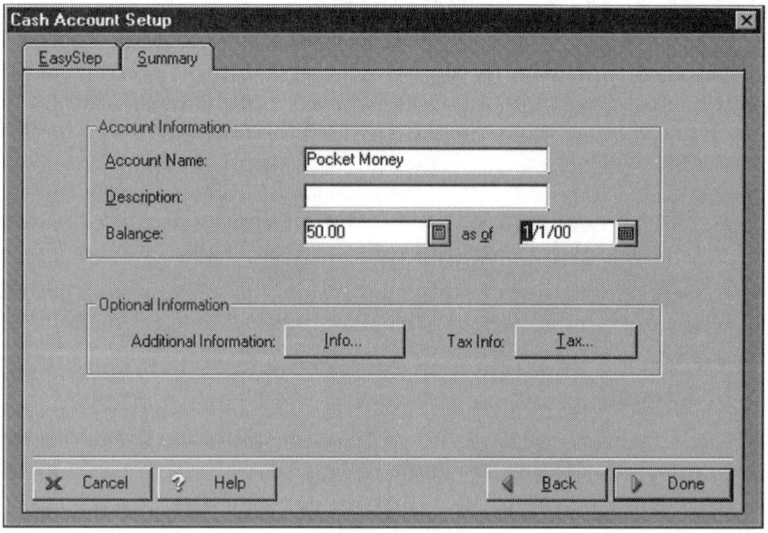

Figure 15-2:
The Summary tab of the Cash Account Setup dialog box.

5. **Name the account.**

   Move the cursor to the Account Name text box and type a name.

6. **Enter a description for the account by using the Description text box (optional).**

   You can type whatever you want as a description — petty cash, mad money, slush fund, and so on — to help you more easily identify this particular account when you have a bunch of different accounts set up.

7. **Enter the cash balance you're holding.**

   Move the cursor to the Balance text box and enter the balance value by using the number keys.

8. **Enter the account balance date.**

   Move the cursor to the As Of (or date) text box and enter the two-digit month number, the two-digit date number, and the two-digit year number (probably the current date). Or click on the calendar button next to the text box and select the date on the miniature calendar that pops up.

9. **Collect some additional information about the cash account (optional).**

   I don't know why you'd want to do this step, but you can. To collect this extra data, click the Info button. Then, when Quicken displays the Additional Account Information dialog box, enter some additional account information there.

10. **Ignore the Tax button (optional).**

    If you happen to have read much of this book, you are probably well aware of what the Tax button does. It displays a dialog box that lets you indicate whether the account you're setting up is tax-deferred. This same dialog box also lets you indicate that transfers into and out of this account impact your taxable income in some way. I cannot conceive, however, of a reason why you would want to use this button or its dialog box for a cash account. No way.

11. **Click Done.**

    Quicken redisplays the Account window. Well, golly, it shows the new cash account.

Tracking Cash Inflows and Outflows

After you set up a cash account, you can use it to track the cash you receive and spend in the same way that you track the deposits and checks for a bank account.

To record your cash inflows and outflows, use the register window. To display the register window for the cash account you just set up, for example, open the Account List window such as by choosing the Finance⇨Account List command, and then double-clicking the cash account in the list in the window. Figure 15-3 shows the cash account version of the register window. I entered a few transactions — just to give you an idea of the sorts of transactions you might record if you live the way that I do.

To record the amount of money you spend, fill in the Date, Payee, and Spend fields. To record the amount of money you receive, fill in the Date, Payee, and Receive fields. To track the reasons that you're receiving and spending the cash, use the Memo and Category fields.

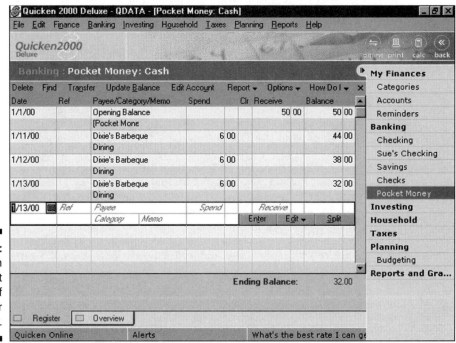

Figure 15-3:
The cash account version of the register window.

Recording Checks You Cash instead of Deposit

By the way, you don't necessarily need to set up a cash account if you like to spend cash (rather than, say, write checks or charge on a credit card). If you just cash a check and you do have a bank account set up, you can record the transaction in another way that may be simpler: Just use the Split Transaction Window to show both the income category (Salary, for example, individual) and how you're going to use the money.

For example, if you cash a $1,000 check and you plan to use the $1,000 for spending money, you may show a positive $1,000 in the Salary category and a minus $1,000 in the Entertainment spending category. Figure 15-4 shows this trick.

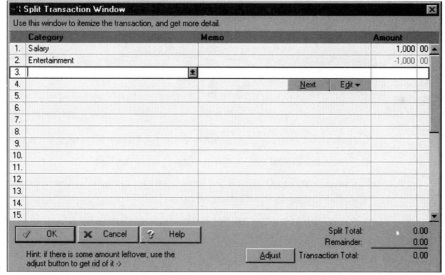

Figure 15-4:
A zero-amount transaction is one handy trick.

Note that the transaction shown in Figure 15-4 produces a transaction that equals zero. This is correct. Cashing a check that you never deposited doesn't affect your checking account balance. But by filling out the Split Transaction Window as shown in Figure 15-4, you do end up recording both the $1,000 of income and the $1,000 of expense.

Don't worry. I won't ask why you're carrying around $1,000 in cash.

Updating Cash Balances

You can update a register's cash balance to reflect what you actually have in petty cash, your wallet, under the mattress, in the cookie jar, or wherever else you keep your cash by taking the following steps:

1. **Display the cash account register.**

2. **Click the Update Balance button.**

   Quicken displays the Update Account Balance dialog box, as shown in Figure 15-5.

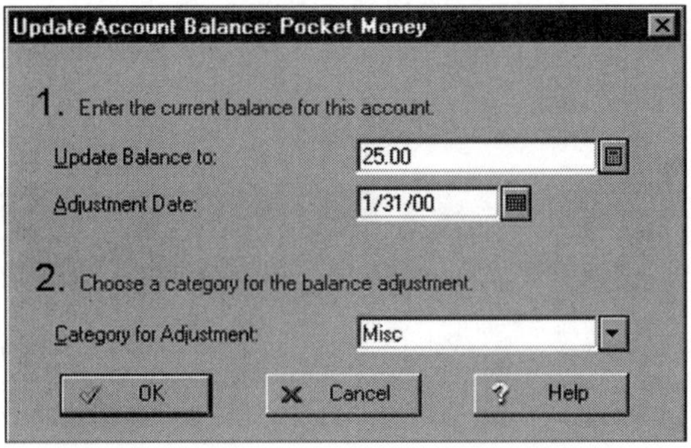

Figure 15-5:
The Update Account Balance dialog box.

> **Update Account Balance: Pocket Money** ☒
>
> **1.** Enter the current balance for this account.
>
> Update Balance to: `25.00`
>
> Adjustment Date: `1/31/00`
>
> **2.** Choose a category for the balance adjustment.
>
> Category for Adjustment: `Misc`
>
> ✓ OK   ✗ Cancel   ? Help

3. **Enter the actual cash balance in the Update Balance To text box.**

4. **Enter a date in the Adjustment Date text box.**

5. **Choose the category that you want to update in the Category for Adjustment drop-down list box.**

   After you click the arrow to the right of the drop-down list box, you get a list of all the categories that you have set up.

6. **After you finish, click OK.**

   Quicken updates the cash account's balance.

And that, my friend, is that.

Part IV
Serious Business

The 5th Wave   **By Rich Tennant**

Arthur inadvertently replaces his mouse pad with a Ouija board. For the rest of the day, he receives messages from the spectral world.

©RICHTENNANT

YOU WILL FORGET YOUR PASSWORD. YOUR HARD DISK WILL CRASH AAAHAHAHAHA

In this part . . .

*1*f you use Quicken in a business, you'll need some information about how to use the program for payroll,
customer receivables, and vendor payables. Sure, you can
learn these things by sitting down with your certified
public accountant, having a cup of coffee, and paying
about $150 an hour.

Or you can read on, pretend that we're chitchatting over
coffee, and save the $150.

Chapter 16

Payroll

● ●

In This Chapter

▶ Creating categories and accounts necessary to prepare payroll

▶ Getting an employer ID number

▶ Getting Social Security, Medicare, and federal income tax withholding information

▶ Calculating an employee's gross wages, payroll deductions, and net wages

▶ Recording a payroll check in Quicken

▶ Making federal tax deposits

▶ Filing quarterly and annual payroll tax returns

▶ Producing annual wage statements such as W-2s

▶ Handling state payroll taxes

● ●

*M*any people use Quicken in their business. Many businesses have employees. Many employees want to be paid on a regular basis. Methinks, therefore, that many readers will find information on preparing the payroll helpful. I should warn you, however, what I am about to discuss gets a bit ugly. Payroll with Quicken is, well, terrible. If you're planning to use it for doing payroll, do yourself a favor and buy QuickBooks Pro (another Intuit product). However, if you're determined to use Quicken 2000 for payroll, this chapter explains how you do so.

Let me mention one other thing here, and I'm embarrassed to say that I almost forgot. While this book assumes you have Quicken Deluxe (and works equally well, by the way, for Quicken Basic), there's another version of Quicken called Quicken Home and Business. Quicken Home and Business, it's relevant to note, includes QuickPayroll. QuickPayroll lets you calculate with-holding amounts and prepare paychecks. If the approach described in this chapter doesn't work well for you, you might want to consider stepping up to Quicken Home and Business.

Getting Ready for Payroll

To prepare payroll checks and summarize the payroll information that you need to prepare quarterly and annual returns, you need to set up some special accounts and categories. You also need to do some paperwork stuff. I describe how to do both things in this section.

Getting Quicken ready

To do payroll in Quicken, you need to set up several liability accounts, a payroll expense category, and several payroll expense subcategories. Fortunately, doing so is not particularly difficult.

I'm going to describe how you do this task for purposes of United States federal income and payroll taxes. If you employ people in one of the states that has a state income tax — California, say — you may also have to deal with state payroll taxes. But you can track and process these the same way you process the federal taxes.

I should say that you may also have other taxes to pay if you employ people outside the United States. But, hey, with a couple hundred countries in the world, your best bet is to get specific advice from someone of authority or expertise in the country of employment.

Setting up liability accounts

You need to set up three liability accounts to deal with federal payroll and income taxes: one named *Payroll-SS* to track Social Security, one named *Payroll-MCARE* to track Medicare, and one named *Payroll-FWH* (for *Federal Withholding*) to track federal income taxes owed. (I should confess that these aren't my names. They're the names that Quicken expects you to use.)

To set up a liability account for any of these payroll tax liabilities, follow these steps:

1. **Choose Finance⇨Account List or click the Accounts Feature Tab.**

   Quicken displays the Account window. You've probably seen this window about a hundred times before. If you want to see the window right now, though, choose the command and look at your screen.

2. **Click the New button in the Account List window.**

   Quicken displays the Create New Account dialog box. If you've been reading this book cover-to-cover, you've seen this baby a bunch of times before. If you want or need to see it now, though, you can just follow along on-screen.

3. **Click the Liability button and then click the Next button.**

   Doing so tells Quicken that you're going to set up a Liability account. Quicken displays the Liability Account Setup dialog box.

4. **Click the Summary tab.**

   Quicken displays the Summary tab of the Liability Account Setup dialog box, as shown in Figure 16-1.

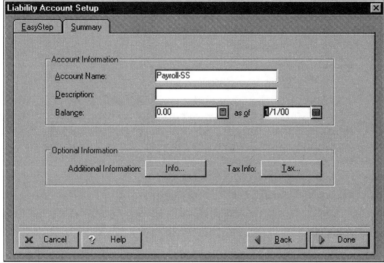

Figure 16-1: The Summary tab of the Liability Account Setup dialog box.

5. **Enter the appropriate account name: Payroll-SS, Payroll-MCARE, or Payroll-FWH.**

   Move the cursor to the Account Name text box and type in the right name.

6. **Enter a description, if you want, in the Description text box (optional).**

   I think the standard payroll tax liability names are pretty obvious, so I just go with them alone.

7. **Enter the current amount you owe for the payroll tax liability.**

   Move the cursor to the Balance text box and enter whatever you already owe. Or, if you're just starting and you owe nothing, type **0**. (If you do owe something but you don't have a clue in the world as to how much, you should figure out what you owe now, before going any further. Sorry.)

8. **Enter the As Of date.**

   Move the cursor to the As Of (or date) text box. Type the date — probably the current date — on which you owe the balance you entered in the Balance text box.

9. **Click Done.**

   Quicken displays a message box that asks whether you want to set up an amortized loan for this liability.

10. **Click No.**

    This choice tells Quicken that you don't want to set up an amortized loan for the liability account. Quicken, only slightly bent out of shape, redisplays the Account List window with your new account now visible.

11. **Repeat Steps 2 through 10 for each of the other payroll tax liability accounts you want to add.**

    Remember that you need at least three payroll tax liability accounts — Payroll-SS, Payroll-MCARE, and Payroll-FWH — for the people you employ in the United States. And if you live in a state with income taxes, you either need to move or set up a fourth account: Payroll-SWH.

The only trick to naming other payroll tax liability accounts is that you need to start each liability account name with the word *Payroll*. No, I didn't just make up this rule arbitrarily. Quicken really has a reason for this policy. The Quicken Payroll report prints information on all the accounts and categories that start with the word *Payroll*.

Setting up a payroll expense category

You also need to set up a payroll expense category, which isn't tough. Here's all you have to do:

1. **Choose Finance⇨Category&Transfer List.**

   Quicken, with no hesitation, displays the Category & Transfer List window. Figure 16-2 shows this puppy.

2. **Click New.**

   Quicken displays the Set Up Category dialog box (see Figure 16-3).

3. **Enter Payroll as the category name.**

   Move the cursor to the Name text box and type **Payroll**, as shown in Figure 16-3.

4. **Enter a description of the category (optional).**

   If you want, you can type a description in the Description text box. Figure 16-3 doesn't show any description; I figured that with a name like "Payroll," I wouldn't get too confused.

5. **In the Type section, select the Expense option button.**

   This choice tells Quicken that you're setting up an expense category. But you probably know this, right?

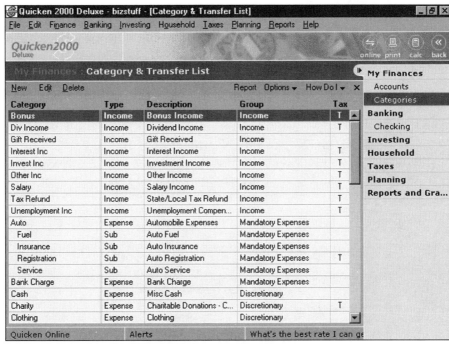

Figure 16-2:
The
Category &
Transfer List
window.

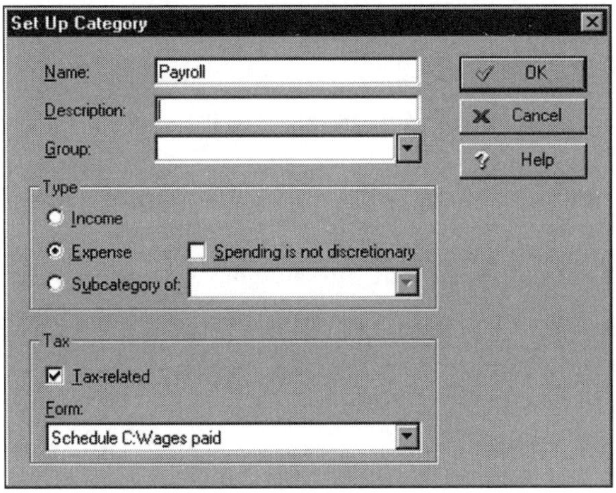

Figure 16-3:
The Set Up
Category
dialog box.

6. Indicate whether the payroll tax is a tax-deductible expense for you.

If you're preparing payroll for a business, select the Tax-related check box
and select the tax form from the Form drop-down list box. If you're preparing payroll for a household employee — like a nanny, say — don't select

the Tax-related check box. This little check box merely tells Quicken to include this category on the Tax Summary report. Household employee payroll expenses aren't tax-deductible — as you probably know.

7. Click OK.

Quicken adds the category to the category list and redisplays the Category & Transfer List window. This part of the mission is almost complete, Commander Bond.

Setting up the payroll subcategories

You need to do one more thing to get Quicken ready for payroll. You need to set up subcategory expenses for employee gross wages, the company's share of the Social Security taxes, and the company's share of the Medicare taxes. Quicken expects you to use *Gross, Comp SS,* and *Comp MCARE* as subcategory names. So that's what I'll use in the following steps.

1. Display the Category & Transfer window if it isn't showing already.

Choose Finance⇨Category&Transfer List. If you can't remember what this window looks like, refer to Figure 16-2.

2. Click New.

Quicken displays the Set Up Category dialog box (refer to Figure 16-3).

3. Enter the appropriate payroll expense subcategory name: Gross, Comp SS, or Comp MCARE.

For example, move the cursor to the Name field and type **Gross** or **Comp SS** or **Comp MCARE**.

4. Enter a description of the subcategory in the Description text box.

Because the subcategory names are a little more cryptic, you may want to use the Description text box to document things such as what Comp SS means. (I recommend Social Security-Employer.)

5. In the Type section, select the Subcategory Of option button.

This option tells Quicken that you're setting up a subcategory.

6. Indicate that the subcategory falls into the Payroll expense category by moving the cursor to the Subcategory Of text box and typing P for Payroll.

Or, because this is a drop-down list box, you can open the list box and select the payroll expense category from it.

7. Click OK.

Quicken adds the subcategory to the category list and redisplays the Category & Transfer List window. It also automatically adds the tax information you specified for the Payroll category.

8. Repeat Steps 2 through 7 for each of the remaining payroll expense subcategories you need.

For employees working in the United States, you need at least three subcategories: Gross (for tracking gross wages), Comp SS (for tracking company Social Security taxes), and Comp MCARE (for tracking employer Medicare taxes).

Congratulations, Mr. Bond. You saved the world again. You created the liability accounts and categories that you need to track the amounts you pay employees and the payroll taxes you withhold and owe.

Getting the taxes stuff right

You also need to do a couple other things if you want to do payroll the right way.

Requesting (or demanding) an employer ID number

First, you need to file the SS-4, or Request for Employer Identification Number form, with the Internal Revenue Service (IRS) so you can get an employer identification number. You can get this form by calling the IRS and asking for one. Or, if you have an accountant friend, he or she may have one of these forms. (See, you do have a reason to invite people like me to your dinner parties.)

In one of its cooler moves, the IRS changed its ways and now lets you apply for and receive an employer identification number over the telephone. You still need to fill out the SS-4 form, however, so that you can answer questions the IRS asks during the short, telephone-application process. (You also need to mail or fax the form to the Service after you have your little telephone conversation.)

If you have an Internet connection, you can actually download a copy of the SS-4 form that I discuss in the previous paragraph as well as the W-4 form and the *Circular E* publication that I discuss in the next paragraph from the Internal Revenue Service's web site at www.irs.ustreas.gov/prod/forms_pubs/.

So what about Social Security, Medicare, and withholding taxes?

You need to do two things before you can figure out how to handle all those taxes. First, you need your employees to fill out a W-4 form to let you know what filing status they will use and how many personal exemptions they will claim. Guess where you get blank W-4 forms? That's right . . . from your friendly IRS agent.

You also need to get a *Circular E Employer's Tax Guide* publication. The *Circular E* publication is the pamphlet that tells you how much you should withhold in federal income taxes, Social Security, and Medicare from a person's salary. You can get this form, as well as the additional federal forms that you must fill out to satisfy the government requirements for hiring employees, by calling those friendly people at the Internal Revenue Service. To get state tax forms, you need to contact the equivalent tax agency in your state.

Paying someone for a job well done

After you tell Quicken to get ready to do payroll and you collect the necessary tax information, you're ready to pay someone.

Figuring out the gross wages figure

Determining how much to pay your employees should be pretty easy. Does Raoul make $15 an hour? Did he work 40 hours? Then you owe him $600 because $15 times 40 equals $600. Is Betty's salary $400 a week? Then you owe her $400 for the week.

Calculating that deductions stuff

Your next step — after you know how much you're supposed to pay Raoul or Betty — is to figure out what Uncle Sam says you must withhold.

To determine this amount, you need both Raoul's and Betty's W-4s to find out their filing statuses and personal exemptions. Then just flip to the page in the *Circular E* that describes withholding for persons claiming those filing statuses and weekly pay.

If Raoul is single and claims just one personal exemption, for example, you need to flip to the page like the one shown in Figure 16-4. Remember that Raoul is paid weekly. I circled the number in the table in Figure 16-4 that shows what Raoul is supposed to pay in federal income taxes.

And Betty? Remember that Betty's pay is $400 a week. If Betty's filing status is married filing jointly and she has three personal exemptions, you need to flip to the page that resembles Figure 16-5. Again, I circled the number in the table in Figure 16-5 that shows what Betty is supposed to pay.

Always use up-to-date information. The numbers you use for federal income tax withholding change annually. Therefore, *don't* use the tables shown in Figures 16-4 and 16-5. They will be long out-of-date by the time you read this.

You determine Social Security and Medicare amounts by multiplying the gross wage figure by a set percentage. Social Security is 6.2 percent of the gross wages up to a specified limit — roughly $70,000 in 1999. The Medicare tax is 1.45 percent of the gross wages. Be sure to check your faithful *Circular E* if you think limits come into play for a particular employee. Note, too, that as I'm writing this, Congress is fiddle-faddling with the tax laws again. But, of course, Congress is always fiddle-faddling with the tax laws.

SINGLE Persons—WEEKLY Payroll Period
(For Wages Paid in 1999)

If the wages are –		And the number of withholding allowances claimed is —										
At least	But less than	0	1	2	3	4	5	6	7	8	9	10
		The amount of income tax to be withheld is—										
$600	$610	94	79	67	59	51	43	36	28	20	12	4
610	620	96	94	69	61	53	45	37	29	21	13	5
620	630	99	84	70	62	54	46	39	31	23	15	7
630	640	102	87	72	64	56	48	40	32	24	16	8
640	650	105	90	75	65	57	49	42	34	26	18	10
650	660	108	93	78	67	59	51	43	35	27	19	11
660	670	110	95	81	68	60	52	45	37	29	21	13
670	680	113	98	83	70	62	54	46	38	30	22	14
680	690	116	101	86	71	63	55	48	40	32	24	16
690	700	119	104	89	74	65	57	49	41	33	25	17
700	710	122	107	92	77	66	58	51	43	35	27	19
710	720	124	109	95	80	68	60	52	44	36	28	20
720	730	127	112	97	83	69	61	54	46	38	30	22
730	740	130	115	100	85	71	63	55	47	39	31	23
740	750	133	118	103	88	73	64	57	49	41	33	25
750	760	136	121	106	91	76	66	58	50	42	34	26
760	770	138	123	109	94	79	67	60	52	44	36	28
770	780	141	126	111	97	82	69	61	53	45	37	29
780	790	144	129	114	99	85	70	63	55	47	39	31
790	800	147	132	117	102	87	73	64	56	48	40	32
800	810	150	135	120	105	90	75	66	58	50	42	34
810	820	152	137	123	108	93	78	67	59	51	43	35
820	830	155	140	125	111	96	81	69	61	53	45	37
830	840	158	143	128	113	99	84	70	62	54	46	38
840	850	161	146	131	116	101	87	72	64	56	48	40
850	860	164	149	134	119	104	89	75	65	57	49	41
860	870	166	151	137	122	107	92	77	67	59	51	43
870	880	169	154	139	125	110	95	80	68	60	52	44
880	890	172	157	142	127	113	98	83	70	62	54	46
890	900	175	160	145	130	115	101	86	71	63	55	47
900	910	178	163	148	133	118	103	89	74	65	57	49
910	920	180	165	151	136	121	106	91	77	66	58	50
920	930	183	168	153	139	124	109	94	79	68	60	52
930	940	186	171	156	141	127	112	97	82	69	61	53
940	950	189	174	159	144	129	115	100	85	71	63	55
950	960	192	177	162	147	132	117	103	88	73	64	56
960	970	194	179	165	150	135	120	105	91	76	66	58
970	980	197	182	167	153	138	123	108	93	79	67	59
980	990	200	185	170	155	141	126	111	96	81	69	61
990	1,000	203	188	173	158	143	129	114	99	84	70	62
1,000	1,010	206	191	176	161	146	131	117	102	87	72	64
1,010	1,020	208	193	179	164	149	134	119	105	90	75	65
1,020	1,030	211	196	181	167	152	137	122	107	93	78	67
1,030	1,040	214	199	184	169	155	140	125	110	95	81	68
1,040	1,050	217	202	187	172	157	143	128	113	98	83	70
1,050	1,060	220	205	190	175	160	145	131	116	101	86	71
1,060	1,070	222	207	193	178	163	148	133	119	104	89	74
1,070	1,080	225	210	195	181	166	151	136	121	107	92	77
1,080	1,090	228	213	198	183	169	154	139	124	109	95	80
1,090	1,100	231	216	201	186	171	157	142	127	112	97	83
1,100	1,110	234	219	204	189	174	159	145	130	115	100	85
1,110	1,120	236	221	207	192	177	162	147	133	118	103	88
1,120	1,130	239	224	209	195	180	165	150	135	121	106	91
1,130	1,140	242	227	212	197	183	168	153	138	123	109	94
1,140	1,150	245	230	215	200	185	171	156	141	126	111	97
1,150	1,160	248	233	218	203	188	173	159	144	129	114	99
1,160	1,170	252	235	221	206	191	176	161	147	132	117	102
1,170	1,180	255	238	223	209	194	179	164	149	135	120	105
1,180	1,190	258	241	226	211	197	182	167	152	137	123	108
1,190	1,200	261	244	229	214	199	185	170	155	140	125	111
1,200	1,210	264	248	232	217	202	187	173	158	143	128	113
1,210	1,220	267	251	235	220	205	190	175	161	146	131	116
1,220	1,230	270	254	237	223	208	193	178	163	149	134	119
1,230	1,240	273	257	240	225	211	196	181	166	151	137	122
1,240	1,250	276	260	244	228	213	199	184	169	154	139	125

$1,250 and over   Use Table 1(a) for a **SINGLE** person on page 34. Also see the instructions on page 32.

Figure 16-4: Raoul's tax deduction stuff.

MARRIED Persons—WEEKLY Payroll Period

(For Wages Paid in 1999)

If the wages are—		And the number of withholding allowances claimed is —										
At least	But less than	0	1	2	3	4	5	6	7	8	9	10
		The amount of income tax to be withheld is—										
$0	$125	0	0	0	0	0	0	0	0	0	0	0
125	130	1	0	0	0	0	0	0	0	0	0	0
130	135	1	0	0	0	0	0	0	0	0	0	0
135	140	2	0	0	0	0	0	0	0	0	0	0
140	145	3	0	0	0	0	0	0	0	0	0	0
145	150	4	0	0	0	0	0	0	0	0	0	0
150	155	4	0	0	0	0	0	0	0	0	0	0
155	160	5	0	0	0	0	0	0	0	0	0	0
160	165	6	0	0	0	0	0	0	0	0	0	0
165	170	7	0	0	0	0	0	0	0	0	0	0
170	175	7	0	0	0	0	0	0	0	0	0	0
175	180	8	0	0	0	0	0	0	0	0	0	0
180	185	9	1	0	0	0	0	0	0	0	0	0
185	190	10	2	0	0	0	0	0	0	0	0	0
190	195	10	2	0	0	0	0	0	0	0	0	0
195	200	11	3	0	0	0	0	0	0	0	0	0
200	210	12	4	0	0	0	0	0	0	0	0	0
210	220	14	6	0	0	0	0	0	0	0	0	0
220	230	15	7	0	0	0	0	0	0	0	0	0
230	240	17	9	1	0	0	0	0	0	0	0	0
240	250	18	10	2	0	0	0	0	0	0	0	0
250	260	20	12	4	0	0	0	0	0	0	0	0
260	270	21	13	5	0	0	0	0	0	0	0	0
270	280	23	15	7	0	0	0	0	0	0	0	0
280	290	24	16	8	0	0	0	0	0	0	0	0
290	300	26	18	10	2	0	0	0	0	0	0	0
300	310	27	19	11	3	0	0	0	0	0	0	0
310	320	29	21	13	5	0	0	0	0	0	0	0
320	330	30	22	14	6	0	0	0	0	0	0	0
330	340	32	24	16	8	0	0	0	0	0	0	0
340	350	33	25	17	9	1	0	0	0	0	0	0
350	360	35	27	19	11	3	0	0	0	0	0	0
360	370	36	28	20	12	4	0	0	0	0	0	0
370	380	38	30	22	14	6	0	0	0	0	0	0
380	390	39	31	23	15	7	0	0	0	0	0	0
390	400	41	33	25	17	9	1	0	0	0	0	0
400	410	42	34	26	(18)	10	2	0	0	0	0	0
410	420	44	36	28	20	12	4	0	0	0	0	0
420	430	45	37	29	21	13	5	0	0	0	0	0
430	440	47	39	31	23	15	7	0	0	0	0	0
440	450	48	40	32	24	16	8	1	0	0	0	0
450	460	50	42	34	26	18	10	2	0	0	0	0
460	470	51	43	35	27	19	11	4	0	0	0	0
470	480	53	45	37	29	21	13	5	0	0	0	0
480	490	54	46	38	30	22	14	7	0	0	0	0
490	500	56	48	40	32	24	16	8	0	0	0	0
500	510	57	49	41	33	25	17	10	2	0	0	0
510	520	59	51	43	35	27	19	11	3	0	0	0
520	530	60	52	44	36	28	20	13	5	0	0	0
530	540	62	54	46	38	30	22	14	6	0	0	0
540	550	63	55	47	39	31	23	16	8	0	0	0
550	560	65	57	49	41	33	25	17	9	1	0	0
560	570	66	58	50	42	34	26	19	11	3	0	0
570	580	68	60	52	44	36	28	20	12	4	0	0
580	590	69	61	53	45	37	29	22	14	6	0	0
590	600	71	63	55	47	39	31	23	15	7	0	0
600	610	72	64	56	48	40	32	25	17	9	1	0
610	620	74	66	58	50	42	34	26	18	10	2	0
620	630	75	67	59	51	43	35	28	20	12	4	0
630	640	77	69	61	53	45	37	29	21	13	5	0
640	650	78	70	62	54	46	38	31	23	15	7	0
650	660	80	72	64	56	48	40	32	24	16	8	0
660	670	81	73	65	57	49	41	34	26	18	10	2
670	680	83	75	67	59	51	43	35	27	19	11	3
680	690	84	76	68	60	52	44	37	29	21	13	5
690	700	86	78	70	62	54	46	38	30	22	14	6
700	710	87	79	71	63	55	47	40	32	24	16	8
710	720	89	81	73	65	57	49	41	33	25	17	9
720	730	90	82	74	66	58	50	43	35	27	19	11
730	740	92	84	76	68	60	52	44	36	28	20	12

Figure 16-5: Betty's tax deduction stuff.

Figuring out someone's net wages

Table 16-1 summarizes the payroll calculations shown in Figures 16-4 and 16-5.

Table 16-1	Payroll for Raoul and Betty		
Item	*Raoul*	*Betty*	*Explanation*
Gross wages	$600.00	$400.00	Their pay
Withholding	$79.00	$18.00	From *Circular E*
Social Security	$37.20	$24.80	6.2 percent of gross wages
Medicare	$8.70	$5.80	1.45 percent of gross wages
Net Wages	$475.10	$351.40	What's left over

Does Table 16-1 make sense? If it doesn't, take another look at the marked information in Figures 16-4 and 16-5 and read my earlier discussion of how to figure out deductions stuff. All I've really done in the table is reorganize some information, calculate the Social Security and Medicare taxes, and show how Raoul's and Betty's gross pay gets nickeled and dimed by the various taxes they owe.

Working with other taxes and deductions

If you have other taxes and deductions to make and you understand how the federal income taxes, Social Security taxes, and Medicare taxes work, you won't have any problem working with the other taxes — no matter what they are.

State income tax withholding, for example, works like the federal income tax withholding. (Of course, you need to get the state's equivalent to the *Circular E* guide.)

In general, you treat other taxes and the amounts the employee pays similarly.

In fact, the only thing that you need to be careful about is what affects your employees' gross pay for income taxes but not their Social Security taxes — things such as 401(k) deductions and certain fringe benefits. If you have these kinds of things to deal with and you need help, just ask your accountant. (Providing general answers that will work for everyone who reads this paragraph is just too difficult — and actually kind of dangerous, too. Sorry.)

Recording a payroll check

After you make the tax deduction and net wages calculation, you're ready to record the check. Doing so is a little bit tricky, but stick with me; I'll get you through it in no time.

If Betty is milling around your computer, whining and saying things like, "Gee, Boss, how much longer? I want to get to the bank before it closes," tell her to cool her heels for about three minutes.

Suppose that you're going to record the check by using the register window for your checking account. (As you know, recording the check into the Write Checks window works the same basic way. The difference is that by using the Write Checks window, you can print the payroll check.)

After you display the checking account register window and highlight the first empty row of the register, follow these steps:

1. **Enter the date of the payroll check in the Date field.**

2. **Enter the payroll check number in the Num field.**

3. **Enter the employee name in the Payee field.**

4. **Enter the net wages amount in the Payment field.**

5. **Open the Split Transaction Window (see Figure 16-6).**

   You can do so by clicking the Split button.

6. **In the first row of the Split Transaction Window, enter the category and gross wages amount in the correct fields.**

   Enter the category **Payroll:Gross**. The amount, of course, should be the gross wages figure (**400.00** in the example).

7. **Enter the employee's Federal withholding tax and account in the second row of the Split Transaction Window.**

   Instead of a category in the Category field, enter liability account **[Payroll-FWH]**, or select it from the drop-down list box (in this case, it would be Transfer to/from [Payroll-FSH]). This tax withheld amount comes from the *Circular E* form (**18.00** in this example).

8. **Enter the employee's Social Security tax withheld and account in the third row of the Split Transaction Window.**

   In the Category field, enter the liability account **[Payroll-SS]**, or select Transfer to/from [Payroll-SS] from the drop-down list box. The amount of the Social Security tax withheld should be 6.2 percent of the employee's gross wages (**24.80** in this example). Type this number in the Amount field.

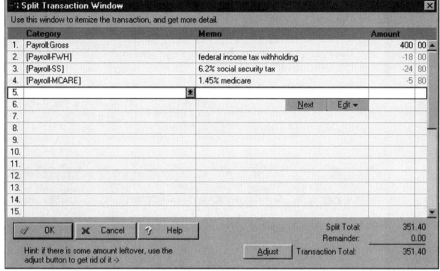

Figure 16-6:
The Split
Transaction
Window
recording
Betty's $400
wages and
her $351.40
paycheck.

9. Enter the employee's Medicare tax withheld and account in the fourth row of the Split Transaction Window.

In the Category field, enter the liability account **[Payroll-MCARE]**, or select the account from the drop-down list box. The amount of the Medicare tax withheld should be 1.45 percent of the employee's gross wages (**5.80** in this example).

Figure 16-6 shows the Quicken register window and Splits dialog box filled out to record Betty's $400 of wages, the taxes poor Betty has to pay on these earnings, and the net wages figure of $350.40. If you have questions about any of these figures, take a peek again at Table 16-1.

10. If you have other employee-paid payroll taxes, record them in the next empty rows, following the same set of procedures.

11. If you plan to print this paycheck on a payroll check that has a remittance advice or payroll stub, move down to line 17, otherwise just move to the next empty line.

(An *advice* is accounting jargon for the little slip of paper that's attached to the actual check form.)

Only the first 16 lines of the Split Transaction Window information print on a payroll stub. So by using lines 17 and higher for the employer portions of the payroll tax, you won't confuse the employee about employee versus employer payroll taxes. If you aren't printing payroll stubs, you can just move to the next empty row.

12. On the next two empty lines of the Split Transaction Window, enter your (the employer's) matching share of the Social Security tax.

If the employee pays $24.80 of Social Security tax, for example, type **Payroll:Comp SS** in the Category field and **24.80** in the Amount field in the first empty line.

Then type **[Payroll-SS]** in the Category field and **–24.80** in the Amount field in the next line to record the Social Security tax liability.

Figure 16-7 shows the Social Security and Medicare payroll tax information.

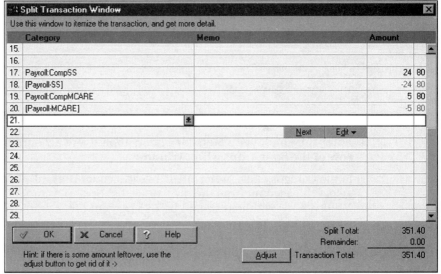

Figure 16-7:
The employer's matching share of Social Security and Medicare taxes.

13. On the next two empty lines of the Split Transaction Window, enter your (the employer's) matching share of the Medicare tax.

If the employer pays $5.80 of Medicare, for example, use the first empty line to type **Payroll: Comp MCARE** in the Category field, or choose the account from the drop-down list box, and then type **5.80** in the Amount field.

Then type **[Payroll-MCARE]** in the Category section, or choose the account from the drop-down list box, then enter **–5.80** in the Amount section in the next line to record the Medicare tax liability.

The accounts you use to show the payroll taxes withheld and owed are liability accounts. By looking at the account balances of these accounts, you can easily see how much you owe the government.

14. **If you have other employer-paid payroll taxes, record these following the employer's matching share of the Social Security and Medicare taxes.**

    You can use this same basic approach to record federal and state unemployment taxes.

15. **After you finish entering the employer-paid payroll taxes, click OK to close the Split Transaction Window.**

16. **To record the payroll check and related employer-paid payroll tax information in the register, click Record Check.**

You did it! You recorded a payroll check and the related payroll taxes. Maybe it wasn't all that much fun, but at least it wasn't very difficult.

Depositing Taxes

Make no mistake. Uncle Sam wants the money you withhold from an employee's payroll check for federal income taxes, Social Security, and Medicare. Uncle Sam also wants the payroll taxes you owe — the matching Social Security and Medicare taxes, federal unemployment taxes, and so on.

Every so often, then, you need to pay Uncle Sam the amounts you owe.

Making this payment is actually simple. Just write a check payable for the account balances shown in the payroll tax liability accounts. If you have written only the one check to Betty (as shown in Figures 16-6 and 16-7), for example, your payroll liability accounts would show balances as follows:

Liability Account	Amount
Payroll-SS	$49.60
Payroll-MCARE	$11.60
Payroll-FWH	$18.00
Total	$79.20

Notice that the Payroll-SS account balance and the Payroll-MCARE account balance include both the employee's and the employer's Social Security and Medicare taxes.

Then you write a check for the $79.20 you owe (see Figure 16-8). The only tricky thing about this transaction is that you transfer the check amount to the payroll liability accounts rather than assign the check amount to a payroll tax category. In effect, you transfer money from your checking account to the government to pay off the payroll taxes you owe.

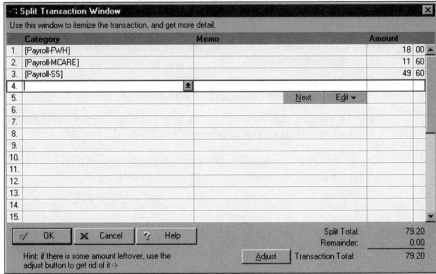

The first time you see this sort of transfer, it can be a little confusing. So take a minute to think about it. If you write the check to the government, your checking account doesn't have the money in it anymore, and you don't owe the government the money anymore. Therefore, you need to decrease both the checking account balance and the liability account balance. In Quicken, you do so with an account transfer (if you're a little shaky on doing the account transfer thing, you may want to take a quick peek at Chapter 4).

When do you make payroll tax deposits? Good question. Fortunately, it's not one you have to answer. The Internal Revenue Service tells you when you're supposed to deposit your money. In my business, for example, I have to deposit payroll taxes within a couple of days of doing payroll. Some businesses have to deposit more frequently or quickly. And some businesses get to deposit less quickly or less frequently.

While I am on the subject of federal payroll tax deposits, I should talk about another general rule related to when you need to make the deposit: If your accumulated payroll taxes are less than $500, you can just pay the taxes the next time you're supposed to remit payroll taxes: the next payroll date, the next month, or whatever. (This is called the *De Minimis* rule — named after the Congresswoman Dee Minimis, I think.) Don't rely on this *rule,* however, without first checking with either the Internal Revenue Service or your tax advisor.

To make a payroll tax deposit, just run your check with a federal tax deposit coupon to a financial institution qualified as a depository for federal taxes (probably your local bank) or to the Federal Reserve bank serving your geographical area. The IRS should have already sent you a book of coupons as a result of your requesting an employer ID number. And one other thing: Make your check payable to the depository or to the Federal Reserve.

Some businesses are either now, or will shortly be, required to electronically remit payroll tax deposits directly to the U.S. Treasury. The IRS should tell you when that's the case. Talk to your bank if you need to do this.

Filing Quarterly Payroll Tax Returns

At the end of every quarter, you need to file a quarterly payroll tax return. (By *quarters* here, I'm referring to calendar quarters. You don't do this four times on a Sunday afternoon as you or your couch-potato spouse watch football.)

If you're a business, for example, you must file a Form 941 — which is just a form you fill out to say how much you paid in gross wages, how much you withheld in federal taxes, and how much you owe for employer payroll taxes.

If you're not a business but you have household employees — such as a nanny — you must file a Form 942. Again, you just fill out this form to say how much you paid in gross wages, withheld in federal taxes, and owe in payroll taxes.

To get the gross wages totals and the balances in each of the payroll tax liability accounts, print the Business Payroll report by choosing Reports⇨ Business⇨Payroll. Quicken will display the Payroll Report, but the dates will probably be wrong so click the Customize button. Quicken displays the Customize Payroll Report dialog box, as shown in Figure 16-9.

Specify the range of dates as the start and end of the quarter for which you're preparing a quarterly report. Then click Create. Quicken produces a payroll report, which you can easily use to fill out the quarterly payroll tax return. Figure 16-10 shows the on-screen version of the Payroll Report. If you want to print a version of this report, click the Print button. As I mention earlier, this report summarizes all the transactions categorized as falling into the Payroll expense category or transferred to an account named Payroll (something).

The Gross amount in the Payroll Expenses section — $400 in the example — is the gross wages upon which employer payroll taxes are calculated.

The company's Social Security contributions and Medicare contributions are the amounts you recorded to date for the employer Social Security and Medicare taxes — so you need to double these figures to determine the actual Social Security and Medicare taxes you owe.

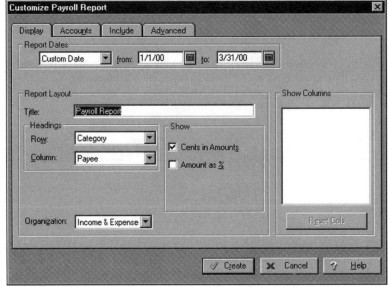

Figure 16-9:
The
Customize
Payroll
Report
dialog box.

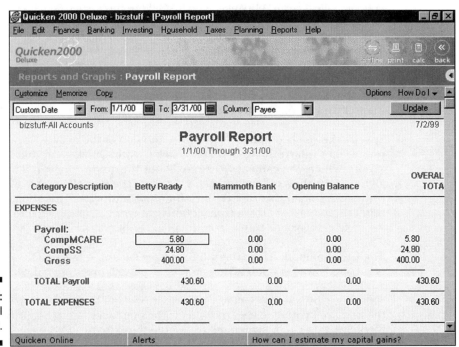

Figure 16-10:
The Payroll
Report.

The Total Transfers line in the Payroll Report represents the federal tax deposits you paid. If you're working off the on-screen report, you need to scroll down to see all the transfer information.

Note: By the way, if your accountant fills out the 941 or 942 for you, you don't even need to read this stuff. Your accountant won't have any problem completing the quarterly payroll tax return by using the Quicken Payroll Report and, in fact — I kid you not — will probably even enjoy it.

Computing Annual Returns and Wage Statements

At the end of the year, you'll need to file some annual returns — like the 940 federal unemployment tax return — and the W-2 and W-3 wages statements.

As a practical matter, the only thing that's different about filling out these reports is that you need to use a payroll report that covers the entire year — not just a single quarter. So you need to enter the range of dates in the Payroll Report dialog box as January 1 and December 31.

The 940 annual return is darn easy if you've been wrestling with the 941 or 942 quarterly returns. The 940 annual return works the same basic way as those more difficult quarterly tax returns. You print the old payroll report, enter a few numbers, and then write a check for the amount you owe.

Note that you need to prepare any state unemployment annual summaries before preparing the 940, because the 940 requires information from the state returns.

For the W-2 statements and the summary W-3 (which summarizes your W-2s), you just print the old payroll report and then, carefully following directions, enter the gross wages, the Social Security and Medicare taxes withheld, and the federal income taxes withheld into the appropriate blanks.

If you have a little trouble, call the IRS. If you have a lot of trouble, splurge and have someone else do it for you. You don't have to be a rocket scientist to fill out these forms, by the way. Any experienced bookkeeper can do the job for you.

Please don't construe my "rocket scientist" comment as personal criticism if this payroll taxes business seems terribly complicated. My experience is that some people — and you may very well be one of them — just don't have an interest in things such as payroll accounting. If, on the other hand, you're a "numbers-are-my-friend" kind of person, you'll have no trouble at all once you learn the ropes.

Doing the State Payroll Taxes Thing

Yeah. I haven't talked about state payroll taxes — at least not in any great detail. I wish I could provide this sort of detailed, state-specific help to you. Unfortunately, doing so would make this chapter about 150 pages long. It would also cause me to go stark raving mad.

My sanity and laziness aside, however, you still need to deal with the state payroll taxes. Let me say, though, that you apply to state payroll taxes the same basic mechanics you apply to the federal payroll taxes. For example, a state income tax works the same way the federal income tax works, employer-paid state unemployment taxes work the same way the employer-paid federal taxes work, and employee-paid state taxes work the same way the employee-paid Social Security and Medicare taxes work.

If you're tuned in to how federal payroll taxes work in Quicken, you really shouldn't have a problem with the state payroll taxes — at least, not in terms of the mechanics.

Chapter 17

Receivables and Payables

. . . .

In This Chapter

▶ Setting up an account to track customer receivables

▶ Recording customer invoices

▶ Recording customer payments

▶ Tracking amounts your customers owe

▶ Handling customer receivables

▶ Describing vendor payables

▶ Handling vendor payables

▶ Tracking vendor payables

▶ Using the Billminder utility

. . . .

*Q*uicken, as a checkbook program, isn't really built for tracking the amounts that clients and customers owe you or that you owe your vendors, but you can do both if you don't have a long list of receivables or payables. This chapter describes how you can handle both situations.

Tracking Customer Receivables

To track customer receivables, you must set up an asset account just for tracking customer receivables. If you know how to set up an asset account, just do it. If you don't, follow these steps:

1. **Choose Finance⇨Account List or press Ctrl + A.**

   Quicken displays the Account List window, which, if you have been following along from the start, is beginning to look familiar.

2. **Click the New button.**

   Quicken asks you to choose the type of account you want to create.

3. Click the Asset button.

Doing so tells Quicken that you're setting up a catch-all asset account to track something besides a bank account, cash, or your investments.

4. Click Next.

Quicken displays the Asset Account Setup dialog box.

5. Click the Summary tab.

Quicken displays the Summary tab, of course. And that's nice, because the Summary tab provides everything you need to set up an asset account. Figure 17-1 shows the Summary tab of the Asset Account Setup dialog box.

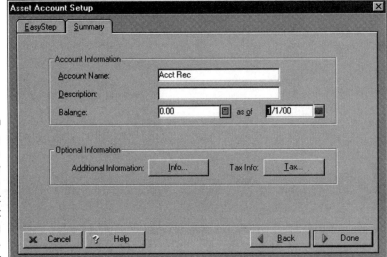

Figure 17-1:
The
Summary
tab of the
Asset
Account
Setup dialog
box.

6. Name the account.

Move the cursor to the Account Name text box and type a name, such as **Acct Rec**, to identify the account as the one that holds your accounts receivable. But one of the fun things about being in your own business is that *you* get to make the decisions about what you name your accounts — so go for it, dude, and be creative.

7. Enter a description for the account (optional).

I don't know — how about something creative, like **Accounts Receivable**? Of course, if the name you choose is descriptive enough, you don't need to use this optional description.

8. Leave the starting balance as zero.

9. **Accept the default date.**

   You don't need to enter a date because you aren't entering a starting balance.

10. **Click Done.**

    Quicken redisplays the Account List window. But, magically, the window now lists an additional account — the accounts receivable account you just created. (Actually, this isn't really magic — but you know that.)

To tell Quicken which account you want to work with, use the Account window. Display the Account List window, select the account you want by using the arrow keys or the mouse, and then press Enter. Quicken selects the account and displays the Register window.

Tracking Customer Invoices and Payments

Because Quicken isn't designed to keep track of lots of receivables and doesn't generate its own invoices (see Chapter 2 for a refresher on what Quicken does and doesn't do), I think that you should just use Quicken to keep a list of your unpaid customer invoices. You can use a Quicken Other account to bill customers and track their invoices, but this approach requires Rube Goldbergian complexity. What's more, if you do want to do all this complex stuff, you're really better off with a real small-business accounting system, such as QuickBooks by Intuit.

Now, back to the chase. . . .

Recording customer invoices

When you bill a customer, you just enter a transaction for the invoice amount in your Accounts Receivable register. You can follow these steps for recording a customer invoice in the next empty slot in the Accounts Receivable register:

1. **Open the Register window for the Accounts Receivable account.**

   Choose Finance⇨Account List and double-click the accounts receivable account.

2. **Enter the *invoice date* — the date you bill your customer or client — in the Date field.**

3. **Enter the invoice number in the Ref field.**

   The invoice number you enter is the number of the invoice you create yourself.

4. **Enter the customer or client name in the Payee field.**

   After the transaction has been recorded, the name appears in the Payee drop-down list box, and you can select the name from the list box any time you activate the list.

   Make sure that you use the same spelling of the customer's name every time you enter it, because Quicken summarizes accounts receivable information by payee name: Quicken interprets *John Doe* and *Jonh Doe* as two different customers. In addition, you must take care with names because Quicken QuickFill works quickly in assuming that you mean a particular account name. If you first enter a customer name as *Mowgli's Lawn Service,* for example, and then later you type **Mowg** as an account name, Quicken assumes that you're entering another transaction for *Mowgli's Lawn Service* and fills the Payee field with the complete name. You can avoid trouble in both these instances by activating the Payee drop-down list and selecting the payee name from the list.

5. **Enter the invoice amount in the Increase field.**

6. **Click Enter to record the transaction.**

   If Quicken reminds you to enter a category, click No. You don't want to use a category in this step because you later categorize the invoice by using an income category when you record the customer deposit.

Figure 17-2 shows a register entry for a $750 invoice to Mowgli's Lawn Service. After you click Enter, the ending balance, shown in the lower-right corner, shows the sum of all the transactions in the register.

Recording customer payments

When you work with customer payments in Quicken, you actually need to do two things. First, you record the customer's check as a deposit in your bank account and categorize it as falling into one of your income categories. Because you can probably record this information with your eyes closed and one hand tied behind your back, I won't describe the process again here. (If you jumped straight to this exciting section, you may want to check out Chapter 4, where I talk all about deposits.)

Second, you must update your accounts receivable list for the customer's payment. To update the list, display the Accounts Receivable account in the Register window and mark the existing invoice the customer has paid by putting a **c** in the Clr (or cleared) field. (You can do so simply by clicking the Clr field.) Figure 17-3 shows that the first $750 invoice to Mowgli's Lawn Service has been paid.

Notice that I've gotten pretty crazy and entered some other invoices, too. It's my job.

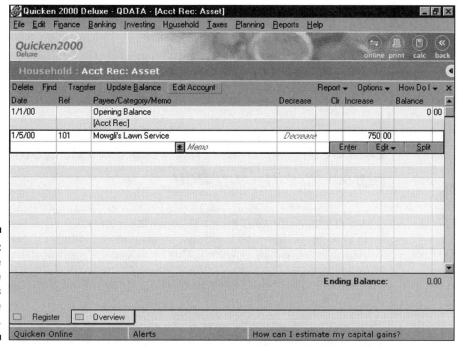

Figure 17-2:
An invoice entry in the Accounts Receivable register.

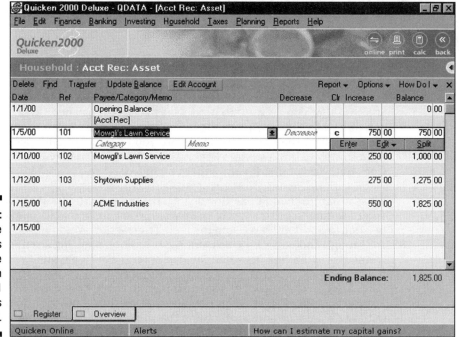

Figure 17-3:
The Accounts Receivable register with invoice #101 marked as cleared.

Tracking Your Receivables

When you look at the Accounts Receivable register at this point, you can't tell the total of what your customers owe you. In Figure 17-3, for example, even though I've marked invoice #101 as paid, the account balance still shows $1,825 (the balance of all four invoices shown).

Discovering a dirty little secret about A/R reporting in Quicken

If you read the last section, you have just discovered an unfortunate quirk in the way Quicken handles accounts receivable: The account balance for an asset account includes all the transactions entered in the register — even those you mark as being cleared. This quirk causes some problems. For example, you can't print an accurate balance sheet report because Quicken uses the account balance from an asset account on the balance sheet report, and this balance is not accurate.

Oh m' gosh — does this mean that you can't track receivables this way? Naw. It does mean, however, that you can't use the accounts receivable account balance for anything because the balance is really a meaningless number. What's more, the accounts receivable, total assets, and net worth figures on the balance sheet reports are also meaningless numbers because the report uses the goofy accounts receivable account balances, too.

Producing an accurate balance sheet

Suppose that you do want to produce an accurate balance sheet. What do you do? You simply strip out the cleared transactions in a receivables register by deleting them one by one. Before you begin your deletions, however, print a copy of the Accounts Receivables register. You may want to keep track of the customer invoices that you billed.

What's that? You don't like the idea of stripping out the transactions? Okay. If you're willing to go to slightly more work, you can fix the accounts receivable balance in another way. Using the Split Transaction Window (see Chapter 15), go through and add split transaction information showing a reduction in the invoice total that results when the customer makes a payment.

For a $750 invoice on which the customer pays $400, for example, the Split Transaction Window includes one line that records a positive number for the initial $750 invoice and another line that records a negative number for the

$400 customer payment. So what you're left with is a transaction that equals $350 — the open balance on the invoice — because that's what the split transaction amounts add up to. Figure 17-4 shows an example of this.

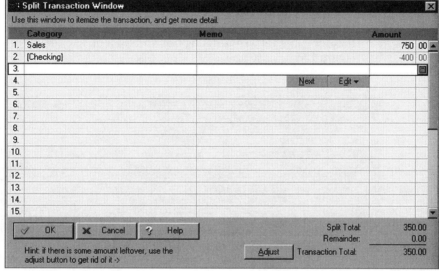

Figure 17-4: The Split Transaction Window can be used to show payments on an invoice.

If you use the Split Transaction window to show invoices being paid, don't mark partially paid invoices as cleared. If you do, they won't show up on the A/R by Customer report. I talk a bit more about this report in the next section.

Getting a list of what customers owe you

You can also mitigate the problem of the inaccurate balance sheet by printing an A/R by Customer business report to summarize which people owe you and how much they owe. (Doing so won't suddenly make an inaccurate balance sheet accurate, of course, but it will let you know exactly who owes you what.)

The A/R by Customer report summarizes all uncleared transactions. To Quicken, however, the first transaction in this register, Opening Balance, looks like a customer — even though it is not a real account. So that this phantom customer doesn't appear on your report, either delete it or mark it as cleared.

To print the A/R by Customer business report, follow these simple steps:

1. Choose Reports⇨Business to display the Business Reports menu.

2. Choose Accounts R̲eceivable Report.

Quicken produces a report that summarizes the uncleared transactions by payee names.

3. Click the Cu̲stomize button if you've already created other asset accounts.

Quicken displays the Customize A/R by Customer dialog box. Click the Accounts tab. Your dialog box should look like the one shown in Figure 17-5.

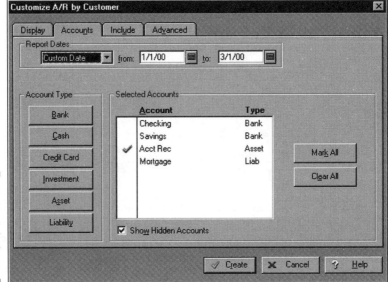

Figure 17-5:
The Customize A/R by Customer dialog box.

4. Select which accounts with uncleared transactions you want on the accounts receivable report.

Then to select an account, click the mouse or press the spacebar. (By the way, if you have only one asset account — the Accounts Receivable account — then the initial selection Quicken makes is correct.)

5. Click Cr̲eate.

Figure 17-6 shows the A/R by Customer report based on the three uncleared invoices shown in Figure 17-3 earlier in this chapter.

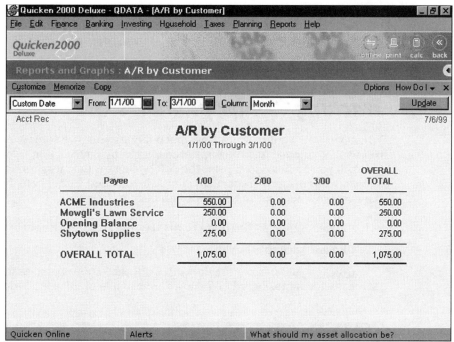

Figure 17-6:
The A/R by
Customer
report.

Preparing to Track Vendor Payables

You really don't have to do anything special to begin tracking the amounts you
know that you'll pay; however, you do need to have a bank account already
set up. (I'm assuming that you do already have a bank account set up. If you
don't — which is almost impossible to believe — refer to Chapters 1 and 2.)

Describing your vendor payables

You describe your vendor payables by filling in the checks you use to pay a
vendor's bills in the Write Checks window. Don't print the checks, though.
Quicken tracks these unprinted checks because they represent your unpaid
vendor invoices. That's it.

I'm super-tempted to describe how you fill out the blanks of the Write Checks
window — the result of the first tenet in the boring old computer writer's
code of honor, "When in doubt, describe in detail." But really — as you probably know — filling out the Write Checks window is darn easy.

If you're not sure about how to fill out the Write Checks window, don't feel bad or think that the process requires an advanced degree. After all, you're still getting your feet wet. If you feel unsteady, peruse Chapter 5 and then go ahead and type away at your keyboard.

Tracking vendor payables

Whenever you want to know how much money you owe someone, just print a report that summarizes the unprinted checks by payee name. Pretty easy, huh? All you have to do is print the A/P by Vendor business report. If you know how to print the report, go ahead. If you need a little help, here's a blow-by-blow account of the steps you need to follow:

1. **Choose Reports⇨Business to display the Business Reports menu.**

2. **Choose Accounts Payable.**

   Quicken summarizes the unprinted checks in your bank, cash, and credit card accounts. Figure 17-7 shows an example of this cute little report.

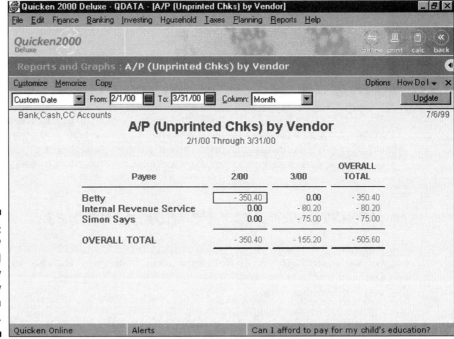

Figure 17-7:
The A/P (Unprinted Chks) by Vendor by Month report.

How Quicken identifies an unprinted check

Here's a little tidbit of information that you may (or may not) find useful. When you describe a check you want to print by using the Write Checks window, Quicken records the check in the register but uses the word *Print* in place of the check number. The word *Print* identifies the check as the one that you want to print and signals Quicken to look at the check and say to itself, "Aha! — an unprinted check!" *Print* is, to say the least, an important word.

If you're someone who has decided to get truly wild and crazy and use the Quicken electronic bill-paying feature, untransmitted payments show up in the register, too. This time, Quicken uses the word *XMIT* to look at and say, "Aha! — an untransmitted electronic payment!" Untransmitted payments, however, don't appear on the A/P (Unprinted Chks) by Vendor report. Go figure.

Electronic payments can be wild and crazy? What a concept! Yes, the entire Quicken program can be just that, if wild and crazy means being fun and adventurous. You know, wild and crazy — as in ordering Thai food and saying, "How spicy? Make it Dragon, please." Or wild and crazy — as in not wearing any underwear. You understand.

Explaining how Quicken handles payables

Before I conclude this wonderfully interesting, terribly exciting discussion about how you track unpaid bills in Quicken, let me make one final, quick point: An unprinted check is counted as an expense only after you print it. Does this news sound like much ado about nothing? It probably is.

But let me take a minute to explain the accounting system that Quicken uses. For example, if you record a $1,000 check to your landlord on December 31, but you don't print the check until January, Quicken doesn't count the $1,000 as an expense in December. It instead counts the $1,000 as an expense in January of the next year.

By the way, the Quicken register shows two balances: the current balance, which shows, well, the current balance (the balance that's in your account even as you read this sentence), and the ending balance, which shows the unprinted checks.

If you know a little about cash-basis accounting versus accrual-basis accounting, you've probably already said to yourself, "Hey, man, Quicken uses cash-basis accounting." And you're right, of course.

This little subtlety between the two accounting systems can cause confusion, especially if you've already been working with a regular, full-featured accounting system that uses an accounts payable module with accrual-basis accounting. In one of these systems, the $1,000 check to your landlord probably gets counted as an expense as soon as you enter it in the system.

Counting on Your Buddy, Billminder

Bill, my affectionate nickname for Billminder, is a separate program in Quicken that will soon become a good friend of yours, too. You can tell Quicken to fix your computer so that the Billminder program runs every time you turn on your computer — a nice feature.

What Bill does is simple: He looks through your unprinted checks for any checks with dates falling on or before the current date. If Bill finds a check with such a date, he displays a message that says, "Hey, dude, you have checks that you need to print." Or, in the case where you have overdue checks, Bill displays a message that says, "Dude, the situation is getting gnarly — you have some seriously overdue checks." (The messages don't use these exact words, by the way.)

To tell Bill you want him to remind you of the checks you need to print, follow these steps:

1. **Choose Finance⇨Reminders.**

   In a surprising move, Quicken displays the Reminder window.

2. **Click the Options button to display the menu showing the Reminders and Billminder submenus.**

   These two menus are where all the action happens — at least from Bill's perspective. Figure 17-8 shows the Options menu with the Reminders submenu open.

3. **Under the Reminders submenu, choose Show Reminders from other files if you have more than one Quicken file you want Bill to keep track of for you.**

   Selecting this command tells Bill that you want to be reminded of checks and events from all files that you have in Quicken.

4. **Under the Reminders submenu, choose Days Shown, and then enter a value in the Days Shown text box.**

   This value tells Bill how many days in advance you want him to remind you of unprinted checks. The value also tells Quicken how many days in advance you want to be queried about scheduled transactions and investment reminder messages.

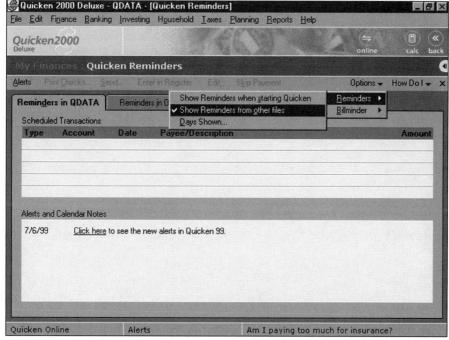

Figure 17-8:
The Options
menu with
the
Reminders
submenu
displayed.

5. **Turn on the Billminder reminder feature by opening the <u>B</u>illminder submenu and selecting the <u>S</u>how Billminder when starting Windows command.**

   Bill also keeps his eyes open for scheduled transactions, investment reminder messages, and notes you post on the Financial Calendar as long as you have them checked in this dialog box. By the way, if you leave your computer on all of the time, don't worry, Bill doesn't just go to sleep after you initially turn on your computer. He'll pop up and let you know what's going on even if it's been months since you restarted your computer.

6. **If you would like to see the Reminders window every time you start Quicken, click the <u>R</u>eminders⇨Show Reminders when <u>s</u>tarting Quicken command.**

   When you start Quicken the next time, you'll see a screen like the one shown in Figure 17-8. It'll tell you whether you have checks to print, scheduled transactions you need to enter, and any calendar notes you should probably be reading.

Note: If you don't want to see the Reminders screen or the Quicken Home Page every time you start Quicken, it's a snap to turn them both off. Just choose <u>E</u>dit⇨Options⇨Quicken Program, click the Startup tab, and then choose None.

To print a check listed in the Reminders window, select the check and click the Print Checks button. To enter a scheduled transaction, select the transaction and click the Enter in Register button. Any calendar notes you've created also show in the Reminders window. Click the Calendar button to go to the date in the financial calendar.

Part V
The Part of Tens

The 5th Wave   By Rich Tennant

"Our plan is to buy the rest of it when we pay off our college loan."

In this part . . .

As a writing tool, laundry lists aren't something that high school English teachers encourage. But you know what? The old laundry list format is pretty handy for certain sorts of information.

With this idea in mind (and, of course, with deepest apologies to my high school English teacher, Mrs. O'Rourke), this final part simply provides you with lists of information about Quicken: answers to ten commonly asked questions about Quicken and ten tips on how not to become a millionaire.

Chapter 18

(Slightly More Than) Ten Questions I'm Frequently Asked about Quicken

- -

In This Chapter

▶ Is Quicken Y2K (or Year 2000) compliant?

▶ What are Quicken's best features?

▶ Does Quicken work for a corporation?

▶ What happens to stockholders' equity in Quicken?

▶ Does Quicken work for a partnership?

▶ Can I use Quicken to track more than one business?

▶ What kinds of businesses shouldn't use Quicken?

▶ Can I use Quicken retroactively?

▶ Can I do payroll with Quicken?

▶ Can I prepare invoices with Quicken?

▶ Can I import data from my old accounting system?

▶ What do you think of Quicken?

- -

*W*hen people find out that I've written a book about Quicken, they always ask a question or two. In this chapter, I list the most common questions and their answers.

Is Quicken Year 2000 Compliant?

The short answer to this question is yes. What Y2K, or Year 2000, compliance means is that Quicken 2000 can handle dates beyond December 31, 1999 without getting goofed up. Quicken assumes, by the way, that if you leave off the first two digits of the year number, you're talking about a year between 1950 and 2049. So, if you enter just 00, Quicken assumes you're talking about 2000. And if you enter 50, Quicken assumes you're talking about 1950. Another way to say this same thing is that Quicken uses the numbers 00 to 49 for the years 2000 to 2049, and it uses the numbers 50 to 99 for the years 1950 to 1999.

You can enter dates that fall before this period of time. To do this, enter the full year number. For example, to enter the date September 15, 1935 you enter 9/15/1935. Quicken replaces the 19 with an apostrophe, recording your date as 9/15/'35.

One other tidbit worth mentioning is that Intuit's Y2K Ready Standard is available from their web site, `www.intuit.com/support`. If you're, like, totally paranoid about all this stuff even after reading my soothing words, go ahead and visit their web site and read what they have to say. You can also write Intuit to get a copy of their Year 2000 Ready Standard if you don't have an Internet connection. The address is:

> Year 2000 Coordinator
> Intuit Inc.
> 2650 East Elvira Road
> Tucson AZ 85706

By the way, if you're still paranoid even after reading all this stuff, here's what you want to do. Sometime late in December of 1999, back up your Quicken data files and then store the diskette someplace. Then, print a complete copy of each of your registers. With both an electronic copy and a paper copy of all your records — even assuming the worst possible case — you'll still be able to reconstruct your records.

I'll probably do this. No, I'm not paranoid. But, well, it's not that much work. And it's not a bad idea to do at the end of the year anyway. And then what if the worst does happen . . . wouldn't I look like a dummy if I lost my data?

What Are Quicken's Best Features?

Quicken has gotten more and more complicated over the years. So I think it's maybe fair to spend just a few sentences reviewing its most valuable and least valuable features. As far as what's best or most valuable, I would say that its checkbook feature is still clearly by far and away the most valuable. If there's one feature you should use in Quicken, it's the checkbook stuff. (To do this, set up a bank account for your checking account and then use Quicken to keep track of your balances, income, and spending as described in Chapter 4.)

I also have to say that I think what Intuit, the maker of Quicken, provides at their Quicken.com web site is pretty neat. So I'd give that feature my vote as the second best feature. I don't talk about the Quicken.com web site a whole lot in this book — just a bit in Appendix B. But that's because Quicken.com is something you'll have more fun and more success with just by exploring on your own.

Just because I'm super-compulsive not only about my personal finances but also about yours, too, let me say that I think Quicken's Financial Calculators (these I describe in Chapter 10) are also really valuable. If you're willing and able to do a just a bit of planning right now, it's truly amazing how positive an impact it'll have on your financial affairs a few years down the road.

So this leads rather nicely to what are Quicken's least valuable features. I'm not sure. I think that this really depends on the person. Nevertheless, I will tell you what I think is Quicken's least useful feature in my case. I think the online banking stuff is overrated. Yeah, it sounds good in theory. But once you factor in the extra complexity of having to make a successful Internet connection in order to get your banking done, well, I'm not sure it's worth it. Or, at least, I'm not sure it's worth it if you have to pay for the privilege. (I do online banking, but only reluctantly and because I have to know what I'm talking about for Chapter 6.)

Does Quicken Work for a Corporation?

Sure. But let me talk for a minute about what's unique — at least from an accountant's perspective — about a corporation.

In addition to recording assets (such as bank accounts and receivables) and liabilities (such as mortgages and trade payables), a corporation needs to *track,* or keep records for, the stockholders' equity.

Stockholders' equity includes the amount people originally paid for their stock, any earnings the corporation has retained, cumulative income for the current year, and sometimes other stuff, too.

"Ugh," you're probably saying to yourself. "Ugh" is right. Accounting for stockholders' equity of a corporation is mighty complicated at times. So complicated, in fact, that Quicken can't track a corporation's stockholders' equity.

I'm not saying that you can't use Quicken if you're a corporation, and I'm not saying that you shouldn't. (I do business as a corporation, and I use Quicken.) Just remember that someone — probably your poor accountant — periodically needs to calculate your stockholders' equity.

Fortunately, the financial information you collect with Quicken provides, in rough form, much of the information that your poor accountant needs in order to do things manually.

What Happens to Stockholders' Equity in Quicken?

Quicken doesn't exactly ignore a corporation's stockholders' equity. In an Account Balances report, the difference between the total assets and the total liabilities actually represents the total stockholders' equity. (Quicken labels this total Net Worth. So, to the extent that your total assets and total liabilities figures are correct, you know your total stockholders' equity.)

Does Quicken Work for a Partnership?

Yep, it does. But a partnership that uses Quicken faces the same basic problem as a corporation that uses Quicken. In a partnership, the partners want to track their partnership capital accounts (or at least they should). A partnership capital account simply shows what a partner has put into and taken out of a business.

As noted in the preceding section, Quicken calculates a net worth figure for you by subtracting total liabilities from total assets. So, to the extent that your total assets and total liabilities are accurately accounted for in Quicken, you know roughly the total partnership capital.

To solve this problem, you — or someone else — needs to track what each partner puts into the business, earns as a partner in the business, and then takes out of the business.

Can I Use Quicken for More Than One Business?

Yeah, but be very careful. *Very* careful. You must be especially diligent in keeping the two businesses' financial records separate.

Quicken provides a handy tool for keeping them straight: You can work with more than one file. Each file, in effect, is like a separate set of financial records. You can't record automatic transfers between accounts in different files; instead, you must record each side of the transaction separately. You can, however, keep truly separate business records.

To create a separate file, choose the File⇨New command.

If you've been using Quicken for a while, you can probably figure out for yourself how the File⇨New command works. If you need help, refer to my discussion of this command in Chapter 9.

Separate bank accounts are usually a must. If you keep separate records for two distinct businesses in Quicken, you need to set up separate bank accounts for them. In fact, my attorney tells me that in the case of a corporation, you must set up a separate corporate bank account for the corporation to be truly considered as an independent legal entity. Talk to your attorney if you have questions; attorneys can tell you the specifics that apply to a particular state and situation.

What Kind of Businesses Shouldn't Use Quicken?

You're probably saying to yourself, "Quicken works for corporations (sort of), and it works for partnerships (sort of). Does that mean that it works for just about any kind of business?"

The answer is no. Quicken is a darn good product. In fact, for many small businesses, it's a great product. But it doesn't work in every situation.

The following is a three-part test that you can use to determine whether your business should use Quicken. If you answer yes to two or three of the questions, you should seriously consider moving up to a full-featured small-business accounting system.

✔ **Do you regularly need to produce business forms other than checks?**

If you answer no to this question, you're in good shape with Quicken, which produces checks easily. And if all you need is an occasional invoice, you can create it easily enough on your computer. I, for example, produce a handful of invoices a month. I do them on my word processing program and never have any problems.

If you do produce a lot of forms besides checks, you should probably consider moving up to a small-business accounting system that produces the forms you want. If you've been using Quicken, for example, take a look at QuickBooks for Windows, another Intuit product. Another more powerful but wonderfully designed product you might try is Peachtree Accounting for Windows from Peachtree Software. You should be able to get either program at the local software store. You can certainly get either program by calling one of the mail order places.

✔ **Do you need to track assets other than cash or investments?**

For example, do you have a long list of customer receivables that you need to monitor? Or do you buy and resell inventory? An accounting system is usually helpful in tracking these items. Quicken doesn't do a very good job of tracking these other assets, so you may want to look at one of the other small-business accounting products — QuickBooks, for example.

✔ **Are you having problems measuring your profits with cash-basis accounting?**

I'm not going to get into a big, tangled discussion of cash-basis versus accrual-basis accounting. It wouldn't be any fun for you. It wouldn't be any fun for me, either. Nevertheless, you should know that if you can't accurately measure your business profits by using cash-basis accounting (which is what Quicken uses), you may be able to more accurately measure your business profits by using accrual-basis accounting. To do so, use an accounting system that supports accrual-basis accounting. I should be totally honest with you and tell you that to measure your profits the right way, you (or your accountant) need to use — horror of horrors — double-entry bookkeeping.

If you are a Quicken user but realize that you're outgrowing the checkbook-on-a-computer scene, check out QuickBooks. (No, I don't get a kickback from Intuit.) Here's the deal: QuickBooks looks and feels a lot like Quicken. Plus, it uses the data that you've already collected with Quicken. So you'll find that moving from Quicken to QuickBooks is only slightly more complicated than rolling off a log.

Can I Use Quicken Retroactively?

Yeah. And the idea is better than it might seem at first.

It doesn't take long to enter a year's worth of transactions in Quicken (as long as you have decent records to work with). If you're, like, a millionaire, it might take you a couple of days. (Of course, in this case, you can probably hire someone to do it for you.) If you're a regular, ordinary person, I bet you can get it done on a rainy Saturday afternoon.

After you enter all the information into a Quicken register, you can easily monitor your spending in various categories, track your income and outgo, and reconcile your bank accounts. I know one professional who uses Quicken records to do these things every year. Hey, it's not the most efficient way to do things. And it's not a very good way to manage business or personal financial affairs. But it works. Sort of.

Can I Do Payroll with Quicken?

Yes. See Chapter 16 for more details.

By the way, if you have only one or two salaried employees who always earn the same amount — a nanny, for example — then you can rather easily use Quicken for payroll. But if you have a bunch of employees or even a single hourly employee, you'll probably want to either purchase a full-featured, real-live small business accounting program like QuickBooks or use a payroll service like PayChex or ADP to take care of the whole thing for you.

Intuit makes and sells QuickBooks, as you might guess by its name. You can get QuickBooks from the local software store, from one of the mail order places, or by calling Intuit.

You can look up either payroll service — PayChex or ADP — in the telephone book. Nevertheless, you need to do one, crucially important thing if you choose to use PayChex. When you call, tell PayChex that you were referred by another customer, Stephen L. Nelson, of Redmond, Washington. If you do this — and I'm really not kidding about this — PayChex will give me a $50 gift certificate to Nordstrom. (What I'm thinking here, by the way, is that if I can get 10,000 readers to join the happy PayChex family, I may be able to go on the shopping spree of the century.)

Can I Prepare Invoices?

Not with Quicken Deluxe, but you can, sort of, with Quicken for Home and Business. This may be a symptom indicating that you should consider moving up to a full-featured, small-business accounting system.

Can I Import Data from an Old Accounting System?

Someone had to ask this question, I guess. (Imagine me taking a deep breath here.) Yes, you can import data from your old accounting system. To do so, export the old system's data into a file that matches the Quicken Interchange Format, or QIF, specification. Then import this file into an empty Quicken file.

- ✔ This process isn't for the timid or faint-hearted.
- ✔ I would also claim that it isn't for people who have better things to do with their time.

✔ My advice to you? Go to a movie. Mow your lawn. Read a trashy novel. Forget all about this importing business.

What Do You Think about Quicken?

I think it's great. But I bet your question isn't really whether Quicken is good or not. Heck, the package sells something like two million copies a year. So we both know that the package is pretty good, right? My guess is that what you really want is my opinion about using Quicken in particular business or personal situations.

It's tough to answer this question in a one-way conversation. Even so, let me give you some of the best reasons for using Quicken:

✔ You always know your bank account balances, so you won't ever have to wonder whether you have enough money to pay a bill or charge a purchase.

✔ Reconciling your account takes about two minutes. (I'm not joking. It really does take a couple of minutes.)

✔ You get a firm handle on what you're really making and spending.

✔ You can budget your spending and then track your spending against your budget.

✔ If you're a business, you can measure your profits as often as you want by using cash-basis accounting.

✔ If you're an investor, you can monitor your investments and measure their actual returns.

I hope these answers help. My guess is that if you think a program like Quicken will help you better manage your financial affairs, then it probably will.

Chapter 19

(Almost) Ten Tips on How Not to Become a Millionaire

. . . .

In This Chapter

▶ Ignore the fact that one can build surprising wealth by investing in ownership investments and earning just average returns

▶ Ignore that one can get much and maybe most of the money from tax savings and employer matching.

▶ Don't tap your computer's and Quicken's power to develop powerful, wealth-building insights

▶ Give up because it's too late to start anyway

▶ Get entangled in at least one "get rich quick" scheme

▶ Fake it with false affluence

▶ Give in to the first big temptation of wealth building

▶ Give in to the second big temptation of wealth building

. . . .

*O*kay. You read the chapter title right. But let me explain a couple of things. First, late last year I wrote a book about how to save a million dollars for one's retirement. That sounds a little money-grubbing, I'll agree, but my argument then (and now) is that most people need to accumulate a nice-sized nest egg for retirement since most of us can't or shouldn't really count on things like pensions and Social Security.

 If Congress does nothing — absolutely nothing — to save Social Security, the best studies show that about 30 or 40 years from now that they'll need to reduce benefits to around 75 percent of the amounts they pay today. For example, where today someone might get $1,000 a month, in the future they may instead get $750. Where today someone might get $400, in the future they may instead get $300. While this isn't quite the financial meltdown that some people think, it does mean that you and I really must prepare to augment our retirement income by having our own savings.

So, anyway, as part of promoting this book, which needs to remain unnamed because *Quicken 2000 For Windows For Dummies* is published by IDG Books and this other book was published by somebody else, I spent several weeks on the road doing radio call-in shows, bookstore appearances, and television talk shows. I learned several things though this experience. First, I learned that after one has appeared on some television show, it is, apparently, customary to remove the strange makeup they apply. Especially if you plan to appear later in other public locations like on the street or in a restaurant.

I also learned something else in my travels and talking with people. While everyone is interested in becoming a millionaire or in preparing financially for retirement, it turned out that most people were really more interested in how not to become a millionaire. In other words, they wanted me to explain in financial terms *why* people don't accumulate wealth.

I thought at first that this was a little strange. But then finally somebody explained, "We all know you need to save and invest to build wealth. . .what we don't know enough about are those things that prevent or sabotage our attempts to do this." In other words, people wanted to know what screws most people up in their wealth-building activities — so they don't have to make the same mistakes.

And so this is what I want to do here. I want to share with you my observations and research results about why people who know they should save at least some money for retirement don't end up building wealth. I've observed that there are seven, really common problems or traps that foul most people up.

One of the things that happens when you start talking about compound interest and future values is that inflation makes it hard to make apples-to-apples comparisons. In other words, I can say something like, ". . .and then you'll have $3,000,000." But you then have to wonder, well, but what's that going to be worth with inflation. To deal with this annoying complexity, I'm just going to adjust all the numbers I use in the following paragraphs for inflation. In other words, I'm going to subtract out the inflation and only give you the "adjusted-for-inflation" numbers, denominated in current-day dollars. Note that the Quicken financial planners also let you adjust for inflation by checking the "Adjust for Inflation" box, which appears on most of the calculator dialog boxes.

Ignore the Fact that You Can Build Surprising Wealth by Investing in Ownership Investments and Earning Just Average Returns

Okay, here's the first trap that people encounter. You can build surprising wealth just by investing in ownership investments that produce average returns. By ownership investments, I mean, basically stocks and maybe real estate. Let me give you three quick examples:

- ✔ Just by earning the stock market's average inflated adjusted return of around six percent, a 25-year-old saving $150 a month can build wealth of as much as $300,000 by age 65.

- ✔ Just by earning the stock market's average inflated adjusted return of around six percent, a 35-year-old saving $300 a month can build wealth of as much as $300,000 by age 65.

- ✔ Just by earning the stock market's average inflated adjusted return of around six percent, a 50-year-old saving $850 a month can build wealth of as much as $300,000

I want to stop here. There's a really important truth that, sadly, most people miss this information. But you should consider what this means: You don't have to get fancy. You don't have to spend a bunch of time worrying. You don't need to spend a bunch of money on advisors, newsletters, or commissions. Or even books about using Quicken.

Compound interest is a powerful engine and it creates wealth. And that means you can build surprising wealth by investing in ownership investments and earning just average returns.

Note, too, that you can lock in average returns by choosing a low-cost index fund like The Vanguard Group's Index 500 or Total Stock Market Portfolio mutual fund.

If you choose an actively managed mutual fund or a mutual fund that charges average fees for managing your money, you basically don't have a snow-balls-chance-in-you-know-where of actually earning an average return over time. No. Over the long investment horizons required to prepare for retirement, if you go this route, chances are that you'll actually earn a return equal to the market's return less the expense ratio that the mutual fund manager charges. Expense ratios for actively managed funds run around two percent annually. So rather than a six or seven percent annual, adjusted-for-inflation return, you'll actually typically earn a four or five percent annual adjusted-for-inflation return on actively managed mutual funds.

One final point: People see way more risk in this investing than there really is. If you would have begun investing in stock market in 1926 and then continued systematically investing for 25 years through the crash of '29, the global depression of the thirties, World War II, and then the start of the Cold War, you would have earned about an 8 percent return on your money. Given that the inflation rate was just 2 percent over this same period of time, you could still have built wealth by investing in ownership investments producing average returns.

Ignore that You Can Get Much and Maybe Most of the Money from Tax Savings and Employer Matching

Okay. Let me now move on to a second, really important point. It's all fine and well to say that you just need to invest $300 a month, and that produces the wealth you need. The big question is, where do you get that money?

You've got bills to pay. A rent or mortgage check to write. You want to enjoy at least a few of the material pleasures — like food and drink — that life offers up. Where in the world does someone come up with this kind of money?

Well, the answer is mostly from the taxman and your employer. No kidding. Because of the way that employer-matching provisions work in things like 401(k) and Simple-IRA plans and because of the way our progressive income tax system works, you can get much from your employer and from the government in the form of tax deduction savings. You may even be able to get most of the money you'll need for your retirement savings from these sources.

The following table shows how someone who wants to save $300 a month might come up with the money. And, in fact, the first line of the table shows how much you want to save: $300.

The second line of the table shows how much you might get from your employer in a 401(k) or Simple-IRA plan. Note an IRA obviously doesn't include employer matching (this shows up therefore as zero in the table). But it's common for 401(k) plans to provide a 50-percent match on at least the first portion of your contribution (this shows up as $100 in the table). And basically by law, Simple-IRA's provide a 100 percent match on the first portion of your contribution (which shows up as $150 in the table).

	IRA	401(k)	Simple-IRA
What you want to save	$300	$300	$300
What you can get from employer	0	100	150
What you can get from tax man	100	65	50
What you come up with yourself	$200	$135	$100

The third line of the table shows how much you might get in the way of tax savings. For example, in the case of a $300 a month IRA contribution, you might actually enjoy $100 a month in federal and state income tax savings.

The fourth line of the table shows what you need to come up with yourself. The IRA is the worst case shown in the table. With an IRA and $300 a month of savings, you would need to come up with $200 yourself. The 401(k) plan looks better; with it you need to come up with $135 yourself. The Simple-IRA is the best case in the table. With it, you need to come up with only $100.

I don't want to overload you with data. But please note that this is an incredibly powerful insight. Much and maybe most of the money you need to build wealth can come from other people — specifically the tax man and if you work someplace where there's a 401(k) or Simple IRA plan from your employer.

Don't Tap Your Computer's Power to Develop Wealth-Building Insights

This is hard to describe in general terms. Because, by definition, what the computer lets you do is get very specific. But think about this: Personal financial planning is essentially applied mathematics. What this means is that to make a decision, you're often needing to tally up the costs of benefits of option A versus option B. And then you need to make time-value of money calculations. (Practically speaking, this just means you also need to figure in things like interest expense and investment income.)

The thing is, these sorts of tasks are the perfect applications for the personal computer.

And this becomes very relevant to our discussion of saving money. Because when you use your computer to make better, wiser personal financial decisions, you develop powerful, wealth-building insights that often supply the rest of the money you need for your investing. More specifically, if you need to or should be saving $300 a month and you can get $150 of this from your employer and through tax savings, you still need to come up that last $150 a month. But what I'm saying is that your computer can, should, help you find this money.

I want to give you one example: Have you heard about this notion of early mortgage repayment? It always sounds like a good idea, at least on the face of it. If you add an extra $25 a month to the regular mortgage payment on a typical mortgage, you often save around $25,000 in interest. And maybe more. (How much you save depends on the interest rate, the mortgage balance, and the remaining number of payments.)

Okay, you hear some bit of financial trivia like that, and early mortgage repayment sounds like a pretty good idea. Lots of people — encouraged by financial writers — have started doing this. But is it a good idea? It depends.

Consider this. If you could instead put an extra $25 a month into a 401(k), you end up with about $100,000.

So there you have it: Option "A," which is early mortgage repayment sounds pretty good because $25,000 of interest savings is a lot of money. But Option "B," is clearly better because for no extra pain or hassle, you end up with $100,000, or an extra $75,000.

Weird right? But other important financial decisions and personal financial planning issues often provide you with similar opportunities for free money or extra wealth because you use your computer:

- ✔ ARM Mortgages? Sometimes, these actually make you bear less risk and work better.
- ✔ Buying a home? Sometimes, it isn't a good investment — even when it seems like it is.
- ✔ Car leases? They can be great deals. . .or terrible deals. It all depends on the implicit interest rate charged by the lease.

In Chapter 10, "Compound Interest Magic and Other Mysteries," I talk about how you use Quicken's financial planners to make better financial decisions. The Internet also provides a ton of tools, many helpful, for doing personal financial planning. I don't want to sound like your mother or some cranky uncle. But I urge you to use these sorts of computer-based financial tools to make wiser decisions. A little extra money here, a little there, and pretty soon you've found that last bit of money you need to save to fund a comfortable retirement. No kidding.

Give Up Because It's Too Late to Start Anyway

Okay, here's another common trap that prevents people from saving money for retirement: You can just decide to give up because it's too late to start anyway. But I have to tell you that, mathematically speaking, this is just dead wrong.

Oh sure. There's a tendency to think that wealth-building schemes that rely on compound interest only work for young people. And it is true that wealth building can be very easy for someone who's young. Often someone who is young, only needs to make a single, clever decision in order to build wealth. For example, a 25-year-old, pack-a-day smoker quits and then puts his or her money into cigarettes, they can rather easily build a $1,000,000 by the time he retires. All he needs to do is save his money into an IRA, and select a small-company stock mutual index fund.

And remember: I'm adjusting for inflation, so really this person will probably have between $3,000,000 and $4,000,000 of inflated dollars.

You can't do that if you're 50 years old. I mean, you can't make one decision and expect to let the positive benefit of that single, good decision, to grow to $1,000,000.

But there's another angle in all of this: You aren't limited to making a single, good decision. Oh sure. That's easiest. But I really believe that if you make five or six or seven — maybe even ten good decisions — you can still build substantial wealth by the time you stop working.

I don't think this should surprise you if you're a mature investor. And I don't think it should discourage you. You possess more life-experience and, I dare-say, more wisdom, than someone who's 25. You can use your experience and wisdom to make a greater number of good decisions. And that can produce the wealth you need.

Get Entangled in at Least One "Get Rich Quick" Scheme

Get rich quick schemes don't work except for the person selling the scheme. And, in fact, they drain off energy and money you really should be using to build your investments. You know all this of course. We all do. But I think for all of us, there's a tendency to assume that this one particular great investment or business we're presented with is different. Oh sure, we know that other dummies get suckered. But "fill in blank" is different.

I actually don't think that it's a bad idea to try the occasional flier. If you have some small percentage of your investment money chasing speculative returns, that's okay. But only as long as it doesn't foul up your other, more important, boring but predictable wealth-building for retirement. That's fair, right? If you or I want to try chasing down the hottest new mutual fund or try online day-trading or invest in some friend's start-up business, that seems okay. But we can't allow these get rich quick schemes — which is what each of these are when you get right down to it — to foul up our meat-and-potatoes investing.

Unfortunately, what I observe is that most of the people who get involved in "get rich quick" schemes attempt to use this speculation as a replacement for true, disciplined investing. And I have never seen a "get rich quick" scheme that consistently works.

Let me make one other comment: Many and perhaps even most of the best-selling books about money and about how you should invest, amount to just new get rich schemes. I'm not going to name names here. Neither my attorney nor the publisher will let me. But, come on, any book that promises you that the writer's found some way to magically and consistently double or triple the returns that other investors earn is a get rich quick scheme.

However, there are some wonderful books about how to better manage your money. For example, Eric Tyson's book, *Personal Finance For Dummies*, is a really good book about the basics. And I'm not just saying this to schmooze the publisher. (Both Eric's book and this book are published by IDG Books.) I also love basically everything that Andrew Tobias writes, John Bogle's two books about mutual fund investing, *Bogle on Mutual Funds* and *Common Sense Guide to Mutual Funds,* and Burton Malkiel's classic, *A Random Walk Down Wall Street*. All of these books provide good, fact-based advice that leads you in the right direction.

Fake It with False Affluence

I talked about this a bit in Chapter 2. But it's an important point and worth repeating. When people spend all their money trying to look rich, they don't have any money left over to save and invest. Which means that most people have to decide — either explicitly or implicitly — whether they want to be rich or look rich. Weird, right?

Yet, most millionaires live average lives. They live in average houses located in middle-class neighborhoods. They drive average cars.

And ironically, most of the people who live in big houses or drive expensive cars aren't rich. They may have high incomes. But they aren't rich. And yet that makes sense. You can't become rich if you're spending all your money trying to look rich.

Faking affluence is a trap that goofs up more people than you'd guess.

Give In to the First Big Temptation of Wealth Building

I think that when you boil everything down to its very essence, the big problem is that most people lack the commitment. We all must be culturally programmed this way or something. But most of us — and hey, I'm the same way — stumble over a couple of big temptations. So I want to mention these temptations at least in passing.

Temptation #1: I can tell you, and so can any good financial planner, how to come up with an extra $100 or even $500 a month. I would also say that if you really do use Quicken in a disciplined way to manage your financial affairs, you will find yourself freeing up money. You'll save a little bit of money here. Waste a little less over there. And pretty soon you find yourself with a bit of extra cash. But you must have the commitment to save and invest that money. You and I have to decide that the next $100 or $500 we come up with should go for our investments. If we do, we don't have to worry about financial security in retirement. And if we don't, we should worry. But anyway, that's the first temptation: When you find some extra money, you need to have the discipline to save and invest those funds. And if you do start to do this, you'll rather quickly amass thousands of dollars.

Give In to the Second Big Temptation of Wealth Building

Ironically, resisting temptation #1 leads rather quickly to temptation #2: Once you do have an extra $5,000 or $25,000 or $50,000 in your portfolio, you need to have the commitment necessary to let this money grow. That seems obvious of course. But I've also noticed that a lot of people don't do this. A lot of people, once they amass a nice little pot of money, decide it's time to abandon a strategy that's worked wonderfully well. They decide to buy a bigger house or a boat. Or they change investment strategies, maybe by investing in some friend or family member's new business. Or they turn their money into a hobby — perhaps deciding they're going to try out this online investing thing using their retirement money.

It's your money of course. You get to do with it whatever you want. But I am going to be honest with you and say that if you really want to build up a nice nest egg for retirement, you need to be committed enough to resist the two big temptations described here.

Appendix A

Quick and Dirty Windows

● ●

*I*f you're new to Microsoft Windows — and by Windows I mean Windows 95, Windows 98, Windows 98 Second Edition, Windows NT, and even Windows 2000 — you need to know a few things about the Windows user interface. Although this appendix doesn't reveal anything earthshaking, it does provide a quick and dirty overview of what you need to know to get around.

If you've used other Windows applications, you probably don't need to read this appendix because you already know the material it covers.

I won't bore you with technical details. The information here, though, will enable you not only to operate Quicken but also to converse easily about the newest versions of Windows at cocktail parties, over lunch, or with the guy at the computer store.

If you want to find out more, you may want to read a book such as my *Small Business Windows 95 For Dummies* or *Small Business Windows 98 For Dummies* (IDG Books Worldwide, Inc.).

What Is Windows?

Windows — and when I use the term *Windows* here again I mean Windows 95, Windows 98, Windows 98 Second Edition, Windows NT 4.0, or Windows 2000 — is an operating environment that manages your *system resources* (things like memory, monitor, printer, and so on).

Applications (programs such as Quicken) run on top of Windows. In other words, you first start Windows (by turning on your personal computer) then, after Windows is running, you can start applications such as Quicken.

Windows provides a standard graphical interface. In English, Windows provides a common approach for using *visual elements* — icons, buttons, check boxes, and so on. (This appendix describes how the major pieces of this graphical interface work.)

Windows enables you to run more than one application at a time. You may, for example, run Quicken, a tax preparation package, and even a Windows accessory program such as the Calendar. You don't need to do this stuff, but, hey, you can if you want.

Starting Windows

Starting Windows is easy. You just turn on your personal computer. If you can find the on-off switch, you're set.

By the way, if for some reason you can't find the on-off switch or it doesn't seem to work, don't feel silly. Ask someone who has used the computer before. Sometimes the on-off switch is on the front of the computer and is labeled "on-off" (which makes good sense, of course). But all too frequently, I'm afraid, manufacturers stick the on-off switch on the back of the computer or label the switch something really stupid, such as 0 and 1. Sometimes, too, people plug a computer and all its peripherals (such as printers, modems, and all that junk) into a power strip that needs to be turned on to turn on the computer. So just ask someone. (If you bought the computer, of course, you can just telephone the place you bought it from.)

Just so you don't feel like a complete imbecile, I have to tell you something. I once had to call someone to learn how to click this stupid mouse that I got with my laptop computer.

Figure A-1 shows what a typical Windows 98 desktop looks like. The desktop is what you see after Windows 98 has started. Note, though, that the Windows 95, Windows NT 4.0, and Windows 2000 desktops look similar.

Starting Programs

To start a program like Quicken, you click the Start button so that Windows displays the Start menu. Then you click the Programs menu option so Windows lists all the programs that you, Windows, or someone else has installed. And then you click one of the listed programs to start that program.

Some programs — such as Quicken — don't appear as options on the Programs menu. They appear on Programs submenus. If you click Start and then choose the Programs menu option, you'll see a Quicken item, for example. Choosing the Quicken item from the Programs menu displays the Quicken submenu, which lists a bunch of different options (which depend on the version of Quicken you've installed). To start Quicken, you choose Programs⇨Quicken⇨Quicken 2000.

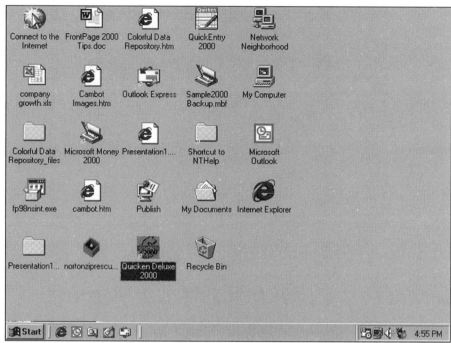

To practice this starting business, try starting the WordPad application that comes with Windows by following these steps:

1. **Click the Start button.**

2. **Choose Programs⇨Accessories⇨WordPad.**

When you follow these steps, Windows opens the WordPad program. Figure A-2 shows the WordPad application window. (An application window is just the window that a program like WordPad or Quicken displays.)

A tidbit about the taskbar

At the bottom of your screen, Windows displays a *taskbar*. It provides the Start button, which I talk about earlier, so you can start another program. (With Windows, you can run several programs at the same time.) And the taskbar provides buttons that you can click to move between the programs you're running. If you look closely at it while you're running WordPad, for example, you'll see a taskbar button for the WordPad program. You'll also see a taskbar button for any other program you're running at the same time. You probably will be glad to know that *multitasking,* which is what running multiple programs is called, is this easy to do — just click the buttons on the taskbar to switch from one running program to another.

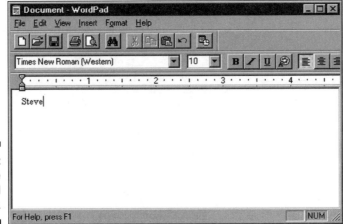

Choosing Commands from Menus

To set something in motion in Windows, you usually need to choose *commands* from menus.

I don't know why they're called commands. Perhaps because you often (but not always) use them to command Windows and Windows applications to do things. "Windows, I command thee to start this application," or "Quicken, I command thee to print this report."

Most application windows have a *menu bar* — a row of menus across the top of the window. Predictably, not every menu bar contains the same menus. But they're often darn similar. Some of the commands on the Quicken menus, for example, mirror commands on the WordPad menus.

This menu similarity isn't some nefarious conspiracy. The common command sets make things easier for users.

If you choose to read the next section, don't worry about what particular commands or menus do. Just focus on the mechanics of choosing commands.

Choosing commands with the furry little rodent

I think that the easiest way to choose a command is to use the mouse.

To select one of the menus by using a mouse, move the *mouse pointer* — the small arrow that moves across your screen as you physically roll the mouse across your desk — so that it points to the name of the menu that you want to select. Then click the mouse's left button: Windows or the Windows application displays the menu. (Pointing to some object like a menu name and then pressing the mouse's left button is called *clicking* the object.) Now click the command that you want to choose.

If you inadvertently display a menu, you can deselect it (that is, make it go away) by clicking anywhere outside the menu box.

Choosing commands by using the Alt+key combinations

Another way to choose a command is to use an *Alt* key (cleverly labeled Alt, these keys are usually at either end of the spacebar):

1. **Press the Alt key.**

   Doing so tells Windows or the Windows application that you want to choose a command.

2. **Press the underlined letter of the menu that you want to choose.**

   Doing so tells Windows or the Windows application which menu contains the command you want. For example, if you want to choose the WordPad application's File menu, you press the F key because that's the underlined letter. WordPad proudly displays the menu in question (see Figure A-3).

3. **Press the underlined letter of the command you want to choose.**

   Each of the commands on a menu is usually underlined, too, so you can tell the program which command you want to choose by pressing the underlined letter of that command. For example, if you've chosen the File menu, you can choose the last option, Exit, by pressing the letter X. (You can try choosing Exit if you want, but then restart WordPad so you can continue to follow along, okay?)

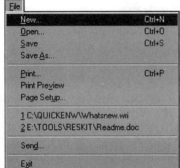

Figure A-3:
The
WordPad
File menu.

Windows and Windows applications offer yet another way to choose menu commands. After you press the Alt key, use the left- and right-arrow keys to highlight the menu that you want. Then press Enter. Windows or the Windows application displays the menu. Use the up- and down-arrow keys to highlight the command that you want to choose. Then press Enter.

For example, press Alt to activate the menu bar. Press the right-arrow key to highlight the Edit menu. Press Enter to display the Edit menu of commands. Press the down-arrow key seven times to highlight the Find command. Then press Enter.

If you want to deselect a menu but still leave the menu bar activated, press the Esc key once. To deselect the displayed menu and, at the same time, deactivate the menu bar, press the Esc key twice.

Using shortcut-key combinations

For many menu commands, Windows and Windows applications offer shortcut-key combinations. When you press a shortcut-key combination, Windows or the Windows application simultaneously activates the menu bar, chooses a menu, and chooses a command.

Windows (and Windows applications such as WordPad and Quicken) display the shortcut-key combination that you can use for a command on the menu beside the command.

Using one of the menu selection techniques that I describe earlier, activate the Edit menu (see Figure A-4). Do you see the rather cryptic codes, or whatever, that follow each of the command names? Following the Undo command, for example, you can just barely make out the code Ctrl+Z. And following the

Paste command, you can see the code Ctrl+V. These are the shortcut-key combinations. If you simultaneously press the two or three keys listed — the Ctrl key and the Z key, for example — you choose the command. (Shortcut-key combinations often use funny keys such as Ctrl, Alt, and Shift in combination with letters or numbers. If you're not familiar with some of these keys' locations, take a minute to look over your keyboard.)

Disabled commands

Oh, jeepers. I almost forgot to tell you something. Not every menu command makes sense in every situation. So Windows and Windows applications disable commands that would be just plain kooky to choose. To show you when a command has been disabled, the program displays disabled commands in gray letters. In comparison, commands you can choose show up in black letters. Take another look at Figure A-4. Several of the commands on that menu are disabled. That's why you can barely read some of their names.

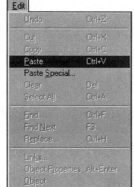

Figure A-4:
The
WordPad
Edit menu.

Working with Dialog Boxes

Windows (and Windows applications like Quicken) use a special type of window, called a dialog box, to communicate with you. In fact, after you choose a command, Windows and Windows applications often display a dialog box to get the information they need to carry out the command.

Dialog boxes have five unique design elements: text boxes, option buttons, check boxes, list boxes, and command buttons.

Text boxes

Text boxes provide a space into which you can enter text. To see what a text box looks like, start WordPad (if you haven't already), type **This is the day**, and choose Edit⇨Find. WordPad, responding nicely to your deft touch, displays the Find dialog box (as shown in Figure A-5). The text box is the box to the right of Find what.

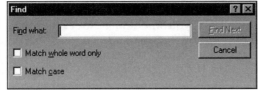

Figure A-5:
The Find
dialog box.

If the *selection cursor* — the flashing line or outline that selects the active element of a dialog box — isn't already in the text box, you need to move it there. Then type in the text. If this "active element" mumbo jumbo seems too technical, just press Tab a bunch of times and watch the dialog box. See that thing that moves around from box to button to box? It selects the active element.

You can move the selection cursor several ways:

- Click the text box.
- Press Tab or Shift+Tab until the selection cursor is in the text box (pressing Tab moves the selection cursor to the next element; pressing Shift+Tab moves the selection cursor to the preceding element).
- Press the Alt+key combination (for example, press Alt+N to move the selection cursor to the Find what text box).

If you make a typing mistake in the text box, use the Backspace key to erase incorrect characters. Other editing tricks are available, but I won't describe them here. (Remember that this chapter is just a quick and dirty overview of Windows.)

You also can move the *insertion bar* — the vertical line that shows where what you type gets placed — by using the left- and right-arrow keys. The left-arrow key moves the insertion bar one character to the left without deleting any characters. The right-arrow key moves the insertion bar one character to the right without deleting any characters.

Figure A-6 shows the Find what text box after I typed some text.

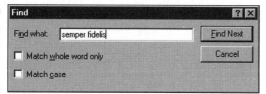

Figure A-6: A text box with some text.

Check boxes

Check boxes work like on-off switches. A check box is "on" if the box is selected with an X. A check box is "off" if the box is empty (Figure A-6 shows the Match case check box turned off, while Figure A-7 shows the Automatic word selection box turned on).

To turn a check box on or off with the mouse, click the check box. If the check box is on, your click turns the check box off. If the check box is off, your click turns the switch on.

You also can use the spacebar to select and deselect a check box. After you move the selection cursor to the check box, press the spacebar to alternatively select and deselect the check box. Toggle, toggle, toggle.

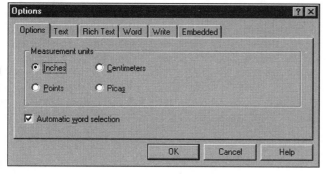

Figure A-7: A dialog box with some option buttons.

Option buttons

Option buttons are sets of buttons representing mutually exclusive choices. The Options dialog box, which appears when you choose the WordPad View⇨Options command, uses one set of option buttons, the Measurement Units buttons: Inches, Points, Centimeters, and Picas (refer to Figure A-7).

You can select only one button in a set. Windows or the Windows application identifies the selected button by putting a *bullet,* or darkened circle, inside the button. In Figure A-7, for example, the Inches button is selected. The easiest way to select an option button is to click the button you want.

Command buttons

Every dialog box includes command buttons. *Command buttons* tell Windows or a Windows application what you want to do after you finish with a dialog box.

Figure A-7, for example, shows two command buttons: OK and Cancel. If you use the Options dialog box to make some changes, you click OK after completing the rest of the dialog box. If you don't want to use the Options dialog box after all, you choose Cancel.

To choose a command button, either click it or move the selection cursor to a command button and press Enter.

List boxes

List boxes list a series of possible choices. To see an example of a list box, choose the File⇨Open command. Windows or the Windows application displays the Open dialog box (as shown in Figure A-8).

Windows and Windows applications use two types of list boxes: a regular list box, which is always displayed, and a *drop-down* list box, which Windows won't display until you tell it to. Drop-down list boxes look like text boxes with a down-arrow button at the right end of the box.

To open a drop-down list box — such as the Files of Type list box, shown in Figure A-8 — click the down-arrow button (or you can move the selection cursor to the list box and then press Alt key).

After it's opened, a drop-down list box works the same as a regular list box. After you select an item from the list box (by using the mouse or the arrow keys), press Enter.

If you exit Quicken the wrong way

If you exit Quicken by turning off (or resetting) your computer, the index file that Quicken uses to organize your financial records gets, well, wasted. Quicken rebuilds the index when you restart, but this process takes a few seconds.

Don't exit Quicken or Windows by turning off your computer. Doing so may not cause serious problems (let me say, though, that Windows isn't as forgiving as Quicken), but it is bad form — akin to eating the last potato chip.

Unfortunately, a list is sometimes too long for the list box to completely display. When this minor tragedy occurs, you can use the PageUp and PageDown keys to page through the list.

You also can use the *scrollbar* — the vertical bar with arrows at either end. Just drag the square scrollbar selector up or down. You also can click the arrows at either end of the scrollbar, or you can click the scrollbar itself (this last trick moves the scrollbar selector toward the place where you clicked).

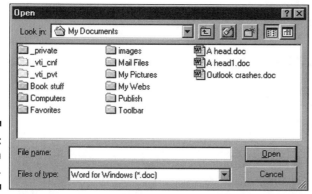

Figure A-8: The Open dialog box.

Stopping Quicken for Windows

To stop a Windows application like Quicken for Windows, either click the application's Close box — the button with the X in it that appears in the top-right corner of the application window — or choose File⇨Exit.

A Yelp for Help

Help, a separate application within Windows, has a number of powerful tools to help you learn about Windows and Windows applications such as WordPad and Quicken. To access Help, select the Help menu or click the ? icon.

The Help menu (see Figure A-9) lists seven commands: Index, Current Window, Show Me Videos, Onscreen Manual, Product Support, Internet Business Solutions, and About Quicken. Different versions of Quicken have different Help menus and supply different commands. But for the most part, they all work pretty much in the same way. So in the following paragraphs, I briefly describe how each command shown in Figure A-9 works.

Figure A-9:
The Quicken
Help menu.

Index command

If you choose the Help⇨Index command, the Help program displays a dialog box (see Figure A-10) that has three tabs: Contents, Index, and Find.

The Index tab lists all the Quicken help topics in alphabetical order. To use the index, type the first few characters of the topic you're interested in or curious about into the text box. If you want to learn more about creating new accounts in Quicken 2000, for example, you may type the word **new**. Then review the list of Help topics shown on the Index tab's list box. If you see one that matches the topic you have questions about, double-click it. Help then displays a dialog box that lists the specific Help topics related to the index entry. You *double-click,* or quickly click twice, the one you want. And that's that.

Note: If you have the time, you can also use the Index tab by scrolling through its (lengthy!) alphabetical list of all Quicken Help topics until you find the one you want.

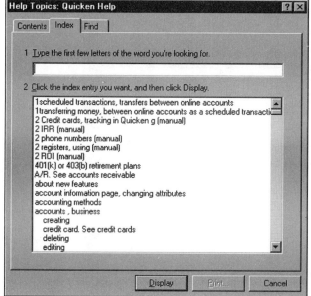

Figure A-10:
Select the
Help menu's
Index
command to
display the
index of
Help topics.

You can click the Contents tab to view a list of the major Help topic categories. To display the topics that fall within a particular category, double-click the Help topic category. Help expands the list shown so that it shows the topics with each category (see Figure A-11). Double-click the topic to display the Help information on that topic.

You can click the Find tab (shown in Figure A-12) to search through the help topics. When you first click the Find tab, Find launches a wizard that sets up the database of topics. After Help creates the database, you use the Find tab by entering key words into the first text box, selecting a related word from the second list box, and selecting the help topic from the last list box.

Current Window command

You can also get Help information specifically related to the active window (the window that appears on top of any others). To do so, either press F1 or choose the Help➪Current Window command to start the Help program. I really don't need to say any more about this command. If you have questions about it, just try it.

Figure A-11:
The Contents tab lists major Help topics.

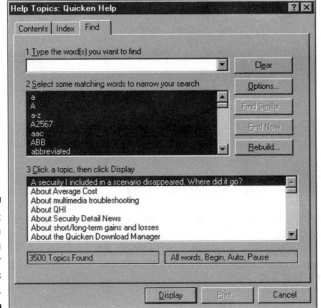

Figure A-12:
The Find tab lets you search for Help topics by keyword.

Show Me Videos command

The Show Me Videos command displays a window you can use to see videos about how the Quicken product works. Quicken supplies videos about a variety of topics including Installing Quicken, a Quick Tour of Quicken, Converting Data, and so on. To play the Show Me Videos, you need to insert the Quicken CD in your CD-ROM drive.

Onscreen Manual command

Oh, this is a big surprise. Choose the Onscreen Manual command and Quicken opens up an electronic manual. While I'm understandably jealous of you getting help about Quicken from some other writer, I want to encourage you to take at least a look at the Onscreen manual. That truth is that sometimes having someone else describe how you accomplish some task in just a slightly different way makes all the difference.

Product Support command

The Product Support command displays a dialog box that simply describes the various ways that you can get help from Intuit, including the Quicken troubleshooting feature, Intuit's Worldwide Web support, and fax support. Basically, I guess, the folks at Intuit are looking for some way to get you help — without actually having to talk to you in person. (This practice sounds terrible, but if you end up having to talk with someone, Intuit will probably spend more paying people to talk to you than they make from your purchase.)

The Intuit Business Solutions command

The Intuit Business Solutions command is basically just a pitch for Intuit's product line. "If you liked Quicken, you'll love QuickBooks Pro!" All seriousness aside, this command actually does give you a quick overview of the additional features you gain by moving up to one of Intuit's more advanced programs.

The About Quicken command

The About Quicken command displays a dialog box that gives the application's complete name, Quicken for Windows. To remove this dialog box from the screen, click OK.

Quitting Windows

To quit Windows, click the Start button and choose the Shut Down command. Then wait until Windows says that turning off your computer is OK. When you get the go-ahead, flip the power switch.

Appendix B

Quicken, the Internet, and You

●●

I thought that I should say something about Quicken and the Internet before wrapping up this book. After all, Quicken is big. The Internet is big. And, perhaps more to the point, the newest versions of Quicken connect in some pretty neat ways to the Internet and its vast sea of information.

Getting into the Internet Club

This book isn't about the Internet, so I'm just going to give you the bird's-eye view here about how you connect your computer to the Internet. If you want to connect to the Internet, you need four things: some hardware, an account with an online service or Internet Service Provider, a web browser, and vast quantities of patience.

If you want to make the most common and inexpensive connection to the Internet, you need a piece of hardware called a modem to connect your computer to a telephone line. When purchasing a modem, it makes sense to get one that runs as fast as possible, namely 56.6 Kbps. Unless you have more time on your hands than you know what to do with, the extra money you put into a faster modem will be well worth it. You can probably install a modem yourself (following the manufacturer's instructions). Or you can pay some chiphead, oh I don't know, maybe $20 or so to install it for you.

Other, faster types of Internet connections are also available. These connections are becoming more popular and affordable for home users and small businesses. So if you expect that you, your kids, your spouse, or your coworkers will want to spend a lot of time on the Internet, you may want to investigate a high-speed connection such as ISDN, a cable connection, or ADSL. For more information about these connections, ask your phone company, your cable company, or make a trip to the local library.

You need an account with an online service or Internet Service Provider (ISP) so that you can connect your computer (via a modem and a telephone line) to their computer, which connects to the Internet. If you already have an account with an online service (like America Online, CompuServe, or the Microsoft Network) or an ISP, you're all set. If you don't yet have an account, you need to get one. I always get into lots of trouble saying this, but if I were you, I'd just go with one of the big online services previously mentioned. Or, barring that option, go with whatever your neighbor has and is satisfied with. By the way, after you pick an online service or ISP, follow whatever instructions they provide for setting up their software and making an Internet connection.

You also need a web browser. A *web browser* is the program you use on your computer to view information that is stored someplace on the Internet. Man, oh man, you may be thinking at this point. Where do you get a web browser? Well, not to worry, my friend. Your copy of Quicken came with a copy of Microsoft Internet Explorer 5, which is one of the popular web browsers. If you want to make use of the web browsing integration in Quicken, and don't already have Internet Explorer 4 or later, just install Internet Explorer 5 from the Quicken CD. For other web browsing you do, it doesn't matter which web browser you use. If you're using an online service to connect to the Internet, it probably provided you a copy of a web browser.

You also need lots of patience. Technically speaking, patience isn't actually a requirement for connecting to the Internet. The connection is easy. No, patience is required for using the Internet. So I suppose that this point should really be made somewhere, a little farther along in our discussion . . . but no, I think the point belongs here. If you're going to get into this thing, you may as well know from the very start that actually grabbing information from the Internet often takes a painfully long time.

The Internet in a nutshell

In a nutshell, the Internet is just a bunch of computers — some big and some small — that are cabled together so that the people who use these computers can share information. With the Internet's help, some bloke on computer A, for example, can grab information from computer B. The only thing that sometimes gets just a tiny bit confusing is that you can share all sorts of different types of information (text, pictures, sounds, and so forth), and you share information in lots of different ways. If you want to learn more about the Internet, I recommend you beg, borrow, or steal a copy of *The Internet For Dummies,* 5th Edition, by John Levine (IDG Books Worldwide, Inc.). Oh, what's that? You're right. You shouldn't steal. Stick to begging and borrowing.

Configuring Quicken for an Internet Connection

Once you have your modem, online service or ISP account, and a web browser, you're all set to rock and roll. You can connect to the Internet in the usual way (probably by starting the web browser directly or by starting the online service connection). Or you can make your connection from within Quicken.

Before you connect to the Internet from within Quicken, you need to choose the Edit➪Internet Connection Setup command. When you do, Quicken starts a wizard that asks you some questions about your online service or ISP account and your web browser (see Figure B-1). You just answer the questions by clicking buttons and selecting entries from a list box.

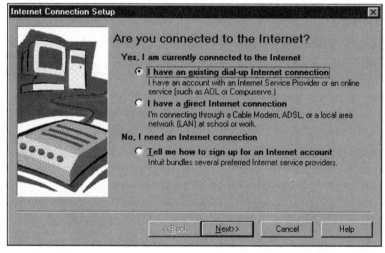

Figure B-1:
The first
dialog box
of the
Internet
Connection
Setup
wizard.

Surfing the Web

Once you've run the Internet Connection Setup wizard, you can connect to the Internet by choosing the Finance➪Quicken on the Web➪Quicken.com command. Quicken makes the connection and opens the Quicken.com home page, as shown in Figure B-2.

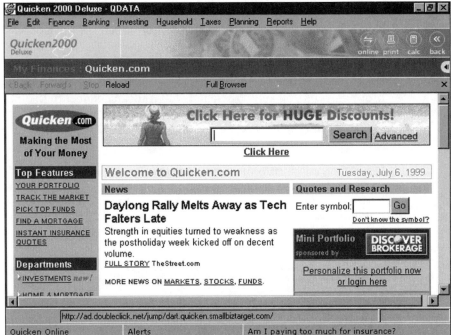

Figure B-2:
The
Quicken.com
home page.

To view a web page like the one shown in Figure B-2, you scroll up and down by using the scrollbars or the PageUp and PageDown keys. (Go ahead and try it.) You can also move to another web page by clicking a hyperlink. A *hyperlink* is a piece of text or a picture that points to another web page. You can tell where hyperlinks are because your mouse pointer changes to a "hand-with-pointing-finger" thingamajig when you point to a hyperlink. When you click the hyperlink, your web browser retrieves the other web page. Figure B-3 shows the web page that appears when you click the Investments hyperlink.

Click the Back button to move back to the web page you last visited. If you've clicked the Back button, you can click the Forward button to return to where you were before clicking Back. Click the Stop button to tell Internet Explorer to stop trying to load a page. Click the Reload button to grab a new copy of a page. You might need to do this if a page changes frequently or if it loaded incorrectly.

Quicken.com is made up of dozens and dozens of cool web pages — and more are being added all the time. So, your best bet for figuring out what is available is personal exploration. In other words, just go wild clicking those hyperlinks. (Note that you can move back and forth through web pages you've already viewed by clicking the Back and Next buttons.) I should also tell you that because the Quicken.com web pages change frequently, the web pages you'll see will almost certainly look very different from what the previous two figures show.

My name is URL, not Earl

This chapter is a quick-and-dirty description of the Internet. And you know that. But even so, let me point out that clicking a hyperlink isn't the only way you can move to a web page. You can also enter the page's uniform resource locator, also known as an URL, into the Address box of the web browser. You've undoubtedly seen hundreds of URLs even if you didn't recognize them. URLs, which often start with text `http://www`, or `www`, now routinely appear in advertisements and in television commercials. If you're watching a television commercial for Honda cars, for example, you may see `http://www.honda.com` at the bottom of the screen. And if you're flipping through a travel magazine and see an advertisement for Palm Springs, you may see `http://www.palm-springs.org` at the bottom of the advertisement. These cryptic text strings are URLs.

To fit more web page on your screen and shorten the time you spend scrolling, click the Full Browser button.

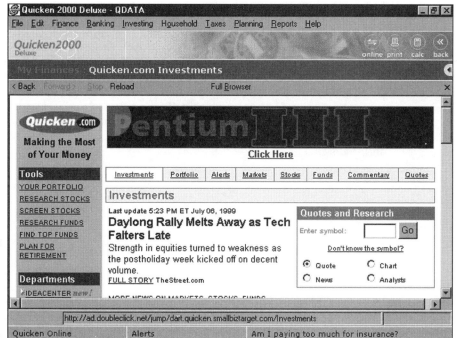

Figure B-3:
The
Quicken.com
Investments
page.

Covering the Bases

You don't need to spend a bunch more time reading what I have to say about the Internet. You have better things to do. Walk your dog. Kiss the kids goodnight. Catch a rerun of *Baywatch*. Nevertheless, before I wrap up this lightning-quick discussion, you should know a handful of additional things:

- ✔ Many banks, mutual fund companies, insurance companies, and government agencies also publish web pages with information that's useful or interesting to people who want to better manage their personal finances. (My personal favorite, just so you know, is www.vanguard.com.)

- ✔ Finding information on the Internet is tough — a real-life example of searching for a needle in a haystack. Therefore if you get serious about using the Internet, you'll want to learn to use a search service like AltaVista. (The URL for AltaVista is www.altavista.digital.com.) Note that you can use a search service like AltaVista to locate the web sites of banks, mutual fund companies, insurance companies, and government agencies who publish web pages. For example, if you tell AltaVista that you want to look for web pages related to the Internal Revenue Service, you'll easily locate the IRS's web site.

- ✔ The Deluxe version of Quicken includes quite a bit of Internet connectivity. In some versions of the Quicken product, for example, you'll see a "Best of the Web" button on the financial planning calculators. If you click this button, Quicken starts your web browser and then displays web pages at the Quicken.com web site that talk in more detail about the financial planning decisions related to making a particular calculation. The Deluxe version of the Quicken product also includes other Internet connectivity features such as its Market Watch tool (a feature that lets you monitor share prices and news stories about investments you own).

And that's that.

Appendix C

Glossary of Business, Financial, and Computer Terms

• •

1-2-3: The Lotus 1-2-3 spreadsheet program. The original "killer" application, 1-2-3 almost single-handedly turned IBM-compatible personal computers into standard business and financial management tools. Quicken, by the way, lets you create electronic versions of its reports that can be read by 1-2-3 and other spreadsheet programs.

940 Payroll Tax Form: The annual federal unemployment tax return. There's also a 940EZ version that is supposed to be EZ-er to fill out.

941 Payroll Tax Form: The quarterly federal payroll tax form that tells the IRS what federal employee payroll taxes (Social Security and Medicare) you've collected and remitted.

942 Payroll Tax Form: The quarterly payroll tax form that tells the IRS what domestic employee payroll taxes an employer has collected and remitted.

account: In Quicken, a list of the increases and decreases in an asset's value or in a liability's balance.

account balance: The value of an asset or the outstanding principal owed for a liability. For example, the value of a checking account is the cash value of the account. The balance of a mortgage liability is the principal you still owe.

account transfer: An amount you move from one account (such as a checking account) to another (such as a savings account).

account type: Quicken provides different versions, or types, of accounts There are 12 for keeping records of the things you own (checking, saving, money market, cash, brokerage, IRA or Keogh, 401(k), dividend reinvestment plan, other investment, house, and vehicle) and 2 for keeping records of the amounts you owe (credit card and liability).

accounts payable: In a business, the amounts you owe your trade creditors— your landlord, the office supplies store, the distributor from whom you purchase your inventory, and so on. People who prefer monosyllabic speech often refer to accounts payable as *A/P*.

accounts receivable: In a business, the amounts your customers or clients owe you. People who prefer monosyllabic speech often refer to accounts receivable as *A/R*.

Activity Center: In an effort to organize what had become an increasingly complicated and confusing set of features, Quicken 2000 now organizes all of its features into big bunches that it calls Activity Centers. Each Activity Center gets a QuickTab along the right edge of the Quicken program window. And many of the menus available in the menu bar are named after Activity Centers. *See also **Feature tab.***

amortization: The itsy-bitsy principal payments you make over the course of repaying a loan. Eventually, these principal reductions pay off the loan.

ASCII: An acronym standing for the American Standard Code for Information Interchange. People usually use the term to refer to files — in other words, ASCII files — that contain just regular old text: letters, numbers, symbols from the keyboard, and so on.

backing up: Making a copy. If something terrible happens — fire, hard disk failure, thermonuclear exchange — you still have a copy on floppy disk.

balancing an account: The steps you take to explain the difference between what your records show as a balance and what the bank's records (statement) show. Also referred to as *reconciling an account.*

Billminder: A program that comes with Quicken, Billminder looks through your postdated checks whenever you start your computer. If there's a check that needs to be paid, Billminder tells you.

bookkeeper: Someone who keeps the "books," or financial records.

Brokerage account: An account specifically set up to track a brokerage account that you use to invest in securities. Unlike a mutual fund account, a brokerage account includes a cash element. *See also **Account Type.***

budget: A plan that says how you will make and spend money.

Capital accounts: The money a sole proprietor leaves in or contributes to the sole proprietorship. Also, the money a partner leaves in or contributes to a partnership.

capital gain: What you earn by selling an investment for more than you paid for it.

capital loss: What you lose by selling an investment for less than you paid.

category: In Quicken, how you summarize income and outgo. For example, you may use a category such as Wages to summarize your payroll check deposits. And you may use categories such as Housing, Food, and Fun to summarize your checks.

category list: The list of categories you can use. While setting up the first account in a file, Quicken suggests category lists for home users and for business users.

certified public accountant: Someone who's taken a bunch of undergraduate or graduate accounting courses, passed a rather challenging two-and-a-half-day test, and worked for at least a year or two under a CPA doing things like auditing, tax planning and preparation, and consulting.

chart: A picture that shows numbers. In Quicken, you can produce pie charts, bar charts, line charts, and so on.

check date: The date you write your payment instructions, or check. Technically, the check date is the date on which your payment instructions to the bank become valid.

check form: The preprinted form that you use to provide payment instructions to your bank: "Okay, Mammoth National, pay Joe Shmoe $32 from my account, 00704-844." Theoretically, you could use just about anything as a check form — a scrap of paper, a block of wood, and so on. In fact, rumor has it that someone once used a cowhide. It's easier for your poor bank, though, if you use check forms that follow the usual style and provide OCR characters along the form's bottom edge.

Circular E: Instructions from the IRS to employers. This publication tells how much federal income tax to withhold and other stuff like that. Call the IRS and request a copy if you need one.

cleared: When a check or deposit has been received by the bank. An *uncleared* transaction hasn't been received by the bank.

commands: What you use to tell Quicken what it should do. For example, "Quicken, I command thee to print a report." Note that while you can use menu commands to navigate within Quicken, you can also use the QuickTabs, their Feature tabs, and the hyperlinks that appear within windows. Just thought I'd mention this.

controller: A business's chief accountant — and usually the brunt of most accountant jokes. Also known as a *comptroller*.

corporation: A legal business entity created by state law, owned by shareholders, and managed by directors and officers. As a business entity, a corporation has unique advantages and some disadvantages. Ask your attorney for more information.

Credit card account: A Quicken account specifically set up to track credit card charges, payments, and balances. *See also* ***account type.***

deleted transaction: A transaction that Quicken has removed from the register. *See also* ***voided transaction.***

directory: Basically, a drawer (like a filing cabinet drawer) that DOS uses to organize your hard disk. *See also* ***folder.***

disk: The thingamajig in your computer on which DOS stores your programs (such as Quicken) and your data files (such as the Quicken file for your financial records). A hard disk (inside your computer) can store a great deal of information; floppy disks (nowadays 3½-inch), which can be removed, store a lot less data than a hard disk.

exit: To shut down, terminate, or stop a program. By the way, you want to always do this the right way, which means by using the File menu's Exit command or by clicking the Quicken program window's Close button. Don't just turn off your computer.

Feature tab: Have you figured out where those QuickTab things are? They're the boldfaced words that appear along the right edge of the Quicken program window. Each of these QuickTabs, pretty much, names an Activity Center, which is just a bunch of related Quicken features. Okay, once you know all this, I can tell you that Feature tabs are those indented words underneath the QuickTab that you can click to jump to some Quicken feature, tool, whistle, or bell. *See also* ***Activity Center, QuickTab.***

file: Where data is stored. Your Quicken financial records, for example, are stored in a set of files.

filename: The name of a file in which Quicken stores data. Actually, what Quicken calls a filename is actually the name used for several files. You don't need to worry about this unless you create multiple files.

financial wizards: People who believe that they know so much about the world of finance that it is actually their God-given duty to share their expertise with you. *See also* ***wizards.***

Find: A tremendous bargain, as in: "At $22,000, the five-bedroom house was a real find." In Quicken, also an Edit menu command that you can use to locate transactions. *See also* ***search criteria.***

fiscal year: A fiscal year is just the annual budgeting year. Most of the time, a fiscal year is the same as the calendar year, starting on January 1 and ending on December 31. But some businesses use a different fiscal year. (Why they do that is way, way beyond the scope of this book.)

folder: What Windows uses to organize your hard disk. Some people call folders *directories*.

formatting: Hey, this word is too complicated for a book like this, isn't it? Let me just say that formatting means doing some things to a disk so that you can write files to that disk. It can also mean setting up some nice typesetting "looks" in your printed documents.

Help: A program's online documentation — which can almost always be accessed by pressing F1. Also, a verbalized cry for assistance.

hyperlink: A bit of clickable text and sometimes a clickable picture that you can use (by clicking of course) to move to some other feature of Quicken or some other web page. Quicken 2000, as you may have noticed, scatters hyperlinks everywhere. And I mean everywhere.

Internal rate of return: An investment's profit expressed as a percentage of the investment. If you go down to the bank and buy a certificate of deposit earning 7 percent interest, for example, 7 percent is the CD's internal rate of return. I don't want to give you the heebie-jeebies, but internal rates of return can get really complicated really fast.

Internet: The Internet is basically just a collection of computers that people cabled together so that the people who use these computers can share information. This might seem irrelevant to you and me as mere Quicken users, but the newest version of Quicken lets you connect to the Internet so you can grab financial information and do things like online banking and Online Bill Payment. Quicken also has its own web site, Quicken.com, that works with Quicken and provides all sorts of cool personal finance news and advice.

Liability accounts: An account specifically set up for tracking loans, payments, the principal and interest portions of these payments, and the outstanding balance. *See also **account type**.*

memo: A brief description of a transaction. Because you also give the payee and category for a transaction, it usually makes sense to use the Memo field to record some other bit of information about a check or deposit.

menu: In Quicken, a list of commands. In a restaurant, a list of things you can order from the kitchen.

menu bar: Although it sounds like a place where menus go after work for a drink, a menu bar is a horizontally arranged row, or bar, of menus.

missing check: A gap in the check numbers. For example, if your register shows a check 101 and a check 103, check 102 is a missing check.

Mutual fund account: A Quicken account specifically set up to track a mutual fund investment. Except, wait a minute, Quicken doesn't actually provide an account type for mutual fund accounts. Hmmm. Somebody at Intuit deserves to be spanked with a wet noodle. But just so you know, you can use the Other Investment account type for mutual funds.

My Finances: The My Finances Activity Center is essentially just another document window that Quicken displays. To see this document window, you click the My Finances QuickTab. The My Finances window, by the way, is actually a web page with hyperlinks that point you to Quicken features and even web pages on the Quicken.com web site.

online banking: An extra service you can buy from your bank. With online banking, you record a payment in your Quicken register and then transmit the payment information to your bank so it can make the actual payment. Online banking also lets you electronically transfer money between your accounts and grab your statement electronically. Online banking is cool, but unfortunately, only a handful of banks offer the service. Drats!

Online Bill Payment: An extra service you can buy from the folks who bring you Quicken, Intuit. With Online Bill Payment, you record a payment in your Quicken register and then transmit the payment information to Intuit's computer or your bank. Intuit or your bank then uses this information to make the actual payment.

online investing: Quicken 2000 lets you automatically download transactions from many and maybe even most of the online brokerage services right into your investment accounts. If you're buying and selling securities, downloading these transactions (rather than entering them by hand) saves you time. A particularly valuable feature for people who want to see how quickly they can lose everything they own through day trading.

partnership: A business entity that combines two or more former friends. In general, each partner is liable for the entire debts of the partnership.

password: A word you have to give Quicken before Quicken gives you access to a file. The original password "Open sesame" was used by Ali Baba.

payee: The person to whom a check is made payable. (If you write a check to me, Steve Nelson, for example, I'm the payee.) In Quicken, however, you can fill in a Payee field for deposits and for account transfers.

power user: Someone who's spent far more time than is healthy fooling around with a computer. Power users are good people to have as friends, though, because they can often solve your worst technical nightmares. However, note that most people who describe themselves as power users aren't.

QIF: An acronym standing for *Quicken Interchange Format.* Basically, QIF is a set of rules that prescribes how an ASCII file must look if you want Quicken to read it. If you're a clever sort, you can import category lists and even transactions from ASCII files that follow the QIF rules.

Quicken: The name of the checkbook-on-a-computer program that this book is about. You didn't really need to look this up, did you?

Quicken.com: The Intuit Corporation web site especially for Quicken users. Visit this web site, my friend. It's really good.

Quicken Deluxe: A super-charged and multimedia version of Quicken that includes a bunch of extra whistles and bells including multimedia help information, a really neat program for locating great mutual funds (called, cleverly enough, Mutual Fund Finder), and a Home Inventory System program. This book is about Quicken Deluxe.

Quicken Quotes: Quicken Quotes is an online service that you can use to grab up-to-date price information on stocks and bonds. This book doesn't talk much about Quicken Quotes.

QuickFill: A clever little feature. If Quicken can guess what you're going to type next in a field, it types, or *QuickFills,* the field for you. QuickFill types in transactions, payee names, and category names.

QuickTabs: QuickTabs are the clickable labels that appear along the right edge of the Quicken application window. You can click a QuickTab to display an Activity Center.

QuickZoom: A clever, big feature. If you have a question about a figure in an on-screen report, double-click the figure. Quicken then lists all the individual transactions that go together to make the figure.

Register: The list of increases and decreases in an account balance. Quicken displays a register in a window that looks remarkably similar to a crummy old paper register — your checkbook. To print a copy of the register that you see on your screen, press Ctrl+P and then press the Enter key.

report: An on-screen or printed summary of financial information from one or more registers.

restore: Replace the current version of a file with the backup version. You may want to do this after a fire, hard disk failure, or thermonuclear exchange. *See also **backing up.***

savings goal accounts: Quicken includes this pseudo-account called a *savings goal account.* In effect, a savings goal account is a compartment in a banking account where you can "hide" or set aside money that you're saving for a special purpose: A new car. A boat. A trip to Montana. Whatever.

scrollbars: The vertical bars along the window's right edge and the horizontal bars along the window's bottom edge. Use them to scroll, or page, through your view of something that's too big to fit on one page.

search criteria: A description of the transaction that you want to locate. *See also* ***find.***

sole proprietorship: A business that's owned by just one person and that doesn't have a separate legal identity. In general, businesses are sole proprietorships, partnerships, or corporations.

split transactions: A transaction assigned to more than one category or transferred to more than one account. A split check transaction, for example, might show a $50 check to the grocery store paying for both groceries and automobile expenses.

stockholders' equity: The money that shareholders have contributed to a corporation or allowed to be retained in the corporation. You can't track stockholders' equity with Quicken.

subcategory: A category within a category. For example, the suggested Quicken home categories list breaks down utilities spending into a Gas and Electric subcategory and a Water subcategory.

supercategory: A group of categories that you monitor as a group. You create supercategories so that you can monitor them using a progress bar.

tax deduction: For an individual, an amount that can be deducted from total income (such as alimony or Individual Retirement Account contributions) or used as an itemized deduction and deducted from adjusted gross income (such as home mortgage interest or charitable contributions). For a business, any amount that represents an ordinary and necessary business expense. Be sure, however, to consult with your tax advisor if you have any questions about what is or isn't a valid tax deduction.

Tax-deferred account: Some accounts aren't taxable — Individual Retirement Accounts, for one example, and 401(k) plans for another. To deal with this real-life complexity, Quicken lets you tag any account as being tax-deferred. As a practical matter, however, it'll probably be only investment accounts and the occasional bank account that are tax-deferred.

techno-geek: Someone who believes that fooling around with a computer is more fun than anything else in the world.

transposition: Flip-flopped numbers — for example, 23.45 entered as 24.35 (the 3 and 4 are flip-flopped as 4 and 3). These common little mistakes have caused many bookkeepers and accountants to go insane.

voided transaction: A transaction that Quicken has marked as void (using the Payee field), marked as cleared, and set to zero. Voided transactions appear in a register, but because they are set to zero, they don't affect the account balance. *See also **deleted transaction.***

W-2 and W-3: A W-2 is the annual wages statement that employers use to tell employees what they made and to tell the IRS what employees made. When employers send a stack of W-2s to the IRS, they also fill out a W-3 form that summarizes all the individual W-2s. W-2s and W-3s aren't much fun, but they're not hard to fill out.

Windows: The Microsoft Windows operating system. Quicken 2000 for Windows relies on Windows to do a bunch of system stuff, such as print. Refer to Appendix A for more information.

wizard: A little program that walks you through the steps to completing some tasks that some programmer thinks you're too dense to figure out on your own. While this sounds bad, it actually isn't. Quicken supplies a bunch of cool wizards, including wizards for setting up accounts and setting up how you want to record a paycheck, planning for retirement, planning for your kid's college expenses, reducing your debts, and so forth.

Zen Buddhism: A Chinese and Japanese religion that says enlightenment comes from things such as meditation, self-contemplation, and intuition — not from faith, devotion, or material things. I don't really know very much about Zen Buddhism. I did need a Z entry for the glossary, though.

Index

• S •

IDG BOOKS WORLDWIDE
BOOK REGISTRATION

Register This Book and Win!

We want to hear from you!

Visit **http://my2cents.dummies.com** to register this book and tell us how you liked it!

- ✔ Get entered in our monthly prize giveaway.
- ✔ Give us feedback about this book — tell us what you like best, what you like least, or maybe what you'd like to ask the author and us to change!
- ✔ Let us know any other *...For Dummies*® topics that interest you.

Your feedback helps us determine what books to publish, tells us what coverage to add as we revise our books, and lets us know whether we're meeting your needs as a *...For Dummies* reader. You're our most valuable resource, and what you have to say is important to us!

Not on the Web yet? It's easy to get started with *Dummies 101*®: *The Internet For Windows*® *98* or *The Internet For Dummies*®, 6th Edition, at local retailers everywhere.

Or let us know what you think by sending us a letter at the following address:

...For Dummies Book Registration
Dummies Press
7260 Shadeland Station, Suite 100
Indianapolis, IN 46256-3917
Fax 317-596-5498

™

...FOR DUMMIES

BESTSELLING
BOOK SERIES